THE HISTORIC
HOME OWNER'S
COMPANION

THE HISTORIC
HOME OWNER'S
COMPANION

Matthew Saunders

B.T. BATSFORD LTD · LONDON

To
JS and JS
and
my
friends

ISBN 0 7134 4230 1

Typeset by
Servis Filmsetting Ltd, Manchester
and printed by
The Bath Press
Bath, Somerset
for the publishers
B.T. Batsford Ltd
4 Fitzhardinge Street
London W1H 0AH

CONTENTS

PREFACE

England, closely followed by Scotland, Wales and Ulster, is undergoing a quiet, bloodless revolution, albeit one of degree rather than kind.

By the end of the 1980s this revolution will, in less than a decade, have doubled the number of buildings of special architectural and historic interest protected by statutory listing. By that time the owners of perhaps 500 000 buildings or more will find themselves possessed of structures that the State directs shall not be demolished nor altered out of character other than by its express sanction, and which shall be kept in reasonable repair to the satisfaction of the local planning authority. In return for the circumscription of freedom, listing will bring tax advantages under the VAT regime, a permissive right to direct financial assistance, some protection for the building from demolition for road widening and other developments, some safeguard of the setting and, most probably, an enhanced value on the open market. The immediate effect is likely to be disappointingly undramatic. However, the dormant legal and economic implications for each owner will surface whenever works of demolition, alteration and extension are envisaged.

This book is for those at the receiving end of this considerable extension in State power – the private lay owners of listed buildings. It does not deal with non-domestic property and it is not geared to the professional, who will know much more than is given in its pages. For that matter it is not a DIY Manual. Rather it is a review of the problems, opportunities and delights offered by historic buildings and by the protection at law that they enjoy. I assume throughout the book that the owner will call on the services of professionals whenever trouble presents itself. Indeed it remains vital that he does so. And yet I hope that he will be able to speak, after reading this book, as an educated client. There is no Glossary, as technical terms are explained in the text and index. If there is difficulty in understanding, one of the dictionaries mentioned in the Bibliography should be able to elucidate. The full name of societies referred to by their initials only is given in the chapter on 'Useful Addresses'. Bibliographical references are explained either in the General Bibliography or at the end of the relevant chapter.

As my concern is with standing occupied houses the book is limited to the present millenium and shares the definition of 'historic' accepted by the listing authorities in England as applying to any structure put up before 1939.

As architectural conservation is fast-moving in the expansion of knowledge about historic buildings and the discovery of new techniques for their repair, the astute owner should certainly keep himself informed in the future. Subscription to one or more of the national amenity societies and to one or more of the magazines *Traditional Homes, Period Home* and *Heritage Outlook* will keep him up to date.

I shall have succeeded in my purpose if appetites are whetted, let alone fulfilled, by the following pages.

Many people, a goodly number without their knowing it, have helped in the writing of this book. However, special thanks must go to Mrs Christopher Dalton who has had the daunting task of typing the manuscript almost twice over; and Timothy Auger, of Batsford, who had sufficient faith to commission the book in the first place. To Timothy Bidwell, Jim Boutwood, Kit Martin, David Park, Anthony Rossi, Rob Walker and Gilbert Williams who have read through selected chapters I owe the traditional but essential disclaimer that all errors still unspotted remain my own. Extra special thanks is owed to David Pearce who braved the complete manuscript and passed comments both perceptive and helpful, and Richard Reynolds who saw the book through the various stages of production. To my father I owe immense gratitude for help with the index. My thanks too goes to D.T. Rathbone, Austin Vernon Associates, Kellett and Thompson, Saunders Boston, Graham Jones and Ian Harper for permission to reproduce their drawings in Chapter 24, and to the Brick Development Association and the Society for the Protection of Ancient Buldings who have permitted quotations from *The Conservation of Brick Buildings* and *Chimneys in Old Buildings* respectively.

Matthew Saunders
London, October 1986

1 FINDING YOUR PROPERTY

There should be little difficulty in discovering historic buildings in good condition through the books of estate agents. The price, of course, is another matter. A list of such agents divided by counties is given as an appendix to the Period Property Register (see below).

It is the 'problem' buildings which the normal channels sometimes neglect. Indeed, so often it is precisely because the existing owner is unwilling to sell or lease a neglected farmhouse, barn or country house, that it has fallen into dereliction in the first place. If you can rise to the challenge of taking on such a property the following may be able to assist:

1 The Ancient Monuments Society (see Useful Addresses) has published an annual register of listed buildings threatened by application to demolish in England and Wales since 1978. Each list includes about 500 properties. It does not follow that entry thereon means that the properties are either standing or that they are on the market but this may be a useful starting point. The lists are £1 each p & p included.

2 The Civic Trust for the North-West (see Useful Addresses) has published a quarterly digest of vacant buildings in its area since 1983. The charge for the digest and the four quarterly supplements in the first year is £46, £40 per annum thereafter. The Trust can also prepare feasibility studies on particular buildings. February 1986 saw the first issue of its Property Portfolio.

3 The Historic Buildings Bureau (Scotland), The Scottish Development Department, New St Andrew House, Edinburgh EH1 3SZ, tel. (031) 5568–400. Ext. 4618. The Bureau publishes a quarterly list of listed buildings in Scotland on the market. It is not illustrated. The City of Glasgow maintains an illustrated inventory of surplus and disused historic buildings within its area for inspection by potential users and developers. A similar list is maintained by Renfrew.

4 The Historic Buildings Council for Wales (see Useful Addresses) is willing to advise on listed buildings in need of new uses in the Principality.

5 The Home Buyer's Consultancy (HBC), 14 Buryfields, Lydiard Millicent, Swindon SN5 9NF, tel. (0793) 770764. Can advise on property in the Cotswolds and North Wales.

6 The Historic Buildings and Monuments Commission (see Useful Addresses). Although the foundation of the Commission in April 1984 unfortunately coincided with the abolition of the lists issued by the Historic Buildings Bureau (England) the HBMC has established the post of Conservation Officer (presently occupied by John Fidler), with the specific task of ferreting out threatened buildings and encouraging the introduction of suitable new uses and the implementation of programmes of repair.

7 'Listed Houses', 23 St John's Hill, Shrewsbury SY1 1JJ, tel. (0743) 246826. This service, operated by Dr Michael Sayer, covers Shropshire, Hereford and Worcester, the Severn and Wye Valleys and the Welsh Borderland. It is concerned primarily with the larger property.

8 *Period Property Register*, issued by the Historic Buildings Company, Chobham Park House, Chobham, Surrey GU24 8HQ, tel. (09905) 7983/7196. This is a nationwide inventory of listed buildings on the market. It is issued monthly, by post, and is illustrated. The standard charge for entry is £25 and that for the purchase of the lists in the UK £25 for 12 issues or £15 for 6.

9 The Society for the Protection of Ancient Buildings (see Useful Addresses) publishes a quarterly list of properties for sale available to members only. There is no charge for inclusion. Its Wind and Watermills Section also publishes a list.

FURTHER INFORMATION
A number of magazines contain regular advertisement features on historic buildings for sale. Perhaps the leader in this field is *Country Life*.

2 Choosing Your Professional Adviser

'What professional adviser?' I hear you say. 'If I do the repairs myself there are no fees, there is no VAT, I can carry out the work to my own timetable and reduce the "middle man" element in the purchase of materials. If my property is a vernacular one, designed through the oral language of folk tradition rather than the caprice or inventiveness of an individual designer, why should I now bring in the "polite" architect?' These points are valid to a certain extent but they are also deceptively simplistic. The best professional sees you through the quagmire of planning permission, listed building consents and building bye-laws. He keeps abreast of the latest developments in techniques and materials through the technical literature, most of which is only sent to the offices of registered practices. If he is an architect, his design skills are the result of seven years' training, a long process where up to 30 per cent of students will back out before the end. And it is some comfort, if things go wrong, that he should have a professional indemnity insurance policy behind him.

The leading building profession is undoubtedly that of architect. No one can call himself an architect unless he is registered under the terms of the Architects Registration Acts of 1931 and 1938, and he can only be so registered if he is suitably qualified. Membership of the Architects Registration Council of the United Kingdom (ARCUK) is thus compulsory and at the end of 1984 the total on the approved list was 29 143. Membership of the Royal Institute of British Architects (RIBA) is not compulsory, but those who are Associates or Fellows of the RIBA subscribe to a code of Professional Conduct, to conditions of engagement and a recommended fee structure (although this does not apply to works having a total construction cost of less than £20 000 or more than £5 000 000). The conditions are summarized in a free booklet entitled *Architects Appointment* available from RIBA Publications (see p. 14)

The fee structure, where it is not based on a time charge, is graduated on a falling scale dependent on the total cost of the project. Unfortunately, but understandably, these are proportionally more expensive the less costly the project. Fees below the recommended rates can be negotiated between architect and client and there is no ban on their being waived altogether. Moreover they can be legitimately reduced by asking for a 'partial service' and can be paid in instalments. *Architects Appointment* states that in repair and restoration work fees are normally charged on a time basis and continues 'where architects appointment is in connection with works to a building of architectural or historic interest, or to a building in a Conservation area, higher fees may be charged'. Unfortunately VAT is chargeable on architects' fees.

Finding your architect has been made somewhat easier by a recent decision of the Institute to allow members to advertise. There has not been a rush to take advantage of the new provision, but the easiest way to evaluate the many candidates is either by consulting the free service offered by the Clients Advisory Service of the RIBA (see p. 14) or by referring to the Directory of Practices also published by the RIBA (see p. 14). The Advisory Service is free and the book is decidedly expensive (although a large number are sent out free to potential clients) but it is able to offer more information on the specific experience of the given practice with details and photographs of completed works. However, not all the 6000 architectural practices subscribe to it. A development late in 1984 was the joint publication by the Association of Consultant Architects and the Architectural Press of the first illustrated Directory of Architects (£10.50 including p & p from the Architectural Press, 9 Queen Anne's Gate, London SW1H 9BY). There is still a great deal to be said for the traditional method of a personal recommendation and a visit to completed works.

All the national amenity societies would be delighted to nominate architects experienced in the care of particular historic building types or those conversant with special philosophies and problems.

Other professionals employed either as an alternative to the architect, or in addition to him, include the Quantity Surveyor, responsible for the Bill of Quantities by which the work is costed, and the

Building Surveyor. Anyone can call himself a surveyor but to use the adjective 'Chartered' he must be a member of the Royal Institute of Chartered Surveyors (RICS) (see p. 14). There is an alternative Guild of Surveyors. The surveying profession, like the architectural, has dropped the mandatory scale of fees. The particular skill of the Building Surveyor is in the surveying of existing structures – although they do carry out design work sometimes, to the chagrin of architects. The architect's brow will become even more furrowed when you mention the various titles of those who offer 'architectural services' but are careful not to describe themselves as 'architects'. The Architectural Assistant, Architectural Technician and Architectural Draughtsman are all standard members of the design team but when they set up independent offices and undercut RIBA fees they become rivals, not employees, and excite much resentment. Blanket condemnation of such people would be unjustified but in resorting to them the public should know that such practitioners

often lack the full training that a qualified architect has to undergo. Analysis of building failures may require the additional services of a structural engineer and if a case goes to Public Inquiry, or proves otherwise contentious, the services of one of the 750 planning consultancies may prove useful. The use of the term 'Chartered Town Planner' denotes that the person in question is a member of the Royal Town Planning Institute.

No architectural practice in the country has its own labour force. The job of the architect, surveyor and structural engineer is to direct and supervise the builder. However, it should not be forgotten that the builder too can be a professional with his own Chartered Institute (see p. 14). Many a smaller rural firm possesses a wealth of knowledge in the repair of vernacular structures way beyond that

Typical architectural drawings from A Short Dictionary of Architecture *by Dora Ware and Betty Beatty, 1944, George Allen & Unwin Ltd*

FIG. XI

METHODS OF SHOWING A BUILDING

PERSPECTIVE

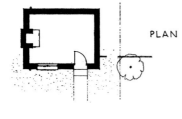

PLAN

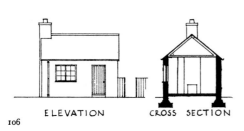

ELEVATION   CROSS SECTION

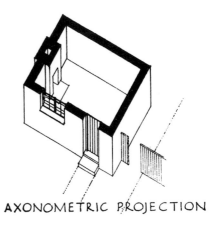

AXONOMETRIC PROJECTION

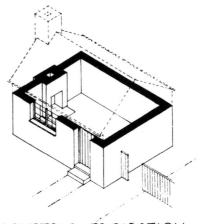

ISOMETRIC PROJECTION

which any architectural school can impart. It must equally be borne in mind however that no qualifications at all are needed to set up as a builder and there are 'cowboys' in operation. Once again, ask to see examples of works already executed and satisfied customers. Payment to builders is normally by a daily rate, 'labour and materials' or a fixed price. Members of the National Register of Warranted Builders set up in 1981 have, among other things, to supply a selection of three recent satisfactorily completed jobs, which are checked by the Registration Board.

Once the professionals have been selected the engagement is either by the exchange of letters or by a Pro Forma Memorandum of Agreement. There are standard clauses in contracts of builders too lengthy to summarize here. However, it is perhaps worth mentioning the provision known as 'retention'. This normally involves holding back 5 per cent of the contractor's fees until the client is ready to move in, when half of the retained sum is released, the rest being held back for three months, on smaller jobs, during the period of 'defects liability'. In that time, any faults that emerge which are identified by the architect have to be set right at the expense of the contractor.

Any architect worth his salt will of course be able to expound on his own plans, but again, it may save embarrassment to know that an accepted set of drawings for an architectural project should comprise a Survey showing the existing state of the building and a set of Proposal Drawings which, if they are comprehensive, will include Floor and Roof Plans, Sections (cross and longitudinal) and Eleva-

tions. A full survey may be expensive and incur costs over and above the percentage fee. However, in many restoration projects they are essential. Working drawings will show the details of construction. The broader context is provided in a Site Plan and Block Plan. Plans should be scaled: 1:50 is normal although 1:100 would allow several small elevations on a single sheet. Amendments added after the initial drawings should be itemized in a Revision Box at one side. All measurements are now metric rather than Imperial. The more sophisticated drawings known as Axonometric or Isometric which give a bird's-eye view are really only suitable for large-scale projects. The same is true of photogrammetry, a particularly accurate method of measuring an existing building using the processes of photography. The draughtsman will provide his own marginalia explaining drawing conventions and verbal abbreviations. This is essential because there is no universally accepted code in this respect. The drawings, which remain the copyright of the architect unless otherwise agreed, are backed up by written specifications.

Until very recently the surveying of a standing structure could be a very destructive process, with the stripping off of wallpaper, plaster and panelling. Now increasingly sophisticated surveying systems are offered by a number of specialist firms who use the X-ray and fibre optic techniques that have already proved their value in medical detection (see articles by John Fidler, particularly in *Building Conservation*, October 1979, and the 1980 Transactions of ASCHB; see Useful Addresses). Such techniques remain too little known, and much unnecessary destruction is still occurring.

FURTHER INFORMATION

The *Register of Architects* is available from ARCUK, 73 Hallam Street, London W1N 6EE, tel. 01-580-5861. Terms strictly cash with order.

The RIBA *Directory of Practices* (now *Architects 86, 87* etc.), published annually, is available from: RIBA Publications Ltd, Finsbury Mission, Moreland Street, London EC1V 8VB, tel. (01) 251-0791.

A guide to 150 architectural practices specializing in conservation in Scotland (1985) is available from: Scottish Development Agency, Rosebery House, Haymarket Terrace, Edinburgh EH12 5EZ.

ADDRESSES

RIBA: Royal Institute of British Architects, 66 Portland Place, London W1, tel. (01) 580-5533.

RIAS: Royal Incorporation of Architects in Scotland, 15 Rutland Square, Edinburgh EH1 2BE.

RSUA: Royal Society of Ulster Architects, 2 Mount Charles, Belfast BT7 1MZ.

There is no special architects' institute for Wales.

RICS: Royal Institute of Chartered Surveyors, 12 Gt George Street, London SW1P 3AD.

CIB: Chartered Institute of Building, Englemere, Kings Ride, Ascot, Berkshire SL5 8BJ, tel. (090) 23355.

3 Listing and Legislation

Before any sensible policy for the conservation of historic buildings can be prepared they need to be identified and protected. This is the role of the statutory lists of buildings of Special Architectural or Historic Interest, which were begun in 1944 and are now approaching completion. By 31 December 1985 the total had reached 367 720 and it will certainly exceed 500 000 when the resurvey is complete by the end of the decade; an indication of the comprehensiveness of the criteria and the richness of Britain's heritage. The present tallies in Northern Ireland, Wales and Scotland are respectively, 6500, just over 10 000 and about 30 000 (35 000 in 1980 if the non-statutory C grade is included).

The lists are issued by the Department of the Environment, the Welsh Office and the Scottish Office. Some 90 000 buildings were picked up in the survey launched during and after World War II and many more in the re-survey begun in the late sixties on liberalized criteria which brought in a larger number of Victorian buildings, others more of 'group value' than intrinsic interest, and vernacular structures, the importance of which had been overlooked as a result of the discouragement of internal inspection in force up till 1968. To prevent the loss of buildings while the survey is incomplete, structures can be protected through the emergency device of 'spot listing'. This process can in theory be completed within hours of a telephone call (to Fortress House, Savile Row, London w.1., tel. (01) 734–6010). However, bureaucracies dislike being forced into quick decisions and Whitehall encourages District planning authorities to serve Building Preservation Notices on threatened secular buildings. This provides a stay of execution for six months during which time the Department investigates the building's qualities and decides whether or not to confer permanent protection through listing. Most BPN's are confirmed but where they are not compensation can be payable to the aggrieved owner. Second BPN's can be served on the same building after the passing of 12 months. Once the re-survey is complete the Department issues a collated and bound list of protected buildings within a given area. These are deposited with the local planning authority, the County Council and occasionally the local library. The full lists for England are available in the National Monuments Record (see Useful Addresses). Because of their colour they are termed 'greenbacks'. The full listing includes identification on a map, the master copy of which is kept at the Department. This is not included within the 'greenback' where classification is by address and a description known as a 'schedule'. Items of particular interest are identified but omission does not mean lack of protection. Indeed listing extends to all immoveable objects and structures erected before 1948 within the curtilage, or grounds, whether or not they are mentioned in the schedule and whether or not they are of interest. Additions and corrections to the 'greenbacks' are made quite frequently, ranging from mass additions to upgrading, or just amending an address. Even the rechristening of 'Mon Repos' to 'Casa Mia' in theory requires a formal amendment. The legal duty to inform the owner lies with the planning authority, although the Department will also write directly with a standard letter and offer an explanatory leaflet.

The 'schedule' is not sent automatically but do ask for a copy of it. Verification of listing is a formal legal document and should be kept with the deeds and produced on sale for the purposes of a solicitor's search. A copy is deposited in the register of land charges. For obvious reasons no forewarning is provided; nor is there a right of appeal (although an application for listed building consent to demolish on the grounds that the building should not have been listed in the first place is a roundabout way of achieving the same purpose). Even those on the alert can be surprised by listing, particularly as internal inspection is not arranged in every case. (Where a householder refuses entry an investigator can if required return accompanied by a policeman and demand the right to inspect but this power is rarely, if ever, employed.) Although the lists will be issued under the name of the Secretary of State for the Environment, they will have been compiled by the staff of the Historic Buildings and Monuments Commission or of those County Councils or private architectural practices which were brought in during the early eighties to complete the re-survey.

De-listing, although rare, is possible. This is normally carried out at the time of the re-survey when buildings are found either to have been demolished, with or without the benefit of listed building consent, or grievously altered. Rebuilding in replica can lead to de-listing but this is not automatically the case. The Moot Hall in Norwich, for example, rebuilt in facsimile in 1967, remains in the Grade II* category. Most of the Wren churches in the City of London rebuilt after the War are Grade I. Buildings like Iscoed in Wales, a large mansion of *c*.1765 and the home of General Sir Thomas Picton, which had fallen into decay, were taken off the lists in the 1950s, but nowadays an owner in such a case would be expected to apply for listed-building consent to demolish rather than go for de-listing. Boarded-up and derelict buildings can be added to the list. The criterion for listing is architectural interest and not structural condition. The latter becomes a factor in any subsequent application to demolish but not in the decision to list. De-listing can also follow mistaken attribution to a famous architect, although this is not automatic. The Gate House at Chalfont St Giles, Buckinghamshire, of 1903 was listed in September 1982 on the under-

250 High Street, Rochester, Kent. De-listed after the destruction of all but the ground floor façade by fire

standing that it was designed by Sir Edwin Lutyens. When further research reascribed it to James Edwin Forbes, by comparison an 'unknown', this became one of the grounds of appeal by the owners against the refusal of permission to carry out works of susbstantial alteration and extension. However, the Secretary of State was not impressed. Indeed not only was the building retained on the lists but permission for the alterations was refused. (Scholarly accuracy is not just a matter of academic interest: in 1977 a Director of Wates, the building firm, who had paid £385 000 for a house he believed was designed by Lutyens only to discover afterwards that the designer was Philip Tilden, sued the vendors and estate agents for misrepresentation – and was awarded substantial damages.)

Buildings on the list are placed in one of three grades: II, II* and I in England and Wales, A, B and C in Scotland. These have legal force only in 'call-in' decisions (see p. 26) but they provide a useful indication of quality. Buildings in Grade I are the most select and are by definition of 'outstanding interest'. A full list of such properties was published by SAVE in 1980. The total is presently just over 5000. Those in Grade II*, estimated at around 10 000 in 1968 and probably now about 20 000, are 'particularly important'. The vast majority of buildings are in Grade II and are categorized as being of 'special interest'. Grade IIIs, which had no statutory force, were abolished in 1968–69. The bulk of these have been upgraded to Grade II in the course of the re-survey but others remain without formal protection through transference to the 'local lists' which merely indicate buildings of interest which it would be desirable to see conserved and suggest the potential for Conservation Areas (see p. 23). As Anglican churches in use are outside the scope of listed building control, although included on the lists, they were at first either given no grade at all or categorized by a different and parallel grading of A, B or C. The most up-to-date lists have however abolished this differentiation, and they now receive the same grading as secular buildings.

Apart from the outstanding churches, Grade I encompasses the great country houses like Hatfield, Kedleston and Blenheim, town planning set pieces such as Bedford Square, and the Royal Crescent at Bath, and outstanding public monuments including the great Victorian town halls of the North such as Leeds. The re-appraisal of the vernacular tradition can precipitate spectacular leaps: Gatehouse Farm at Gransmore Green at Felsted in Essex was upgraded in 1977 from the non-statutory Grade III to the all but inviolate Grade I when it was found to contain

Iscoed House, St Ishmaels, Camarthenshire. De-listed in the 1950s as a result of dereliction, a move which would now be unorthodox. The structural condition of the building is immaterial to its listing as long as the bulk of the historic fabric remains

The Chapel, Cornbury Park, Oxfordshire. The subject of an unsuccessful application to demolish in 1973; one of the very few Grade I buildings so threatened (Photo, Country Life)

substantial fabric from its origins (c.1300) as a medieval open hall. The increased reverence for the architecture of the seaside may also surprise some. In 1982 the West Pier at Brighton was moved into Grade I, as was the Blackpool Tower, the following year.

Historical association, independent of architectural quality, can be highly valued. Thomas Hardy's Max Gate in Dorchester, designed by the great man and the scene of his death in 1928, is Grade I although it has found no champions for its architectural quality. The identification with an historic character must have been long-term. In the words of the Chief Inspector at the time of writing, 'the transient association of lodgers or tenants is always looked at critically'.

Of the several hundred interwar buildings placed on the lists Grade I status has only been conferred on Lutyens' Midland Bank in Poultry in the City of London (although others like the Peter Jones Store

*Grade I: This highest category includes structural pioneers
such as Oriel Chambers, Liverpool of 1864–65, an early
example of masonry cladding to a metal skeleton*

*Seaham Hall, Durham. Rejected as a candidate for listing
despite Byron's marriage to the daughter of the house
(Photo, James Greenhalgh)*

Listing is not confined to buildings. The railings at the Infirmary, Gloucester (demolished), the cast iron urinal in Birmingham and the Gun Cannon used as a bollard at Grovelands House, in the London Borough of Enfield are all Grade II

in King's Road are Grade II*).

The range within Grade II is extraordinary. If stone has been placed purposely on stone or brick on brick, the structure is listable. The listing of granite setts and headstones has been criticized, the first because it was argued they are not above ground, the second because they are monolithic and therefore not strictly speaking 'constructed'. However the lawyers do now seem satisfied. The listability of chest tombs and other monuments which have in any sense been assembled has not been questioned. Forty-seven lamp-posts in Beverley are protected, as are their equivalents in Taunton which are held to be the earliest example of public electric lighting. The most photographed lamp-posts in London, those outside No. 10 Downing St, are Grade II. Elsewhere the lists include garden walls (boundary walls of importance are often listed in their own right), sundials, icehouses, bridges, canal locks, statues, war memorials, horse troughs, bandstands, telephone boxes and pillar boxes.

At Hanley Castle in Worcestershire, a former privy near Herberts Farmhouse constructed in the

Grade II late Georgian housing in Chichester

Victorian bravura, as here in Exeter, can be rewarded by listing

late seventeenth century over an arched conduit is protected. Although Weaver's Mills at Swansea, the earliest storeyed structure in concrete, was demolished in 1983 it had been accorded the protection of listing. The first bridge in the material, in New Cleveland Street, Hull (built 1902) was listed in March 1978. Technological advance was recognized too in the Grade II* listing conferred in 1976 on 99 Kells Lane, Gateshead, the home of Sir Joseph Swann from 1869 to 1883 and the scene of his most important experiments in dry plate photography and incandescent electric lighting. A building of no general interest may be listed if it houses important early features surviving from a predecessor or transferred from elsewhere.

In October 1983 an untouched Victorian tea and coffee shop interior led to the Grade II* listing of 13 Stricklandgate in Kendal. The average Grade II, however, is less remarkable. As all buildings put up before 1700 which survive in anything like their original condition qualify for listing the unusual move would be for a timber-framed building to be excluded. The standard brick Georgian terrace is Grade II, including those examples of artisan's housing shown (left) in Chichester, West Sussex.

The selectivity which the Department still applies to the selection of nineteenth-century buildings for the lists does lead to some odd exclusions. Victorian landmarks like the Angel Islington, Alexandra Palace in North London and Redhill Market Hall in Surrey are all unlisted and all have been subject of proposals to demolish, the first two escaping by the skin of their teeth, the third succumbing.

Listing cannot be advanced in England beyond the Second World War, the most recent structure protected perhaps being Waterloo Bridge which was only completed after the end of the War. In Scotland, however, there is a rolling 30-year rule. In Wales, in 1986, the Dunlop Factory at Brynmawr of 1954 was listed II*.

A development in 1984 was the publication of the first chapters of the *Register of Parks and Gardens of Special Historic Interest* in England. Despite the similarity of wording and the use of an identical system of grading, the Register differs fundamentally from listing in that it is only advisory. Nevertheless, the Historic Buildings and Monuments Commission, the publisher and compiler, hopes that it will deter destruction by ignorance. It is intended to publish the full Register by 1987.

Complaints about the secrecy and suddenness of listing persuaded the Government in 1980 to introduce for the first time provision for legal immunity from listing in the Local Government, Planning and

Bartholomew Street, Newbury, Berkshire. All the buildings shown are Grade II except for the late Victorian

'The Globe' Public House and its neighbours nearest the camera

Lord Street, Gainsborough, Lincolnshire. A street without any building of particular merit, but of a variety that the DoE has tried to safeguard by listing the third, fourth,

fifth, sixth and tenth buildings from the left (the tenth being to the left of the lamp-post)

The Great Unlisted. The rather splendid Neo-Georgian office of Kay & Company in Worcester constructed in the 1930s would undoubtedly have been listed Grade II* if it had been original. As a pastiche it was omitted from the lists compiled for the City in the early 1970s. The assessment of nineteenth-century buildings is more critical than for earlier centuries. The criteria for interwar buildings are stricter still. (Photo, Geoffrey Hopcroft)

The Market Hall at Redhill, Surrey designed in the 1860s by the Francis brothers, demolished in 1984, was unlisted.

Authorship by the renowned architect, Curtis Green, did not bring listing for the London Life Assurance offices in King William IV Street in the City of London. The building was, however, saved by its inclusion within a Conservation Area and the façade has been incorporated into the redevelopment.

Land Act. Where a planning application has been made to redevelop a site, the owner, or indeed any other party, can apply for a certificate from the Department, which would prohibit the listing of any building affected. Such immunity lasts for five years. Demolition can still be brought under control by inclusion within a Conservation Area, and so far as many as half the buildings drawn to the attention of the Department under this procedure have been listed – so it is certainly double-edged.

There are two further ways that buildings of interest can be protected. Firstly, there is the process of scheduling as an Ancient Monument. As this is now primarily a method of protecting sites of archaeological importance and cannot be applied to buildings that are residentially occupied or ecclesiastical buildings in use, its relevance for our purposes is limited. The number of scheduled sites is also a mere 13 000, some 3% of the number of listed buildings (although there are plans for an accelerated resurvey). However, where some structures are both scheduled and listed, the double protection that is possible is confusing, particularly because scheduling, as the older process, takes precedence in law. As a result the HBMC descheduled the Royal Exchange in 1985 so that its listing would be paramount. As an archaeological device it has great use in extending coverage to non-architectural features within a building such as historic machinery and can even cover moveable items like cars, ships and planes of historic interest. It can protect very broad areas – the historic motor-racing circuit at Brooklands is scheduled. The attendant legal system, which had hitherto relied on a system of notification and gentlemen's agreements, acquired some of the strength of the parallel listed building procedure as a result of the 1979 Ancient Monuments and Archaeological Areas Act, which came into full force in 1981. An owner intending to alter or destroy an ancient monument must now apply for Scheduled Monument Consent directly from the Department of the Environment, which issues the scheduling in the first place and retains the master list for all scheduled sites. In 1983, of 612 applications, 206 were granted subject to conditions and only 11 refused. The local planning authority has no statutory role. The classic English compromise of 'guardianship', a process whereby the burden of maintaining an ancient monument (normally a standing or ruined structure) is carried by central Government but the legal ownership resides with the owner of the land, survived the 1979 Act. Some 400 monuments are now in guardianship and displayed to the public by the Historic Buildings and Monuments Commission (see Useful Addresses) which came into force on 1 April 1984.

The other method of protection apart from listing is the Conservation Area. This concept dates from the Civic Amenities Act of 1967. Thereafter it was possible to confer protection on complete districts with historic character in need of preservation and enhancement. Subsequent acts, of 1972 and 1974 respectively, brought demolition of buildings and the felling of trees within such Areas under statutory control. As a planning device the Conservation Area is wholly a preserve of the local planning authority, other than in Northern Ireland where declarations are made by the DoE. The Secretary of State can in theory declare one but he has yet to exercise this power on the mainland and the former ability of county councils to declare Conservation Areas was recently withdrawn. Unlike listing, there has been no grading of Areas since the abolition in 1980 of the additional status of the more important examples as 'outstanding'. The grand total is now some 5500 (at the last count late in 1981) and between them they bring under control probably as many if not more buildings as are covered by listing. The historic cores of great cities such as Bath, York and Chichester are so designated, as is much of the City of Westminster and 28 per cent of the City of London. As it is not a statutory necessity that areas should be centred on listed buildings or indeed buildings at all, designation has been used to cover historic landscapes as in Staffordshire. There is no reason either why the Areas should be historic in the traditional sense. Both Silver End in Essex, built between the Wars by Crittalls (the window manufacturers), to house their workers, and Kerry Avenue in Harrow with houses by Gerald Lacoste and Douglas Wood, are now Conservation Areas. So are planned townscapes like Hampstead Garden Suburb.

Sanctions within a Conservation Area are mixed. Apart from the non-architectural control which includes the necessity to apply for permission to lop, top or fell any tree over 3in in diameter, there is no veto over internal works except where the building is also listed. Permission is not required to demolish any structure under 115 cubic metres in size or a building affected by a Demolition Order or operative Clearance Order under the 1957 Housing Act. As with listing, redundant Anglican churches are also exempt. Generally speaking, however, permission to demolish a building within a Conservation Area is required. Even though the majority of such buildings will be unlisted this consent is termed 'listed building consent' which leads to understandable confusion with the procedure for statutorily protected listed buildings. Even if you possess 'LBC' for demolition in a Conservation Area you need another explicit consent if the building is subsequently listed. The confusion is the greater because the criteria for a grant of consent are different. Where the intrinsic merit of a listed building can be sufficient to give it protection – and the quality of a replacement building can be considered irrelevent – permission to demolish an unlisted building should be judged in the light of the effect it would have on the character of the Conservation Area. The Department specifically advises planning authorities not to entertain such applications without details of any plans to redevelop. Damaging alterations such as the isolated pebble-dashing of units within an otherwise unaltered terrace are not brought under control except where the local authority has obtained the permission of the Minister to declare what is termed an 'Article 4' Direction. This has the effect of suspending the rights of 'permitted development' given under the General Development Order.

Under such a direction loose control can become very tough. A relaxation in the GDO in 1980 which allowed domestic extensions of up to 15 per cent to be exempt from planning control did not apply to existing Conservation Areas. However, where permission for such an extension within such a Conservation Area has been refused, compensation can be payable. Conservation Area Advisory Committees, through which residents and professionals advise planning authorities on the various applications received, can widen the democratic involvement in decision making.

It would be quite unfair to give the impression that all is controls within Conservation Areas. Schemes of enhancement (the undergrounding of telegraph wires, the painting and cleaning of façades and so on) together with the prevention of overdevelopment by preserving the character of the area all maintain or increase the value of property. Benefits as well as controls also accrue from listing but it is to the latter that we must now return for examination in some detail.

Whenever a listed building is the subject of a proposal to demolish in whole or part, to extend or to alter in a way that would affect its 'character', application must be made for 'listed building consent'. Before 1968 only proposals that 'seriously' affected the character were subject to control. The coverage is now much wider. 'Character' is a deliberately nebulous phrase. Works of basic maintenance are generally exempt but cleaning external surfaces need not be. Works of repair as a rule don't require consent, except where there is any element of rebuilding. Small extensions, under 70 cubic metres or 15 per cent of the volume of the property up to a maximum of 115 cubic metres, and new boundary walls which constitute 'permitted development' for the purposes of the General Development Order and do not require planning permission are not permitted without consent where the building is listed. ('Change of Use' requires planning permission but not listed building consent.) However, this extra limitation on freedom does bring with it the right in certain circumstances to compensation. This may be payable by the local planning authority where listed building consent has been refused for the alteration or extension of a listed building and the changes would otherwise be 'permitted'. For compensation to be payable, however, the case must have reached the Secretary of State – for a refusal of consent or a grant subject to conditions – and the aggrieved person must be able to show that the value of his interest in the land is less than it would have been had listed building consent been granted. A DoE consul-

Woodperry House, Oxfordshire. The application in 1984, the second such, to remove the painting of Westminster Abbey from the overmantel to allow its sale was refused by the planning authority which held the painting to be a fixture and important to the character of the house. (Photo, E. Michael Price)

tation paper in 1986 proposed to abolish this provision. Consent is required for the demolition of any structure, including statues and urns, within the curtilage, although not when built after 1948. As applications for listed building consent do not attract any fee, unlike those for planning permission, at least the applicant is not out of pocket for wishing to improve the appearance of his property. Where the development is of a larger scale and requires planning permission as well as listed building consent, two separate applications must be made and a fee is payable on the former.

Consent is required for internal works to listed buildings. The precise extent of the control is a matter for the local planning authority and does not extend to moveable features. Fixtures, works to which require consent, do include, on the basis of past cases, paintings incorporated into overmantels and historic wallpaper, spice cupboards and bread ovens within fireplaces and pieces of sculpture fixed to the wall or ground and designed for the setting. An important example of the latter arose over the Midland Hotel in Morecambe, Lancashire, a Grade II* composition designed between the Wars by Oliver Hill. In 1980 application was made to remove a large piece of sculpture designed by Eric Gill, for re-siting in the V & A, which promised to supply a replica for the hotel. As the Gill sculpture was regarded as an integral part of this important building, listed building consent was refused. Permission had earlier been given for the sculpture to be removed on temporary loan for exhibition purposes at the Hayward Gallery.

It would take a bold and oppressive local authority to dictate internal colour schemes except where the building is particularly important – but external colour where the building is part of a wider group can be covered. One of the most famous cases in this connection arose around 1970 when the local authority took enforcement action to ensure that the front doors on the Royal Crescent at Bath, one of the greatest set pieces of townscape in the country, were painted the same tone. This control over the minutiae contrasts with the weaker say over the setting. Although the authorities are empowered to protect such settings in the general planning process, this is difficult. Permission is not required, for example, to dig a mine under a listed building even if this results in its breaking its back. The Albert Docks in Liverpool, the largest agglomeration of Grade I structures in the country, depend a great deal for their effect on the Venetian combination of buildings and water. And yet the removal of the latter would not require consent.

Applications for listed building consent must initially be lodged with the local planning authority. Except where the proposal involves alterations only to the interior of Grade II buildings, all applications must be advertised in the local paper and by a notice placed on the site. Objections or representations made as a result are taken into account. Some local authorities ensure that any proposal which attracts representations must be determined by the elected Members and not left to the Chairman to decide between meetings. In Scotland all applications affecting listed buildings are published in the Edinburgh Gazette and in at least one local paper. In England and Wales wherever there is an element of demolition (an important court case of May 1981 gave demolition a very broad definition including the removal of courses of brick and tile to allow an extension) six bodies must be consulted and their views taken into account. These are the Ancient Monuments Society, the Society for the Protection of Ancient Buildings, the Georgian Group, the Victorian Society, the Council for British Archaeology, and the Royal Commission on Historical Monuments (see Useful Addresses). The latter's job is to record threatened structures but the role of the other five is to state the case for retention; in effect to act as defence counsel for the building. From 1 October 1984 the Historic Buildings and Monuments Commission has to be informed of all applications that affect Grade I and II* buildings and those Grade II structures which have been grant-aided by Central Government. Many authorities also consult the local amenity societies, which are coordinated by the Civic Trust in the same way as local archaeological societies are centralized through the Council for British Archaeology. Should the proposal be benign, it of course receives warm support.

The many excellent conservation teams maintained by county councils are also consulted by some districts. In Scotland the statutory consultees are the Scottish Civic Trust and the Scottish Architectural Heritage Society (formerly the Scottish Georgian Society). Each application is meant to be determined within two months. However, where this target has not been met the only sanction open to the applicant is an appeal to the Minister against 'non-determination'. Applications not determined within the statutory period are deemed to have been refused. If the local authority declares itself 'minded to grant consent' for the works proposed, except in cases of alteration to Grade II buildings which have not received grant aid, the application is referred, together with the representations received, to the Secretary of State, who decides whether the issue should be thrashed out at a Public Inquiry. At present all LBC applications in Scotland have to be referred to Edinburgh. Unfortunately it is not unknown for the Department to take six months to decide whether or not to hold an Inquiry and then a further six months or more to come to a decision. The HBMC Investigators can offer informal criticism but these have no sanction, and if the Secretary of State does not 'call in' the case for his own determination he lets it go through unchallenged. Where cases come to the Secretary of State either through the 'call-in' procedure or through appeal against the decision of a local planning authority, he can consider the case on the basis of written representations, but normally where the issues and/or the building is important there will be a Public Inquiry. Although structured like a court of law with the consecutive presentation of evidence, rights to cross-question, and in most cases the presence of lawyers, the Inspectors, who chair the proceedings and make recommendations to the Secretary of State, generally value relative informality. Questions from the audience are welcome. The large-scale and apparently interminable Public Inquiry can attract attention but most of them last half a day or a day and the decision is handed down within a matter of months rather than years. (Although some planning appeals are decided on the spot by the Inspectors they can only make recommendations in the case of listed building consent applications and the decision comes after the closing of the proceedings from the Department.) Council decisions are nearly always defended at inquiries by officers rather than councillors.

A guide to the procedure at Public Inquiries is published by the DoE. It is useful to remember, particularly given the presence of lawyers and the heat which can be generated, that no privilege attaches to the proceedings and that the rules of libel and slander apply. There is no appeal against the Secretary of State's decision but it can be challenged within six weeks on legal grounds by application to the High Court.

In coming to a decision on proposals to alter or extend, the Secretary of State and the local planning authority have regard to the acceptability of the proposal in relation to the 'character' of the listed building. Some authorities will do their best to ensure that professionally qualified persons experienced in the care of historic buildings prepare and execute the plans. In cases of demolition the Department takes the view that there is a presumption in favour of retention and the onus is on the applicants to prove why that should be set aside. Where the building is disused the Secretary of State expects evidence to be shown that genuine efforts have been made to dispose of the property, preferably freehold or on a long lease. The presumption is rarely set aside where the building is shown to be capable of 'beneficial use'. As with planning permission, decisions cannot be influenced, in theory, by alternative proposals for the site, by a threatened loss of value or 'bad neighbour' problems.

Almost any conditions can be attached to a grant of consent, provided that they are relevant and reasonable. Since 1980 there has been a standard time limit of five years. Scheduled monument consents have the same life. Buildings remain listed even after a grant of consent to demolish and the listing is only expunged by the act of demolition. Another standard condition grants the Royal Commission on Historical Monuments one month in which to record the building. Demolition can be accepted in principle but postponed, where there are proposals to redevelop, until planning permission has been granted and a contract for the redevelopment signed. Directions can be made about the salvage of features of interest but the Secretary of State is unwilling to direct the details of such efforts as a third party (antique dealer, public museum, etc.) should not benefit financially from a planning decision.

Where consent has been refused, or granted subject to conditions, the owner of the land may serve a notice requiring the authority to purchase his interest in the land. This Compulsory Purchase Order in reverse is known as a Purchase Notice. If the local authority resists and cannot find a statutory undertaker willing to stand in as purchaser, then the Secretary of State will decide the issue. The determining factor is whether or not the land has 'become incapable of reasonably beneficial use in its existing state'. The Department may, rather than confirm the notice, grant listed building consent.

As the listed building consent procedures rely on the strength of law, illegal action can bring serious consequences. Penalties for works carried out without consent are – on summary conviction – imprisonment of up to three months or a fine not exceeding £1000 or both and, on indictment, imprisonment of up to twelve months or a fine or both. There have been fines of £10 000. A case which attracted considerable publicity, the demolition, allegedly by mistake, of Monkspath Hall, Solihull in Birmingham resulted early in 1981 in a fine on the bulldozer driver of £1500 and on the company, of which he was a director, of £2000. Late in 1984 the local authority was still trying to ensure that the farmhouse was rebuilt by suing the company's insurers for £300 000 in open court. The private prosecution brought on behalf of the Society for the Protection of Ancient Buildings in 1981, pre-empting a similar move by the Secretary of State himself, following the demolition of the Grade II* listed Welby Almshouses at Denton in Lincolnshire, resulted in a fine of £1000 and the award against the owner of £2000 in costs. The lesser offence of causing damage to a listed building has attracted, since 1967, a maximum fine of £100. However, there is at present a weakness in the law which means that the carrying out of unauthorized works to listed buildings is not an arrestable offence. In such circumstances the local authority has to take out an injunction by starting a 'relator action'.

Parallel to the criminal process of prosecution, local authorities have enforcement powers to secure the physical removal of the offending alterations or extensions. But these are rather cumbersome. North Hertfordshire District Council itself had to apply to the Secretary of State for listed building consent to remove additions put on without permission at 106 High Street, Codicote. Clearly where complete demolition has taken place, enforcement requiring complete reconstruction seems both draconian and counterproductive. And difficult too: when Elgin Lodge in Melton Mowbray was taken down the local authority took the view that consent to remove the dismantled materials from the site was not required, and once these had disappeared reconstruction using the original fabric became impossible. In the case of 48 Arlesey Road, Ickleford, Hertfordshire where a sixteenth-century timber-framed building had been completely reconstructed, although the owner was fined £100 on two counts, the Secretary of State rejected the subsequent Enforcement Notice in 1978 on the grounds that it was quite impossible to recapture the original character and fabric of the building. The situation has been alleviated somewhat by the Local Government and Planning (Amendment) Act of 1981 which allows local authorities to require works to be carried out to mitigate the effect of illegal action if restoration is impossible. This may mean the planting of a suitably placed creeper or a fence to conceal the damage.

Where there is an element of danger, the serving of a Dangerous Structure Notice through the local magistrates court inevitably speeds up the process. Under the Housing and Planning Act of 1986 the previous right to demolish after the serving of a DSN without listed building consent has been abolished. A 1980 High Court decision (involving 57–62 High Street, Stroud) has made it clear that local authorities should try to ensure that the danger is removed by methods other than demolition if this is at all possible – and magistrates orders do specify that the danger can be alleviated by repair as much as by dismantling. The exact wording is 'take down, repair or otherwise secure'. The local authority can charge the owner for removing the 'danger' where it has to act itself. In default of payment a legal incubus can attach to the property possibly creating difficulties on resale. Where the local authority is the owner of the building in question, only the Secretary of State can act to halt hasty action.

The law has stings in its tail other than to combat contravention. These are the powers resident with the local planning authority to secure action when listed buildings are in disrepair. Under Section 101 of the 1971 Town and Country Planning Act (Section 97 in the equivalent Act of 1972 for Scotland) urgent but cheap works can be carried out on unoccupied listed buildings or on structures within a Conservation Area (where the Secretary of State shall direct). The Housing and Planning Bill of 1986 proposed to allow Notices in respect of the unoccupied sections of otherwise occupied structures. The costs can be recovered from the owner but these should be of the order of several hundred pounds and 'the financial circumstances of the owner should be taken into account at the outset'. The so-called Repairs Notice operates under Section 115 (Section 105 in Scotland). This applies to occupied or unoccupied listed buildings but not to unlisted structures within a Conservation Area. Under this provision the county or district council serves a notice on the owner 'specifying the works which they consider reasonably necessary for the proper preservation of the building'. Unlike Section 101, the only means of enforcing the notice is compulsory purchase under Section 114 (Section 104 in Scotland). This has to be confirmed by the Secretary of State and if he is satisfied that the owner has deliberately let the building decay in order to redevelop the site, the local authority may be able to acquire it at a substantially reduced price, together with land necessary for access and the amenity and management of the site. Before serving a Repairs Notice and in anticipation of having to follow through with the CPO some councils make a contract with a third party, such as a building preservation trust or a housing association, which guarantees to take the building off their hands.

The powers of Compulsory Purchase contained in Section 114 cannot be executed cold. They can only follow the serving of a Repairs Notice. It is a rare procedure and the recent success of Braintree District Council in securing a CPO in 1981 on the largely collapsed barn at Coggeshall in Essex (built c.1180) in order to secure its repair was notable as the climax of a long and difficult battle. The Secretary of State has powers of compulsory purchase but he has never taken advantage of them. He has similar powers to serve a Repairs Notice but has only done so in one instance, that of the Grade I Barlaston Hall in Staffordshire. Strong words have been uttered by Ministers where local authorities have neglected properties (for example Hendford Manor, Yeovil and Hylands House, Chelmsford) with the same effect.

There are two areas where the law can be unhelpful when it is intended to re-occupy an empty listed building. Where a property has been the subject of a Closing Order under the Housing Act it is illegal to live in it until a scheme of repairs acceptable to the council has been fully carried out. Moreover, it appears illegal to live in a part of a house which may be in a good condition whilst repairing the remainder. As a result a Closing Order might lead to dereliction, although cottages and houses thus affected can receive grants and as a challenge they are well worth the trouble, provided one is wary of these bureaucratic snares.

The second impediment concerns the inflexible application of the Green Belt laws. Where a replacement structure is to be provided in such a setting local authorities can insist that the existing structure, whether a house, farmhouse or a public house, be demolished unless it is listed. Some local authorities have insisted on the demolition of such a replaced building even if it is in good condition and has changed hands. Yet others have prevented the reoccupation of derelict houses.

None of the information in this chapter relates to buildings owned by the Crown, to churches and chapels in use or to redundant Anglican churches. All three have different procedures although in the first and last cases there is provision for a non-statutory Public Inquiry where the decision of the Secretary of State is not binding and there is no power to subpoena witnesses or award costs.

In this chapter there is no discussion of the various building and fire regulations which can have a significant effect on the appearance of listed buildings: as they are technical matters they are entirely the preserve of the professional. In any case they apply generally to new structures (freestanding or an extension) and only affect standing buildings where an existing situation is to be made worse. Exceptions or 'waivers' can be obtained. The Building Regulations were revised late in 1985.

If in doubt about the extent of the law, do make contact with the Conservation Officer at either District or County level who would be pleased to advise or, in difficult cases, seek professional legal advice.

FURTHER INFORMATION

The Royal Town Planning Institute and the Department of the Environment both publish useful leaflets on aspects of planning.

Cambridgeshire County Council publish an invaluable and regularly updated *Guide to Historic Buildings Law* (revised 1984).

The most recent survey of the law is Roger W. Suddard's *Listed Buildings, the Law and Practice*, Sweet & Maxwell 1982. There is also *Urban Conservation and Historic Buildings: A Guide to Legislation*, Architectural Press 1984.

For details on the law in Scotland see *New Uses for Older Buildings in Scotland*, HMSO 1981, chapter 4.

The Town and Country Planning Association issues a general guide on Conservation Areas and listed buildings.

For more general information see Sir Desmond Heap's *Outline of Planning Law* (eighth edition 1982).

The Architectural Press publish a very useful *Guide to the Building Regulations* (1985).

4 FINANCE

Most historic buildings are in good condition and in productive use. Schemes of repair and conversion are for the most part self-financing and in the more prosperous areas of the country the market for 'period' properties retains a buoyancy seemingly unaffected by the recession. Nevertheless, market forces leave a significant minority of historic buildings stranded and a public subsidy is essential to prime the pump.

The principal source of financial help from central government is that offered by the Historic Buildings & Monuments Commission for England and by the Secretary of State on the advice of the Historic Buildings Councils for Scotland, Wales and Northern Ireland. This system of grants operates through five distinct but complementary tiers which between them protect outstanding secular buildings, places of worship in use, historic towns and Conservation Areas, and scheduled monuments. In all cases the system is in the form of grants rather than loans and there is a refusal to entertain retrospective applications for work already executed.

The first tier (under Section 3A of the National Heritage Act 1983), offering grants to 'Outstanding Secular Buildings' is the most generous. In 1983–84, the final full year of the Historic Buildings Council for England, which preceded the HBMC, the grants offered totalled £8.6 m. This compared with £7.2m from HBMC in 1984–85. Applicants are normally expected to substantiate their application by supplying details of assets and income and there is a presumption against help towards the repair of properties purchased up to four years before the application to discourage those without adequate means taking on buildings which they could not hope to save except through inordinate outside assistance. Applicants can be private, public or corporate.

Money can be given towards the cost of acquisition, the preparation of survey reports and the payment of consultants' fees, but the lion's share goes towards meeting the costs of essential structural repairs.

Works of regular maintenance and decoration are ineligible and inexpensive minor works are unlikely to be considered. Those in receipt of public money are expected to show a willingness to allow public access, although this can be by appointment only and does not affect properties where it is the exterior which is the most important feature. Hotels and theatres are 'open' in the normal course of events.

There are provisions for the repayment of grants if the property is resold soon afterwards to provide some insurance against those anxious to make a killing at the public's expense. Generally, however, the object of the system is to save the building and there is no resentment if, as a result, a private individual makes a suitable profit. Now that the general level of grants is only 40 per cent of cost (albeit the total cost including VAT and professional fees) the likelihood of profiteering is remote. (Local Authorities generally have to make do with 25 per cent). The range of buildings grant-aided is very enterprising. The year 1983–84 saw provision for the first time of funds for large-scale engineering structures. One of the projects promised grant aid in 1984 was the reconstruction of the famous Penguin Pool at Dudley Zoo in the West Midlands designed by Lubetkin in 1936–37, and in the same year the likewise modern New Hall of the Royal Horticultural Society (1928) was offered £112 000. Recipients have included cemetery chapels, railway stations, windmills, mills, wallpaintings and theatres as well as country houses, eighteenth-century terraces and early cottages.

In comprehensiveness the grant aid system is as liberal as that of the listing programme and the definition of 'outstanding' is hidebound by neither conventional wisdom nor the grading of the building in the statutory lists – some beneficiaries being Grade II only. Nevertheless paucity of funds has meant that the mass of listed buildings, which are Grade II and not 'outstanding' by any national criteria, are not assisted. On a number of occasions where Grade IIs have been helped they are upgraded to II*.

The second tier offers protection to outstanding buildings in use as places of worship, and is beyond the scope of this book.

The third tier covers the so-called 'Town Scheme', a term at once banal and confusing. Under these Schemes, key buildings within defined areas in historic settlements – be they villages, towns or cities – are earmarked for local and central government assistance in the execution of structural, and normally external, repairs. Under such Schemes, of which there were 189 by 31 March 1985, 25 per cent of the costs comes from central government, 25 per cent from either the district and/or the county council, and 50 per cent from the owner. Since 1980 the running of some of the Schemes has been entrusted to local authorities and applications should be addressed to them even where it is the HBMC which retains administrative control. Town Schemes grew principally out of that created in Bath in 1974 to deal with the integrated repair of its many outstanding terraces.

A Town Scheme on a massive scale, far larger than all others, is that administered through the Edinburgh New Town Conservation Committee, established to protect the Georgian New Town of 1770–1830. In 1979 it received around £250 000 per year from central and local government to be handed out in grants, decided on the basis of the rateable value of the property and on the nature of the repair. In order to encourage people to avoid superficial repair the Commission tends to give a 60 per cent grant for small repairs but an 85 per cent grant towards comprehensive works.

The fourth tier deals with Conservation Areas where the amount offered in 1984–85 was £4.07m. Prior to 1981 only the tenth or so of Conservation Areas designated as 'outstanding' were eligible but now there is no such limitation. Such Section 10 grants are available to private individuals, voluntary bodies or local authorities and are normally 25 per cent. These grants are complementary to the Town Scheme grants in that they can finance conversion as well as repair. In places like Barnard Castle in Durham and Barnack in Cambridgeshire, where the roofscapes depend for their character on the re-use of traditional materials block grants have been made through local authorities, in these two cases for the renewal of stone tiling. Less conventionally attractive areas in industrial cities have also benefitted. Outstanding in this connection is the conservation of the Lace Market area of Nottingham. In 1981–82 the largest single conservation grant went to Liverpool (£257 265) followed closely by Newcastle (£246 914).

Fifthly, there are the grants to scheduled Ancient Monuments. These can be generous – the barn at Leigh Court, Hereford and Worcester received £500 000 in 1984–85.

Money from central government goes towards historic buildings through a number of other channels. The allocation of the HBMC covers not only grants it offers to outside bodies (which totalled £17.3m to historic buildings in 1984–85) but also the cost of maintaining the 400 ancient monuments directly in its care. The State now provides 60% of the costs of the Redundant Churches Fund which was allocated a maximum of £6 million with an added inflation factor in the quinquennium beginning 1 April 1984 and now cares for 200 disused anglican churches. The National Heritage Memorial Fund established in April 1980 closed 1982–83 with over £26 million, having spent or promised £10 million in that year for specific projects. In 1985 it received a special grant of £25 million to 'save' Kedleston, Weston and Nostell Priory. The successor to the ill-starred National Land Fund, the NHMF, like its predecesor, is funded by Government but is able to treat the grants-in-aid as capital. Its brief is to assist others to purchase nationally important buildings, works of art and tracts of land for the nation. Since 1980 donations by the Fund have included £30 000 towards the repair of the bells at Durham Cathedral, £86 000 towards the repair of the great Neo-Classical house of Castle Coole in Northern Ireland, £50 000 towards the restoration of Captain Scott's ship the *Discovery*, £10 000 towards the purchase of Blackpool Grand Theatre, a £10 000 loan to help in the public purchase of fifteenth century Kings House in Salisbury Close, £20 850 to secure a portrait of the architect Pugin for the Palace of Westminster, £6250 to Cheltenham Art Gallery as a contribution towards the purchase of furniture designed by Voysey, £1m towards the endowment of Canons Ashby House in Northamptonshire now in the hands of the National Trust, £50 000 towards restoration work at the eighteenth-century landscaped garden at Painshill Park in Surrey, £12 300 towards the purchase of the Manchester 'Spanish and Portuguese' Synagogue for conversion

into a Jewish Museum, £500 000 towards the restoration of the Pier at Clevedon, Somerset, and half that amount towards the repair of the great Victorian church of All Souls, Haley Hill, Halifax which would certainly have been demolished but for this generosity.

The definition of 'heritage' is catholic, as is evidenced by the grants for the raising of the *Mary Rose*, the purchase of the manuscript of Tennyson's *In Memoriam*, the conservation of films at the National Film Archive, the purchase for the British Museum of the greatest work by the master clockmaker, Thomas Tompion, and the saving for the National Library of Scotland of the papers of Field Marshal Earl Haig.

Government monies also help more indirectly. The Manpower Services Commission has underwritten the labour costs in a number of projects, including the conversion of Middleton Hall in Warwickshire to provide a Conservation Centre. Supervision is essential but given the labour-intensive nature of repair work MSC subsidies might prove indispensable.

The Sports Council can assist in conversion to sports use and has sponsored a book on the potential of disused churches in this regard. The grants offered by the Countryside Commission, Tourist Board and COSIRA are explained on p. 158.

There are other programmes within the Department of the Environment remit: Derelict Land Grants were extended early in 1982 to cover the 'clearance of obsolete buildings' and although it is very alarming that such grants can only go towards the cost of demolition rather than conversion, in at least one case money from this source has been directed towards the repair of an impressive listed viaduct to provide a dramatic footpath. Liverpool and the London Docklands have benefited in particular from the considerable monies allocated under the Inner Urban Areas Act 1978, but it is the Housing Programme which overwhelms all others in its size. Through its funding of the Housing Corporation, the source of money for the many housing associations, but above all through its programme of Home Improvement Grants and 'enveloping' the Department has had more effect, both good and bad, on the appearance of the average British street than all its self-consciously conservationist policies can have hoped to achieve.

The difference between Home Improvement Grants and 'enveloping' is strictly that between functional, largely internal, and external, largely cosmetic, repairs. The former system is quadripartite. 'Improvement Grants' are for major works or the provision of additional homes through conversion. Houses over a certain rateable value are ineligible (in 1986 the figure was £225 outside Greater London, £400 inside), although these limits do not apply if the building falls within a Housing Action Area or the occupant is disabled. The grants are discretionary and there are limits on the eligible expense (in priority cases £13 800 in Greater London and £10 200 elsewhere) although higher limits may be allowed for listed buildings. 'Intermediate Grants' are for putting in standard amenities (inside toilet, bath, sink, washbasin, hot and cold water) plus associated repairs and replacements. These grants are mandatory and there is a statutory right to a grant even if there is no wish to enjoy all the amenities. 'Repairs Grants' are for houses constructed before 1919 in need of substantial and structural repair, to the roof, walls, floors or foundations. Routine maintenance work (such as rewiring) or the replacement of worn fixtures do not qualify. As before, ineligibility follows a rise above a certain rateable value and the grants are normally discretionary although if a 'Repairs Notice' under the 1957 Housing Act has been served, they become mandatory. There are eligible expense limits although again these are higher for listed buildings. The final category 'Special Grants' covers the introduction of standard amenities and means of escape in houses in multiple occupation, and associated repairs and replacements. These go to landlords, not tenants, and are discretionary. The percentage of grant varies. As a rule applications submitted in the Spring, early in the financial year, are the best bet.

The grants cannot be used for improving a second home or holiday cottage and if the improved property is sold within five years of the receipt of the grant other than to another owner occupier the money may have to be repaid. It is however possible to pay back grants with interest, voluntarily. Non-residential buildings to be converted to dwellings are eligible but the grants are less generous. In DIY rehabilitation only the cost of materials and other people's labour can be assisted. If a grant is refused there is the right of appeal to the DoE, Welsh Office or Scottish Office as appropriate, but the process can take several months. It should always be borne in mind that where major improvements or conversions have been carried out the rates are likely to be raised at the next revaluation. Further information can be gathered from leaflets obtainable from local authorities and from the DoE in England, the Welsh Office, Scottish Office and Northern Ireland Housing Executive. This further enquiry is strongly advised, as there are regional variations. Although the pro-gramme is funded very largely by central Government applications are made to, and decisions handed down by, the local authority. The Government published a Green Paper in 1985 proposing an extensive remodelling of the Housing grants system.

Compared with the £13.5 m given by the HBMC in 1983/84 the Housing Programme offers a staggering infusion of public money (£900m in 1984/84 and £740m in 1984/85). Whilst it prolongs the life of many buildings of interest which would otherwise be lost, the alterations financed can be architecturally inappropriate. Where the conservation officer works closely with the housing department such changes, many of them needless, can be avoided. There have been unfortunate cases of unnecessary and inappropriate renewal of windows, the rendering of brick façades and the lowering of ancient floors.

The concept of 'enveloping' reverses the equation: it is a purely architectural, or if you will, cosmetic, improvement consisting of the external repair and redecoration of complete streets of privately-owned dwellings, financed by local government for the most part with Central Government money. 'Enveloping' was anticipated in 1974 with the concept of the Housing Action Area and pioneered particularly in Birmingham and Macclesfield. The present scheme was launched in October 1982 and is limited to Housing Action Areas (which at the time covered some 155 000 homes). All schemes have to be approved by the DoE.

Local authorities are not of course just ciphers for Whitehall money. Finances raised from the rates are also available. Indeed, so is the non-rateable income represented by municipal lotteries. £92 000 from this source was given to the Medway Heritage Centre Trust to form a museum within the disused church of St Mary's, Chatham. The rather discredited process of 'Planning Gain' can bring even greater rewards. Under this, a private party is granted planning permission to develop a particularly valuable site on condition that he agrees to donate some of the profits to a communal or charitable purpose specified by the planning authority. Christchurch Spitalfields has benefited from such a deal.

Payments in kind are more common. In Bury St Edmunds in 1983 developers were given the former library in the centre of the city (itself adapted from a Corn Exchange) for conversion to shops provided that they constructed a new library at a cost of £1 million on a less central site.

The Local Authorities (Historic Buildings) Act of 1962 gave District and County councils the power to make grants or loans towards the repair of historic buildings. Buildings of all types are eligible, as indeed are unlisted properties. Hampshire has led the shire counties in generosity in recent years, but an increasing number of local authorities have no money at all to offer. Warwickshire County Council concentrates entirely on loans which can be interest-free and are repayable after five years. Chester, in so many ways a model, established a Conservation Fund in 1970, the first of its kind. It was boosted annually in 1980, 1981 and 1982 by £200 000 a year, the equivalent of more than a penny rate and unlike most Council budgets it accrues interest and does not have to be spent in any one financial year. The planned eighteenth-century town of Whitehaven in Cumbria has also benefited greatly from a penny conservation rate. 'Industrial Improvement areas', of which some 140 have been designated since 1978, offer some small if double-edged assistance to landcapes dotted with rundown mills. Cleaning, painting and repairing mills within such Areas can be assisted but so can demolition.

The growth of Building Preservation Trusts to the point where they now have their own newsletter *Preservation in Action* owes much to funding by local authorities and even more to the secondment of staff. Although some trusts pre-date the Second World War, notably those covering Bath (founded in 1934), Blackheath (founded 1938) and the Cambridgeshire Cottage Improvement Society also of 1938, spectacular growth followed on the foundation of the Architectural Heritage Fund (see Useful Addresses) in May 1976. A child of European Architectural Heritage Year and sponsored jointly by the private sector and Government, the Fund's main purpose is to provide cheap working capital to supplement the reserves of local preservation trusts. The assistance is in the form of loans at the interest rate of 5 per cent which normally cover less than 50 per cent of the cost of a project and are repayable after two years. For such a 'revolving fund' repayment is crucial so that the limited capital can be ploughed back. Most BPT's also operate on the revolving principle and sell on newly restored properties guaranteeing long-term protection of the building through the use of covenants. Enterprises, such as the creation of museums, where there is no intention to resell, can be assisted although a surety for repayment from a bank, local authority or some comparable corporate body is then required. The number of BPT's now exceeds 60. The year 1985 saw the launch of the British Building Preservation Trust, the first to take a nationwide remit and 1984, the first one in Wales (to cover West Glamorgan). On rare occasions existing owners have been persuaded to offload a burdensome property without charge and with a very useful lump sum. The £50 000 from the Post Office which accompanied the donation of Ladybellegate House, Longsmith Street, Gloucester (now fully repaired) to Gloucester Historic Buildings Limited (set up by the local Civic Trust) is a notable example. Similar relief at being able to free itself from the responsibility of an unwanted but nationally important building led British Rail to give £250 000 towards the repair of Liverpool Road Station, Manchester, listed Grade I and the first railway building in the world.

Private charitable trusts have been generous to BPTS and other conservation projects. The Pilgrim, Carnegie, Monument, Dulverton, Manifold, Rowntree and Chase Charitable Trusts stand out. The Leche Trust specializes in the repair of eighteenth-century architecture and artefacts, complementing the Cleary Fund of the Georgian Group, relaunched in 1984. Others have particular local specializations. A full list of the 2400 grant-making bodies, which between them have a total income of over £482m, is available from the latest issue of the *Directory of Grant-Making Trusts* published in 1985 by the Charities Aid Foundation (48 Pembury Road, Tonbridge, Kent TN9 2JD). It is very important to remember, however, that such trusts cannot assist in the repair of privately occupied houses which are not open to the public.

One final source, and a much neglected one, needs to be mentioned: this is the EEC and more particularly the European Regional Development Fund. Schemes assisted have included the conversion of the eighteenth-century Judges' Residence at Lancaster into a museum and the adaptation of a chapel at Llandovery to form a theatre and craft exhibition centre. A small contribution has been made to the costs of a feasibility study on ways of saving the West Pier at Brighton.

In 1984, for the first time in recent years, the tax regime recognized the special status and the peculiar needs of listed buildings and scheduled ancient monuments. As from 1 June 1984 all works of alteration and extension to such buildings, including structures within the curtilage, became zero-rated for VAT where identical works on an unlisted building continued to be taxed at the standard rate of 15 per cent, provided the listed building consent had been obtained. The substantial reconstruction of a listed building, after a fire for example, as long as it is followed by sale or lease for 21 years or more, is also zero-rated. The developer must still normally prove that 60 per cent or more of the cost of the work excluding fees and purchase price is on 'approved alterations'. The ghost of Kafka alone can explain why VAT is still levied on the repair and maintenance of listed buildings, the duty of a responsible citizen, but at least the Treasury has now granted an explicit concession. Some rating authorities are also prepared to acknowledge the drawbacks of living in a structure which the State dictates must be kept. In one Wiltshire town the owners of ancient buildings with particularly thick walls have been granted a rate reduction on the grounds that this reduces their available living space.

FURTHER INFORMATION

Housing Grants, A Guide to Improvement and other Grants by Nigel Hawkins, is published by the Kogan Press, 120 Pentonville Road, London N1.

Grants for Conservation is published by the North-East Civic Trust, 3 Old Elvet, Durham.

Home Improvement Grants: A Guide for Home Owners, Landlords and Tenants is published by the Department of the Environment, 2 Marsham Street, London SW1P 3EB, free of charge. The DoE also publish a pamphlet entitled 'Insulation against Traffic Noise' which summarizes the grants available to cover such work.

For VAT see VAT leaflet, 708/1/85 *Protected Buildings* and amendment of March 1986, available from Customs and Excise.

---

5 STONE AND FLINT

Stone

There lies in Church Street, Great Bedwyn, Wiltshire one of Britain's more extraordinary private museums. The Stone Museum, run by Ben Lloyd, whose family have been masons for centuries, exists to propound a philosophy as well as a craft. For Ben stonemasons convey primeval truths through their work, in intuitive rejection of the corrupting effect of what he terms 'the priest's language'. He believes the true artist, as the cipher for eternal varieties, must be illiterate. The delightful Ben embarrasses those of a more prosaic turn of mind, yet he serves to remind the world that stone remains the most revered of traditional building materials. Fortunately this is far from a reverence for the deceased. Since 1979 some 50 quarries have opened or re-opened and only a handful have closed. Most important sites have plentiful reserves. There are presently some two hundred member companies in the Stone Federation.

It is true that a common use for the stone extracted is to provide aggregate for mortars and road foundations and that lack of domestic choice is necessitating the import of stone from abroad, particularly France (in itself nothing new). And yet the growing insistence on conservation and particularly the great repair programmes launched by most of Britain's cathedrals have led to the re-opening of long-neglected sites. The quarries at Dunston Hall at Salcombe in Devon, owned by the National Trust, have been reworked for the benefit of Exeter. It is still possible to obtain most of the famous stones – Ham Hill and Blue Lias in Somerset, Carstone in Norfolk, Ketton and Ancaster in the Midlands, Purbeck in Dorset, Grinshill in Shropshire and Kentish Rag in Kent are all still available. Portland and Bath command enormous markets. The demand for Millstone Grit in Yorkshire is so insatiable that those in the market for disused stone-faced mills in recent years have included a number of demolition contractors interested only in salvage.

Stonemasons seem to be in good cheer despite the recession. The numbers are sufficient to support a London Association of Master Stonemasons and a competition for apprentices. The Orton Trust (see Addresses) offers training in the redundant church of that name in Northamptonshire in a scheme first started in 1969. There are plans to expand into a

The Stone Museum founded in the nineteenth century and now at Great Bedwyn, Wiltshire, run by Ben Lloyd

second church at Little Oakley. The Cathedral works Organization (see Addresses) at Chichester, founded in 1965, as well as providing supplies of hydraulic lime (see p. 112) and stone hires out its 40 employees including 20 masons and carvers for restoration and cleaning projects elsewhere. Masons employed for decades on the building of the Anglican Cathedral at Liverpool moved from there to assist in the completion of the Cathedral of St John the Divine in New York. The Standing Joint Committee on Natural Stone (see Addresses) runs a course normally in the spring and autumn on the 'Use of Stone in Buildings' in conjunction with the Geological Museum that is of the greatest interest to laymen, potential clients and practitioners. The 'Men of the Stones' (see Addresses) offers advice on quarries, sculptors and masons. And a more general resource centre together with a museum is promised as part of the National Stone Centre, plans for which were announced in 1983. The presently favoured location for that is Colehill near Wirksworth in Derbyshire (see Addresses). Stonemasons now find themselves alongside the far more modern occupations listed in the *Yellow Pages*, and the Crafts Council (see Useful Addresses) is able to supply a national list.

Cleaning

In turning to the treatment of existing stone buildings, the first consideration should go to cleaning, which is itself very often an essential pre-requisite to

a programme of repair. It would also at first sight seem to be an area where the amateur could save money by tackling the problem himself. However. considerable caution is required.

Firstly, the stone might not need cleaning, particularly in rural areas. The word 'patina', although hackneyed by overuse, is expressive of the magical effects which weathering and time can achieve on stone surfaces. The delicate texturing, the bloom of variegated shades, even the streaking caused by rain, can be very attractive. In classical architecture in particular 'chiarascuro', which emphasizes the recessions and projections of a façade through the effects of light and shade, was highly prized. There are even occasions where the less pleasant coatings of dirt at least have the effect of uniformity, disguising later patching. The previous practice of artificially weathering is frowned upon by one particular school of thought although it is the permanent staining caused by some of the agents including tea, in the case of St. Bartholomew the Great, that invokes opposition as much as any philosophical doubts about the 'dishonesty' of the practice. It is still quite usual to apply cowdung, thinly, to stone, brick and render to imitate ageing. Some planning authorities take the view that listed building consent is required for cleaning and they have refused it where a pristine façade would disrupt a wider group. Cleaning can damage the archaeological evidence presented by a façade, by removing traces of ancient paint and the white residue of a long-lost render. Furthermore, different stones and surfaces require different treatment. The great divide is between the calcareous (principally limestone) and the siliceous (principally sandstone, granite etc.). If it is hard to tell into which category the stone to be cleaned falls or there is reason to suspect that both occur in the same building, these are double reasons for resort to the professional. Even water becomes a danger in untutored hands. Water from the heavens or the earth has the inexorable capacity to enter a building and stimulate decay. Its pernicious effects are merely facilitated if it is applied deliberately to a wall where the joints are weak or where there are concealed ferrous metal cramps or bonding timbers.

Having taken the decision to consult a professional, suitable firms can be suggested by the Stone Cleaning and Restoration Section of the Stone Federation, which will provide free estimates and advice and ensure that the work of its member companies is up to standard. There is a written code of practice. Prior to any cleaning operation the firm will plug cracks and open joints, and protect glazing, rainwater goods and any external light fittings and service ducting. Generally lightning conductors are left in situ during water cleaning. A photographic record of 'before' and 'after' can be a great source of pride where encrusted soot gives way to delicate and varied colouring and is also useful to the historian and the architect. Where particular problems are anticipated a small area on the less visible part of the building can be cleaned first as a controlled experiment.

For limestones and marbles the most common and generally the cheapest method is the use of cold water spray, despite the dangers outlined above. For the less durable stones a fine spray intermittently applied is the safest, followed by the use of light brushes or wooden scrapers. A brown tarry stain can be produced on some limestones but this generally does not endure. Water cleaning can reduce the danger of the build-up of salts within the stone, and it is clearly important to ensure that there are no salts present in any tap water used. Water should not be used too generously and not at all in frosty conditions or where there is any doubt over the capacity of the drainage system to cope.

Steam is now generally limited to tackling localized staining. Channelled by the spout of a kettle it can loosen unwanted blobs of oil or paint but it is a fairly crude method; it can induce caustic soda on the surface, and overuse in a confined space carries the risk of much-increased condensation. Grit blasting, normally dry rather than wet, is controversial. It is used on sandstones but poses clear dangers to any surface tooling and is inadvisable on the more friable blocks where the arrises (or edges) might be vulnerable. There are other obvious dangers, some of which, like the blockage of drains and pipes and the health danger posed to operatives, are the responsibility of the cleaning firm. The further problem of noise is less easily overcome and clients should be forewarned of this and the relatively high cost. The problems posed by dry grit in particular led Alban and Martin Caroe in *Stonework: Maintenance and Surface Repair* (1984) to state unequivocally that 'it should never be used on inhabited domestic property'. Grit holds fewer dangers for the more durable granite, slate and the harder bricks provided they do not have polished surfaces. Even more circumspection is required in chemical cleaning. Certain chemicals are used on sandstone, terracotta and unpolished granites, and against lichen, mosses and graffiti; but there is a strongly advocated consensus that acids are always inappropriate on limestone. Mechanical cleaning through power tools is rarely appropriate on historic buildings. Where it is applied the clean surface is often toned by the application of stone dust. Brushes and scrapes can be less damaging. Where the problem is the cleaning and conservation of particular detailing or the removal of efflorescent salts, special poultices can be prepared. Those employing paper pulp are safe on painted surfaces. The problem of reddening that follows calcination of stone after a fire may be one where aesthetics are better sacrificed to archaeology for such markings provide just one of the pieces in the jigsaw for future historians. The external effects of the recent fire at Westminster Hall are still visible. Bird droppings do not advance the frontiers of scholarship and they damage the building and can impair the health of the occupants. Unfortunately it has been found that the strips of gel placed on horizontal ledges as discouragement can cause staining and only remain effective for a year. Wiring in stainless steel or copper, tensioned to make landing difficult, may be more effective. Bird lime, poison, nets, snares and traps are all banned in the EEC. The distressingly common green stains of copper carbonate induced by rain running on to stone from copper, brass or bronze can be removed with ammonia solution and poulticing, although prior treatment of the metal with lanolin can prevent the problem at source. Similarly, rainwater running from limestone dressings can stain red brickwork with white calcium carbonate. The stains are removable with acid and the cleaned brickwork can be treated with some success with a silicone water-repellent. Salts thrown at a stone surface, particularly during snow clearing operations in the winter, should be removed as soon as possible by repeated damping and wiping. It is hardly ever advisable to cover natural stone with oil gloss paints or any other finish which would trap salts although there is a long tradition in Liverpool and Bath of painting ground floors or door surrounds. Painting stone elevations in any case requires listed building consent. Where it has been done it is a difficult choice between removal and inaction for there is little point in the former if the surface of the stone is also taken off. Where the staining comes from lichens or other biological growth, strips of copper inserted into horizontal coursing joints release a mildly toxic wash over the face of the masonry but as always with copper there is the likelihood of a green stain.

Conservation of stone surfaces

There are four fundamentally avoidable inducements to decay. Firstly, the laying of stone on the wrong bed. The planes can be difficult to detect particularly in limestone but in almost all cases, except on projecting features, blocks should be laid with bedding lines appearing horizontally on the building, even on vertical members such as columns. The alternative, face or cant bedding, is found but it can be costly – a decade ago the nineteenth-century porch and baptistry at the Roman Catholic Cathedral of St Mary in Edinburgh had to be completely demolished because the stones had been laid incorrectly.

Secondly, as a standard although not invariable rule, limestone reacts harmfully with sandstone. Sandstone can even be damaged by the calcium sulphate deriving from lime mortar which creates intractable problems because the alternative of cement mortar brings with it so many disadvantages. The juxtaposition of blocks of different stone is simply avoided by comparison and the repercussions of failing to obey can be quite disproportionately calamitous. Much of the vast repair programme at Gilbert Scott's great church of All Souls Haley Hill, Halifax, which narrowly escaped demolition, results from the disintegration of limestone and sandstone banded together and the crystallization of salts which results as water runs from one to the other. Even where sandstone rubble has provided the core to otherwise limestone columns, chemical reaction has resulted from the penetration of water.

Thirdly, the application of too hard a mortar. This is dealt with on p. 112, although it is always worth repeating the golden rule that the mortar should be less hard than its stone so that the moisture that will inevitably enter the wall will evaporate through the former and not the latter. The role of the mortar is 'sacrificial'.

Fourthly, the age-old practice of inserting iron cramps intended to bind stones together has left a structural time bomb for future generations. Even where these were sheathed in lead asphalt or tar, rust has occurred and with it the extraordinary degree of expansion which has split the stone. The problem is the more frustrating because many of the cramps were structurally superfluous. Where they are not, modern practice is to replace them (after detection by X-ray or mine-detector) with non-corrosive materials, such as copper or stainless steel. On many stone buildings small irregularly placed blocks indicate where stone has been cut out to get to the hidden cramps. The use of dove-tailed surface cramps in slate on coping stones is without chemical hazard.

The damaging effects of water, frost, chemicals and crystallizing (and expanding) salts, which lead to discoloration at the least, and complete 'blowing' of the surface at the worst, are much more difficult to tackle. Clearly the individual house-owner has no control over pollution or the weather. Statues can be protected during the winter, as they are abroad, and on some National Trust properties by hibernation in boxes built around them, but this is far less practical for decorative sculpture on a building. Even where this option is feasible the National Trust counsels strongly against the use of straw and tarpaulin or any material which absorbs water and can freeze in contact with the stone.

Where stone is showing signs of decay a number of preservative techniques are available. The oldest is the regular application of limewash, greatly beloved by the SPAB (Society for the Protection of Ancient Buildings). It is not generally speaking suitable for sandstone but is common on limestone and lime-based plasters, on cob and clay lump and on timber-framed structures, particularly the wattle and daub panels. Unlike modern alternatives limewash is clearly visible. It can, through the addition of pigments, be translated into a number of colours but the standard appearance is off-white and it is normally applied regardless of constructional differentiation between materials. For example, it goes equally on to a shell and any stone tracery or quoining, thus tending to cancel out the contrast of colour and texture. Limewash is not obtainable commercially and has to be slaked in a metal bucket or tank from quicklime and tallow or produced directly from putty lime. The chemical reaction is

Wentworth Old Church, Yorkshire. A dramatic
illustration of the effect of crystallizing salts. (Photo,
Christopher Dalton)

violent and great care must be taken. The recipe and guidance as to the slight difference between limewash for internal and external use is obtainable from the SPAB, which publishes a well illustrated leaflet (see p. 43). Coatings of slaked lime are used to repair small cavities and the use of lime poultices and lime water is particularly associated with Professor Robert Baker and his conservation work on the West Front of Wells Cathedral. Generally speaking this involves poulticing for up to three weeks followed by the application of lime water in up to 40 coatings. The topmost surface is composed of a sacrificial 'shelter coat'.

More modern water-repellents and consolidants have evoked fierce controversies, none more so than the silane-based preservatives on which the SPAB has

urged extreme caution. As with timber, epoxy resins are used to grout cracks while resin spot fixings injected by hyperdermic syringe can re-secure loose detailing. Laminations can be cross-stitched using epoxy mortar, pins and wire. As with wood the uppermost surfaces of projecting cornices and architraves have long been protected by the addition of lead flashings.

There will of course be occasions where decay has gone so far that more drastic constructional methods will be advocated by those in favour of a complete facelift. John Piper in his famous (September) 1947

Famous Romanesque sculptures re-erected in the eighteenth century in Herefordshire as the Shobdon Arches now show the devastating effect of unarrested decay

Queen's College, Oxford (Grade I). The pedimental sculpture designed by Sir James Thornhill was completely replaced in 1982 by a replica. Was this justified? (Photo, John Ashdown)

articles in *The Architectural Review* first coined the phrase 'pleasing decay' and there are certainly occasions where to replace is to destroy the poetic character that the centuries have wrought. At Wentworth Old Church, Yorkshire, owned by the Redundant Churches Fund, the Fund was able to take advantage of the nave walls being no longer loadbearing to consolidate rather than to replace, retaining the shell as a *locus classicus* of the devastating effect caused by the crystallization of salts. There are precious examples of carved stonework such as the Shobdon Arches in Herefordshire where the conservation problem cannot possibly be solved by replacement and might as equally be answered by relocation in a museum. The alternative of removal and replacement by a replica is a solution not just reserved to cathedrals. In 1982 the pedimental sculpture at Queen's College, Oxford, designed by Thornhill, was completely renewed although the fragments of the original were preserved by the

College. The City Council did not request an application for listed building consent. There are cases where the comprehensive replacement of non-decorative facings in natural hewn stone of correct colour and texture would be appropriate. In small buildings such as the lock-up at Cirencester where the surface has failed stones can be turned through 180° so that the inner becomes the outer face although needless to say this can only be carried out once.

The alternative to real stone is the artificial or reconstituted counterpart. The use of scagliola from the early sixteenth century (to convey the illusion of marble) and of Coade stone from the eighteenth century have provided a tradition for such substitutes. The latter has shown a remarkable capacity for endurance, normally failing through the rusting of any internal armature rather than through disintegration of the surface. Nowadays the 'stones' composed of crushed stone, cement, bonding and waterproofing agents are cast in moulds from a stone master. They are not necessarily cheaper; they may shrink more than natural stone and are normally limited in use to the replacement of decorative rather

The lock-up at Cirencester, Gloucestershire where it was suggested that the decayed stones be turned through 180°. (Photo, Corinium Museum)

'Bellies' on stone buildings can be original and intended as on this Welsh farmhouse in Powys

than loadbearing features, especially as the average thickness is four inches.

Rather than replace complete blocks with natural or artificial stone it is possible to cut back the surface prior to building it up again with special crushed stone mortars, or what used to be termed 'plastic stone'. As a patching operation it is sometimes referred to as 'dentistry'; it is not suitable where the surface in question will be exposed to severe weather. It is very different from the application of cement, which never weathers satisfactorily and can become completely detached. In a similar category but philosophically more selfconscious is the technique of tile repairs advocated by the SPAB, particularly in its early years where the cutback area is filled by horizontally laid tiles which are either left exposed or given several layers of limewash (see p. 37). Bricks are an alternative. The aim is to ensure that there is no deceit in disguising new as old and to give the completed surface an attractive unevenness. GRC and GRP (glass-reinforced cement, i.e. fibreglass and

plastic respectively) have served as substitutes for
many other materials besides stone; the decorative
panels on Tower Bridge are now in GRP as is the
ornate early Georgian porch at 21 Queen Anne's
Gate, formerly in wood. So is the spire to Wren's St
James's, Piccadilly, as were the bulbous Hindu
finials at the Brighton Pavilion. The materials are
cheap and light but only time can prove their
capacity to weather and endure, and they have taken
a knock in recent years from the replacement in stone
of the fibreglass finials at the Pavilion.

*SPAB repair techniques. The SPAB feels strongly that the
replacement of historic fabric should not 'sham' the
existing, and advocates the use of tiles in stone repair.
There are certainly historical precedents for harmonious
patching, and extensions, in materials other than the
original as at 'Greyfriars' and the Bell Hotel, Stilton,
Huntingdonshire*

FURTHER INFORMATION

The *Natural Stone Directory* (sixth edition 1985) is available from Ealing Publications, Weir Bank, Bray, Maidenhead, Berks SL6 2ED. This lists the 250 quarries in the UK and Ireland, companies importing foreign stone, masonry training facilities and contains an exhaustive catalogue of stoneworkers and masons. There is also a useful introduction to 'The Stones of Britain' by Francis Dimes.

John Ashurst and Francis Dimes's *Stone in Building, Its Use and Potential Today* was the subject of a limited reprint by the Stone Federation in 1984. Other relevant titles include Alban and Martin Caroe's *Stonework: Maintenance and Surface Repair* (1984), Alec Clifton Taylor and Arch Ireson's *English Stone Building* (Gollancz 1985) and Elaine Leary's *The Building Limestones of the British Isles* (HMSO 1983). An equivalent report on sandstones was published in 1986.

Jane Schofield's broadsheet 'Basic Limewash' was published by the SPAB in 1984 (see Useful Addresses). John Fidler's article on GRP appeared in *Traditional Homes*, January 1986.

ADDRESSES

An exhaustive list of addresses appears in the *Natural Stone Directory*.

Cathedral Works Organization: Terminus Road, Chichester, W. Sussex PO19 2TX, tel. (0243) 86280.

College of Masons: 42 Magdalen Road, Wandsworth, London SW18 3NP, tel. (01) 874-8363.

Dry Stone Walling Association: 1 The Old School, Pant Glas, Oswestry, Shropshire SY10 7HS, tel. (0691) 654019.

Men of the Stones: The Rutlands, Tinwell, Stamford, Lincolnshire.

National Association of Master Letter Carvers: 2A Firbank Place, Englefield Green, Egham, Surrey TW20 0ST.

National Association of Master Masons: Crown Buildings, High Street, Aylesbury, Bucks HP20 1SL, tel. (0296) 34750.

National Stone Centre, Chairman of Study Group: Gordon Michell, 1A The Embankment, Putney, London SW15 1LB.

The Orton Trust: 82 The Walk, Potters Bar, Hertfordshire, tel. (0707) 42716.

Standing Joint Committee on Natural Stones: 82 New Cavendish Street, London W1M 8AD, tel. (01) 580-5588.

Stone Federation: 82 New Cavendish Street, London W1M 8AD, tel. (01) 580-5588.

United Kingdom Institute for Conservation, Stone Section (established 1985). Acting Head: Seamus Hanna: The British Museum, Department of Conservation and Technical Services, London WC1B 3DG.

NOTES

The Geological Museum in Exhibition Road, South Kensington, London SW7 can advise on the identification of stone, and the Building Research establishment at Garston, Watford, Hertfordshire can do the same on their suitability for particular applications. The Victoria and Albert Museum can advise on the conservation of stone sculpture. In 1984 the Beer Stone Quarries in Devon were opened for the first time to the general public, in the summer months. People with a special interest are welcome to visit during the winter, although booking is essential. The quarries have been largely unworked since 1890. Further information is available from: Mrs G.D. Gray, 8 Clinton Rise, Beer, Seaton, Devon EX12 3DZ.

Flint

Flints are hard and comparatively easy to collect. This pair of virtues has led to their use not just in building, mainly in the south and east, but as a whitening agent in the manufacture of pottery, as a source of silica for the production of glass, and as the indispensible element in flintlock guns. The fact that flint is easily split (by hammering at the 'bulb of percussion') facilitated its use in 'knapped' form from *c*.1300, particularly in the 'flushwork' seen on many churches and 'polite' secular structures.

The virtues, however, were not absolute. Although 'knapping' does not impede flint's imperviousness to water, moisture does pose problems with mortaring. Particularly in unknapped flints, the round shape and fairly small size would seem to dictate a hard mortar to counter the tendency of individual flints to fall out. However, the harder the mortar the less it allows the escape of moisture; and as flints are completely resistant to water a fairly soft mortar is recommended to prevent the whole wall becoming an impervious moisture barrier. Nevertheless, the very fact that the earliest flint walls were lime-coated or rendered, and a number along the south coast in the eighteenth and nineteenth centuries were tarred, clearly shows that extra protection against driving rain was considered necessary. The aesthetic and functional problems posed by the wide mortar joints, which are often inescapable in the use of unknapped flint, were tackled by the practice of 'galleting', or the application of flint chips.

Availability was comparative too. Flints can be, and still are, found in abundance in fields and beaches, those on the latter very often being more rounded and with a thinner white rind or cortex. However, on some beaches the collection of flints (and the visually similar but geologically different pebbles) is not allowed, and anyway newly-beached flints could retain the sea salts that cause great damage when washed on to masonry and mortar. Farmers, on the other hand, will no doubt readily agree, if asked, to the collection of flints, as field flints can be a great nuisance to machinery. The collecting of flints has never given a sufficient supply, and they were mined in great quantities from the Neolithic period either directly or as a by-product, particularly in the quarrying of chalk (still a principal source). Knapped flints were made until very recently at Brandon in Suffolk, the heart of the flint industry, up to the retirement of Mr James English.

Flint walls will often have 'lacing courses' of brick or tile to prevent settlement during the setting of the mortar and to provide the workmen erecting it with the occasional level bed from which to start. Ingenious decorative effects can be achieved by the use of chequerwork, alternating brick or stone with flint. There is a herring-curing shed in Lowestoft, dating in origin from the sixteenth century, where the ornamentation is in a most appropriate herringbone pattern.

'Knapped' flint with galleted mortar (see pp. 112–16)

FURTHER INFORMATION

Three flint quarries are listed on pp. 35 and 41 of the *Natural Stone Directory*.

A good source of information is Walter Shepherd's *Flint, its Origins, Properties and Uses*, Faber 1972.

6 TIMBER FRAMING

An historic building without some element of structural timber is almost inconceivable. Even where the shell is entirely in stone, brick or cob, it is normally roofed in wood. Even vaulting has a protective timber second roof above it. Many eighteenth-century brick façades were backed by inner skins of softwood timber members and in the more flimsy elevations two skims of plaster or an outer one of weatherboarding encase a timber skeleton of surprisingly thin dimensions or 'scantling'. However this 'stud framing' normally associated with partitions in modern housing has been caricatured as the poor relation and decadent climax to the great tradition of 'timber framing' where it is the timbers which provide the loadbearing structure.

The golden age of timber framing ran from the early Middle Ages to the seventeenth century and the date of its origin is being pushed further and further back, particularly through the researches of Cecil Hewett. Joints are perhaps the most difficult element within a frame to examine closely, analysis often being helped by the use of a pallet knife or some other instrument but Hewett's close examination of the development of jointing has shown conclusively that frames hitherto dated to the late medieval period are in fact Romanesque. He has backdated the earliest timbers within the great Tithe Barn recently repaired at Great Coggeshall in Essex to the middle of the twelfth century.

Architecture is about the bridging and enclosure of space. The two basic principles are trabeation, where the vertical and horizontal members meet at right angles (think of Stonehenge), and that of arcuation where the bridging is through the curvilin-

ear form of an arch. This duality is expressed in timber framing in a division between the 'box frame', by far the most common, and the 'cruck' structure although strictly speaking in the latter it is the curved blades which support the roof, the walls being maintained independently. In 'post and truss' or 'post and lintel' structures the loading is taken through the principal upright members within the walls which define the bays, the remainder of the shell keeping out the weather and housing the bearings for the floors.

At the last count, in 1981, some 3054 'true crucks' had been identified, the adjective being important in differentiating the full blade rising from the earth to the apex of the roof from its bastard offspring which includes the 'base' where the blade only rises to the collar, the 'upper' or 'raised' where the blade does not spring from the ground floor and the 'scarfed' and 'jointed' where the blades are not continuous members. The true form is rare in the south-west and virtually non-existent in the Home Counties and East Anglia although one example was recently found in Norfolk, at Stiffkey. The earliest documentary reference, of 1225, concerns an example in Essex. The earliest allusion in Wales appears in 1305. The blades or forks of a cruck frame are always curved and thus had to be fashioned or converted from a 'crooked' tree (or a trunk plus a branch), a convincing explanation of the name. As crucks do not frame the wall they are normally only visible internally and far more easily missed than box frame members. These too very often suffer from enforced invisibility obscured by later façades added under the dictates of fashion and to disguise the addition of

Late eighteenth-century brick façades, as here in Islington, can conceal an inner skin of timber as well as the wood of the sash boxes and floors

7–13 Silver Street, Ely, Cambridgeshire. The splendid scissor brace roof probably of the thirteenth or fourteenth centuries, unsuspected until the recent repairs carried out by the Ely Building Preservation Trust, and belying its age by an excellent state of preservation

a further floor. In other cases the overhanging of the first (or indeed the second or third) floor by means of a jetty where each successive floor projects beyond the one below has been disguised by underbuilding up to the bressumer (the principal horizontal beam). One of the most distinctive forms of the box frame known as the Wealden House, with its recessed centre and projecting jettied crosswings, has often been camouflaged by subsequent refacings and underbuildings.

The frames were generally in hardwood, examples in softwood as at The Hoop and Grapes Public House in the City of London being particularly uncommon and normally later. By far the most common wood was domestic oak occasionally supplemented even in the Middle Ages from Scandinavia, a source also of softwoods from the thirteenth century (today some 90% of timber used in the UK is imported). Other historic hardwoods in use included elm, poplar, ash, larch, elder and beech (for laths and underground tiling).

The timbers in the earliest and latest frames tended to be thinner than those employed in the later Middle Ages, when the frames were generally 'overstructured', a conservatism that has of course aided survival. In an important study of one particular house in Suffolk (Grundall House, Stanton), of average 'middling' size with a hall and two crosswings, Dr Oliver Rackham has counted 730 timber parts weighing a total of 24 tons with 1250 joints in a structure that on his calculations would have demanded 330 trees. When a new timber framed cottage of 2000 square feet was constructed on traditional lines in Cheshire in the early 1980s some 36 tons of new oak were required.

Guides to the development of the house and souvenirs of the lives lived therein are visible to the attentive eye. In timber the equivalent to mason's marks, by which stonemason's work was identified for purposes of payment, are the 'assembly marks', normally incised Roman numerals enabling the frame prefabricated in the carpenter's framing yard to be reassembled on site. Beams may contain notches and mortices indicating lost partitions or windows or incisions that provided a key for a lost render. External holes, 'scotches' or 'stay notches'

Later façades conceal earlier timber framed cores at Hitchin, Hertfordshire (in buildings now demolished for the inner relief road) and at Leominster, Herefordshire

with splayed sides were probably the sockets for raking shores used to force walls back to the vertical and support it while it was being secured. Like putlog holes which provided the housing for scaffold poles on the exterior of stone buldings, the holes were not always filled after construction. A good many apertures, however, appear to be inexplicable and come most probably from the fact that the timber was imported to the house. Such re-use was quite common and although these would come from other buildings rather than ships as persistent stories have it, the Royal Commission on Historical Monuments has in fact found one ship's figurehead in use in a medieval house in York. The presence of a jowl or swelling at the head of a timber (a shape that comes

from a tree placed upside down to take advantage of the bell shape at the base) implies support for a beam although they can also appear at the foot. Blackened marks with uneven outline on a timber show where rushlights were repeatedly attached, and small holes in the ceiling beam, hooks from which meat was suspended. Weathering on internal beams obviously suggests they were once external; this is hinted at less obviously by the presence of the heart shapes roughly in the centre of the timber on the halved face, as this was the side always put to the outside as being more resistant to weather. Dates and monograms (indicating not just the year of construction but very often the birth of a child or a marriage) can be found almost anywhere, although more normally on lintels of doors and fireplaces. Grooves to the underside of wall timbers point to the presence of window shutters. The earliest timbers of the house are likely to be in the roof space. 1984 saw the discovery of only the second Crown Post roof in Cornwall in Rectory Farmhouse, Morwenstow.

If the roof is intact it will indicate the original division of the house into bays. Soot on the timbers will confirm that it was constructed as a open 'hall house' as most early properties were, the intermediate floor being a later insertion. If the central truss in a former 'hall house' is more elaborately moulded on one face it is this side which would have looked towards the dais. Such elaboration may occur at both ends of the hall in a Wealden house.

Plans are multitudinous but vernacular studies are greatly guided by evidence for a 'screens passage' running transversely across the hall at one end, smoke bays and single and double aisles. A 'lean-to' is often an extension, but by no means always so. It could be a rear aisle or an outshot designed to take stairs, bedroom or pantry. Outbuildings too could be original, whether brewhouse, stable, ashhouse, detached kitchens, well or cider press.

7 THE CONSERVATION OF TIMBER FRAMES

The general vulnerability of wood to fungus and insect infestation and the particular problems associated with the failure of wooden floors and roofs are tackled elsewhere (chapters 11, 13 and 20). But the conservation of timber frames has fostered additional dilemmas. The first is concerned with the degree to which the timber members should be left in their natural form and the exterior revealed. In the nineteenth century the application of black paint, pitch or tar to the members became quite common, especially in the north-west. The resulting magpie effect was known as 'Black and White'. Some of this blackening does seem to be clearly pre-Victorian. The practice of adding bullock's blood and red ochre, as found on some houses in Bedfordshire and in the hall house from North Cray, Kent recently reerected at the Weald and Downland Museum in Sussex, and the much more common device of limewashing (over both the timbers and the infill panels) shows clearly

that the natural finish of oak was not always highly prized (although these finishes were applied for practical as well as aesthetic reasons). Oak changes colour naturally over time to a lighter silvery grey, an effect which can be, and has been, speeded by the application of lime, be it slowly by the regular annual addition of limewash or quickly by coating in hotlime which is scraped off after fifteen minutes, a device used by Lutyens at his house of Munstead Wood in Surrey. A.R. Powys, on behalf of the SPAB, suggested that the blackening of timbers could be reversed by the application of caustic soda followed by water. At Little Moreton Hall, Cheshire the National Trust is relying on time to fade it.

However, all this treatment presupposes that the timber members were meant to be seen in the first place with or without a coating. Where there are carved patterns and members which are clearly decorative rather than loadbearing, exposure was

Weobley, Herefordshire. Oak timbers left in their natural colour

Bridgnorth, Shropshire. The stripping of a later render with sham painted half timbers reveals the original studs underneath

obviously intended. There are many examples of medieval houses rendered and limewashed except for the highly decorated bressumer supporting the jetty. And yet most authorities accept that as a general rule timber frames were covered by a render at least from the seventeenth century. Indeed had that not been the case the great East Anglian traditions of colour washing and pargetting (p. 118) would have been starved of clients in the sixteenth and seventeenth centuries. In the closing years of the timber frame tradition, particularly the eighteenth century, timbers were so thin that a render was often an essential safeguard. Where rendering was applied there are sufficient examples of sham painted timbers, some of them possibly eighteenth-century, to indicate that they were added with some reluctance. The removal of renders to expose timber frames became common from the nineteenth century, running parallel to the fashion for stripping plaster to reveal the masonry of internal church walls. The Modern Movement in our century has given philosophical justification to the 'honest' exposure of structural members.

From the eighteenth century in particular brick became as common as a render. Weatherboarding as an alternative means of external protection is still strongly advocated by F.W.B. Charles (see Bibliography). Tarred or painted, it has been used for centuries as an outer skin for the protection of timber framed barns. Eric Gee has found mention of the word 'wetherbord' in 1515 and a reference of 1321 to a house with weatherboarded gables.

Internal timbers, particularly principal members with chamfer stops at each end and other mouldings, were clearly meant to be seen. There is now a general presumption against their painting or staining although as later coatings may conceal original decoration painted directly on to the wood, any stripping should be carried out very carefully — whether it is to be by a patent liquid or paste, or wire brush or sandpaper. A small area of the beam could be treated initially with extra special care to avoid possible destruction of evidence. Some unsuspecting owners may also find that the timber which they have reverentially treated turns out to be a nineteenth-century boxing of an original beam complete with fake moulding. Once stripped and washed with white spirit, the timber should be examined for infestation and treated accordingly and given a final coating of clarified beeswax and pure turpentine. Waxes or wax-based commercial applications are the more easy to apply in warm weather. Linseed oil is certainly still used but has been criticized because of a tendency to darken the timber and attract dust. In

certain limited circumstances the authorities may insist on the use of a fire-resistant intumescent paint. Unlike its equivalent on cast iron where the surface can appear stippled, it looks no different on timber from ordinary paints and can be clear. Many architects, however, regard it as superfluous, most notably on oak timbers of such a size that a 'charring depth' of one-fiftieth of an inch a minute or more would have little or no effect on the strength of the timber. It is after all the case that the surfaces of wooden ships used to be deliberately charred to increase durability.

The second dilemma raises more hackles: whether to replace decayed and damaged timbers or to repair them. It has always been possible to splice in new timber, particularly in the replacement of decayed beam ends and to strap suspect joints with metal (see later). Now, however, the advent of synthetic epoxy and polyester resins has for the first time permitted the consolidation of heavily decayed timber (or indeed virtually any other material) as an alternative to its replacement. What some see as misguided reverence for the timber itself has been compounded by the offence of relieving it of any structural role by the insertion of steel members to take the loadings of the floor or roof. The timber becomes an artefact rather than architectural component. Antipathy to this idea is personified by Freddie Charles and articulated most fully in his book on *The Conservation of Timber Buildings* published in October 1984. He has used metal supports and recognizes the limited role for resins but his preferred reaction to substantial decay is to replace and to eschew all substitutes for proper timber 'so long as oak trees grow in England'. He normally uses green oak for structural timbers, in common with medieval practice, despite the differences in shrinkage rates between the old and the new and the tendency of tannic acid in unseasoned oak to attack steel nails.

He believes, from his experience, that the carpenters of today are just as skilled as their medieval counterparts and should be given the chance to prove it. (The SPAB joins him in his dislike of the use of resins which it considers are generally irreversible and damaging in the prevention of movement within joints). Insertions can be clearly but discreetly dated and perhaps signed and the predecessors set on one side for possible use in connection with radio carbon and dendrochronological dating. For the latter, which involves the examination of tree rings, a number of timbers are required for comparison, the better ones being quarter-sawn boards retaining some sapwood. As 'matching pairs', for example the two principal rafters in a roof truss, were 'halved'

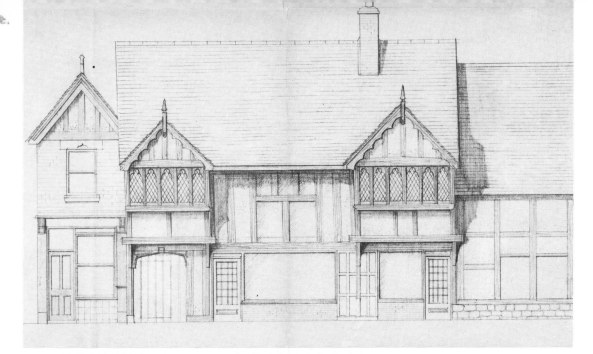

14 Spon Street, Coventry, Warwickshire. In 1984
Coventry City Council proposed to remove the fake half-
timbered façade to reveal the genuine frame beneath which
is shown on the architect's drawing

from a single tree some architects dislike replacing just the one. The use of recycled timber salvaged from demolished buildings, although long-established, can bring its own problems if this is hard to work, archaeologically confusing or infected.

Where the triangulation of principal trusses has been upset by the removal or cutting through of braces or tie beams and other restraining elements the building has 'racked', that is moved longitudinally, so much that it would be impossible to put back the member to the original dimension. In most such 'tumbledown' cottages an equilibrium has been reached and the movement has ceased. Some gables on timber framed properties were constructed with

an outward slope or nod. The contemporary adjective was 'gadered'.

Whereas the differences between the SPAB and Freddie Charles can appear more imagined than real on the question of new timber they diverge completely on the third dilemma; whether timber framed buildings should be moved. The question seems an academic one but the resiting of timber buildings (of inferior construction) was in fact fairly common in

Malt Mill Lane, Alcester, Warwickshire. Restoration can involve stripping down to the frame (Photo prior to restoration, 1964, courtesy National Monuments Record)

A timber-framed barn in Herefordshire where the lack of holes and grooves seems to confirm either that the infill panels have always been open or that they were solid

the past and at least three or four such applications have been submitted every year in the past decade. One of the earliest concerted programmes for the resiting of framed structures in recent years was supervised by Mr Charles and involved the reconstruction of a number of buildings from local sites in Spon Street, Coventry to join medieval examples already there – to re-introduce some historical sense to the centre of a city which was largely destroyed in the War. The same idea gave rise to the so-called Open Air Museums. The SPAB objects to the dismantling and re-erection of timber-framed buildings, particularly barns, on sites abroad where the intention is to add a spurious sense of history by tacking authentic timbers onto modern structures. Where the building to be re-erected is not to be used for museum purposes but as a house it is considered as a new structure and therefore has to comply with modern building and health regulations on window sizes, staircase angles and ceiling heights.

The durability of the timber frame itself is very often in marked contrast to that of the infill panels where these have been provided in wattle and daub – the wattles (known in East Anglia as rizzes and clamstaff in Lancashire) being wooden splints with tapered ends held at their head in auger holes and at their base in a continuous groove, the daub being generally a mixture of chalk, clay and chopped straw.

There may be strengthening horizontal cross ties bound to the wattles by 'withies' of hazel or willow. The whole was faced with lime plaster strengthened by cow hair, spear grass and broken tiles. Some examples, in Wales and Herefordshire, have woven laths left exposed without any plaster. Rarer still are infill panels in wooden boarding or peat shaped like brick (in Shropshire).

More durable materials employed included clay lump, tiles and stone tiles, the latter often being housed in grooves. These were generally concealed by plaster. This was not the case with the most widespread of all substitutes for wattle and daub, brick.

Most brick is later (and criticized for its weight and the difficulty of fitting it into irregular panels), but some 'nogging' in brick as it is termed, does seem to be original. There is an example of large red bricks used on their edge of *c.*1330 in York and it has been argued that the handsome herringbone brickwork at the Ancient House, Thetford, in Norfolk is original. Early examples of wattle and daub have survived but once water has gained a hold its perishability can become irreversible. In the eighteenth and nineteenth centuries substitution was very often by simple laths and plaster. Nowadays, however, many architects have devised their own alternative infill panel, introducing modern insulation material like polystyrene foam, polythene and wood wool slabs between two skins of plaster. The insertion of a tray of lead at the base of each panel overlapping on to the timber (and treated with bitumastic paint to prevent tannic acid attack from the oak) helps to prevent the entry of water. Partly damaged daub can be patched with a mixture in equal parts of clay soil, hydrated lime and fresh cowdung mixed with water and

worked to a paste reinforced with chopped straw or cow hair, followed by a thin coat of lime putty and several applications of limewash (David Pearce, SPAB *News*, Volume 3, No. 2, April/May 1982 p. 21). The sponging of the outer surfaces can prevent a dead look. Any bulging of such surfaces in the manner of a quilt beyond the line of the timbers does not appear to be historically authentic. Where original wattle and daub can be retained without sacrificing the insulatory value of the wall it can be viewed through demountable partitions or doors.

FURTHER INFORMATION

The Council for British Archaeology publish N.W. Alcock's *Cruck Construction: An Introduction and Catalogue* (1981).

More information can be found in the following books: R.W. Brunskill's *Timber Building in Britain* (Gollancz, 1985), F.W.B. and Mary Charles's *The Conservation of Timber Buildings* (Hutchinson, 1984), Richard Harris's *Discovering Timber Framed Buildings* (Shire Publications, 1978) and Cecil Hewett's *English Historic Carpentry* (Phillimore, 1980) Cecil Hewett is the author of a number of other books and articles on timber framing.

An article on 'Infill Panels and the Timber Framed Revival' appeared in The *Architects Journal*, 6.4.1983. More on this topic can be found in the SPAB *News*, July 1982, in an article entitled 'Panel infilling in Timber Framed Buildings'.

SPAB Information Sheet No. 3 'The Surface Treatment of Timber-Framed Houses', *SPAB News*, Winter 1986.

For information on moveable houses, consult J.T. Smith's 'Short-lived and Mobile Houses in Late Seventeenth Century England', *Vernacular Architecture* (vol. 16, 1985, p. 33).

Individual bricks have varied considerably over the centuries in their colour, surface texture and, since the nineteenth century, in the method of production. In their constructional use they are categorized by the bond in which they are coursed and by the presence or lack of a cavity within the walling.

Where there is a telling uniformity is in the size. It is true that Roman bricks were long and thin (and were re-used in a number of medieval buildings) and that the 'great bricks' of the Middle Ages could be as large as $13 \times 6 \times 2$in (length, width, thickness). Nevertheless the bulk of surviving historic brickwork dates from the sixteenth century or later and was the subject of regulatory statute. (The first English brickwork, after the Romans, dates from the thirteenth century, that in Wales, 1567). The directions were capriciously applied but they did establish standard practices. For example, the Act of 1625 regularized bricks to $9 \times 4\frac{3}{4} \times 2\frac{1}{4}$in which was only slightly altered by that of 1776 to $8\frac{1}{2} \times 4 \times 2\frac{1}{2}$in. Until very recently although that Act had long lapsed the standard size of what is termed the 'brick format' (the size of the brick plus half that of the encompassing mortar joint) was $9 \times 4\frac{1}{2} \times 3$in. So predictable were the dimensions that the word 'brick' came to denote size rather than material. In West Yorkshire in the common walling termed 'parpoint' stones were cut to the size of bricks and known simply as stone bricks. Standardization enables the local variants like the Hitch bricks in East Hertfordshire, the small Dutch bricks at Sandwich and Measham Gobs in Leicestershire to stand out. The greater difficulty is to identify the so-called mathematical tiles (see page 60).

Colour arose from the clay, the differing rates of oxidization and the degree of burning. Most early bricks were extracted locally to meet *ad hoc* needs. The first brick companies with nationwide sales did not come into existence until the mid nineteenth century. However, there is a clear divergence between the colour of most local clay and that of the indigenous brick; the firing changes the colour considerably. The most obvious exceptions to this rule are the 'white bricks' (more generally light yellow) common to several of the East Anglian counties, which are produced from clay with a high lime and low iron content. A speckling of black indicates the addition of clinker whilst fly ash and a considerable degree of burning produced the silver-grey or 'vitrified' (blackened) bricks used to such effect to form 'diaper' patterns from the sixteenth century and employed more generally in the eighteenth. Where the heavily blackened bricks were difficult to obtain red bricks were sometimes simply

The juxtaposition of sixteenth-century brickwork (nearest the quoins) with 'harder' bricks of the 1834 rebuilding at Baynards, Cranleigh, Surrey (Grade II*: demolished)

'Parpoint' walling in West Yorkshire constructed in 'stone bricks'. Note the irregular courses and the lack of quoins

painted black and where this has been washed off over the years the configurations now appear curiously incomplete. The inescapable variations in firing also explain the pleasing irregularity of historic brick.

The pleasing irregularity of texture results too from the practice of applying sand to the inner face of the mould within which the brick was formed, to prevent its sticking to the sides. The visual effect is sufficiently envied for modern companies to produce 'sand-faced' and 'sand-creased' bricks by machine. Nevertheless the famous London stock brick is one of several produced by the alternative 'slop-moulded' system where water is substituted for sand. The earliest bricks made in the local fields can still bear the impression of the grass and hay on which the pre-fired 'green' bricks were placed in order to be moulded. Occasionally the imprint of a stray animal will be found on the topmost surface. The most radical change in surface texture was the introduction of glazing on a wide scale from the mid-nineteenth century, particularly for use in connection with terracotta, glazed or unglazed (see chapter 9).

Until the late nineteenth century all bricks were produced from clay (including fired earth or shale). Calcium silicate (sandlime/flint lime) bricks were patented in England in 1866 and Germany in 1881, although the first examples in use did not appear in this country until 1904. Nevertheless, the vast majority of bricks in use are still composed of clay. It is in the method of production that greater change has arisen. The most obvious revolution has come with mechanization. Nowadays only 1–2% of bricks are made by hand although those firms like Bulmers in Sudbury and the Swanage Brick and Tile Co which have stayed loyal to the traditional methods are finding a constant market for the non-standard or 'specials' with which to match existing plain or ornamental brickwork on historic structures. Even if they are hand-made, no bricks at present are baked using the original method of burning timber; the last wood-fired brickworks at Ashburnham Place, Sussex was closed in November 1968. (This has had at least one important visual effect; firing by coal cannot produce the vitrified grey bricks or 'grizzles' and where these were required in the mid-nineteenth century there had to be resort to salt glazing.) Whereas early bricks were formed in a mould (although the more delicate ornamental work was often carved *in situ*) bricks are now for the most part 'pressed' or 'wire-cut'. Both methods were introduced in the mid nineteenth century (wire-cutting being patented in 1841), the former producing the smooth hard 'engineering' bricks associated with names like Staffordshire Blue, Accrington Bloods and Ruabon from Wales. Wire-cut bricks lack the V-shaped indentations known mysteriously as 'frogs' on the upper and/or lower surfaces which help to reduce weight, take the mortar and receive the ends of wallties. Such bricks can however be perforated, also, for the reduction of weight and many different sorts were produced in the nineteenth and twentieth centuries with varying numbers and sizes of hole. In the case of garden walls such holes facilitated the training of plants. Mechanization has helped more conscious differentiation on grounds of quality, 'firsts', for example, being the cutters that can be rubbed. 'Commons' or 'place bricks' although not necessarily weaker were reserved for inferior or invisible locations. Although such bricks were purpose-made from poorer clays, many were inadvertent 'rejects'. The greater precision of modern production has produced with it greater predictability and 'commons' are now a line of production in their own right. The present British Standard categorises bricks as Ordinary, Internal and Special, including Engineering, for extra durability. Semi-engineering are used for foundations and drains.

In almost all cases the choice of bond depends apart from the thickness of the wall upon another differentiation – between the long 'stretcher' and the shorter 'header', the one showing the longest face, the other being placed head-on. Very occasionally bricks were placed 'on edge', showing a third face. Bonds are designed to avoid continuous vertical jointing, which weakens the load-bearing capacity of the wall and can induce differential settlement. A good many were irregular but many were carried through systematically except at the corners where there was often trouble. Before 1500 the English Bond with alternate courses of headers and stretchers was almost universal and retained a considerable popularity well into the sixteenth and seventeenth centuries. By that time Flemish Bond, with alternate headers and stretchers in each course, had become its main rival and was to predominate in the eighteenth century. The first examples date from the fourteenth century although the earliest complete example is Kew Palace (1631). English Garden Bond with either 3 or 5 courses of stretchers to one of headers, is first recorded in 1559. The Header Bond became fashionable under the Georgians. Nowadays the simple Stretcher Bond is largely unchallenged. In a number of areas distinctive local bonds developed. For example, in eighteenth-century Leighton Buzzard, pilaster-like vertical courses or 'chaining' in Flemish Bond were set within a shell otherwise constructed in heavily vitrified Header Bond. In yet further cases where laziness overruled pride, stretchers were grooved to fake headers. Particular techniques of coursing were used on 'tumbled-in' brickwork on a gable and more particularly on window lintels bridged by what is termed, in appropriate contradiction, a flat arch. Until the advent of the distressingly

unadventurous brick-on-end 'soldier coursing' such arches were normally composed of unrubbed or rubbed and gauged brick 'voussoirs' laid in very fine joints often composed in the eighteenth and nineteenth centuries of lime putty. These are nearly all of dovetail shape, each of the bricks slightly splayed away from the centre so that each exerts holding pressure on its neighbour. At least one works at Bracknell which makes 'rubbers' still survives but it is in fact easier to remove the whole of the arch than individual bricks. In the better examples each of the latter will be marked for a particular position in the arch, the symbols being impressed by leather dials nailed to the base of the mould. It was common for manufacturers from the nineteenth century to inscribe their name on every brick and some at parapet level may have been specially inscribed with the owners name for the topping out ceremony. At one brickworks (Smeed Dean in Kent) the foreman would press the bowl of his clay pipe into every millionth brick produced.

Most walls were 'solid' well into the nineteenth if not the twentieth centuries. The inverted commas are appropriate for cavities partially filled with rubble mud or 'hearting' were not uncommon. They were, however, a sign of parsimony, not science. The modern 'cavity wall' is deliberate and now almost universal.

In this system two skins or leaves of brick (or in the case of the inner skin insulating block) are connected by metal ties or transverse bricks but otherwise do not touch. The first ties, of the early nineteenth century, were wrought iron, and occasionally tarred and sanded. Most modern examples are in wire. The intervening air space serves much like a firebreak in a wood to prevent the ingress of moisture and improve insulation, air being more easily warmed than brick. Many such cavities are now being filled with foam or other materials to further improve insulation. The system was presaged by the rat-trap bond which originated in the early nineteenth century and made use of a discontinuous cavity. There is however no statutory ban on solid walling and in London the Building Officers have allowed Mr Quinlan Terry to maintain the integrity of his newly constructed block of 'Georgian' flats in Broadwick Street, Soho by the employment of load-bearing brickwork without cavity or expansion joints. 'Solid brickwork', i.e., walling where if there is more than one skin they abut directly, can be as thin as 3in where the bricks are laid 'on edge'. However the standard historic widths are $4\frac{1}{2}$in (half brick), 9in (one brick) or $13\frac{1}{2}$in (one-and-a-half brick). Generally speaking the walls of façades will be thicker at their base than at the top,

Example of rat-trap bond

Pallant House, Chichester – rubbed and cut brickwork

a fact which means that any untoward increase in the thrust of the roof can, the more easily, push out the uppermost sections of the elevation. It is not uncommon for the ground floor to be one brick thick with the second floor being half a brick (as is clear one brick thickness is measured by the length not the width of the brick). Even where the bond uses headers it was not uncommon in the eighteenth century for these to be 'snapped' (halved) so that they failed to bond the two skins. There is nothing against the use of different materials in the different skins, although there may be differential expansion, as for example between concrete block and brick. Many stone-faced buildings possessed brick inner leaves completely hidden internally and externally.

Repairs

There are many causes of failure in brickwork. Where for example the foundations have failed, or there is 'eccentric' loading of the wall, repairs serve little purpose until the source of the trouble has been tackled. Other causes arise from contradictions in the wall itself.

Firstly there is the movement of the wall from the vertical, normally at the head of the elevation or at its midriff where it is appropriately known as 'bellying'. This can be caused by the parting of the front wall from the party wall or more commonly the failure of the bond between the inner and outer skins. As it was by no means unusual in the eighteenth century for the owner of a terraced house to buy it in carcass form, adding a front elevation designed to his own requirements, the two very often meet at a butt or straight joint with little or no bonding between the two. The danger point arises when the amount of the lean in the full height of the wall exceeds one-third of the thickness of the wall at its base. The Building Research Establishment has stated that repair is normally not required to walls that are out of plumb by under 1in in the average storey height. The two historic methods of tackling this problem offer at the best containment.

The first is the erection of buttresses. But these are clearly inappropriate in certain situations and there is an ever-present risk that the buttress will settle differentially from the wall and, if the junction is by a hard mortar, instead of containing the movement it will sink and pull the wall towards it. The use of metal rods or straps has also been common for centuries and is visually more acceptable. It was possible to pull the wall back somewhat nearer the vertical by heating the centre of the rod which contracted as it cooled down and thus through the pressure of its plated face on the surface exerted inward pressure on the wall. The heating of the bolts alone was an easier alternative. Nevertheless it does seem that most ties were installed for containment alone and were not heated – in order to be effective they required a firm anchoring of a floor or another external wall to which the end of the strap could be fixed. The containment of particular features like a parapet or a chimney by the use of strapping, with or without the use of galvanized hoops, was likely to be more effective. More modern methods range from jacking the wall back to the vertical, re-bonding the two skins, and reducing the impact of point loads bearing on brickwork, for example at floor ends, by the insertion of stone or concrete 'spreaders'.

The second problem of cracking can have a bewildering variety of explanations too technical to be entered into here but some, such as the effect of seasonal changes, are inescapable and need not be alarming. Broadly speaking they are divided into hairline, fine, medium or wide and are the more serious, because it is indicative of greater force, if it is the bricks rather than the joints which are sheared. Settlement where it is uniform can be harmless; it is differential settlement where different parts of the building sink at different rates that introduces the tensions that cannot be accommmodated. It is fairly easy to discern if the movement is still active by the use of non-ferrous pegs fixed either side of the cracks. The once familiar glass telltales are now rather out of favour as they lack calibration and are vulnerable to impact. More acceptable modern substitutes include sliding perspex telltales and vernier crack markers. It follows of course that where movement is still progressing this should be arrested before permanent repairs are effected. Where the cracks are proving troublesome they can be temporarily filled using oil based mastic, better able to withstand movement than mortar. Cracking however is not just the sign of tension but can be indicative of chemical attacks, particularly by sulphates. Analysis and remedy must be a matter for professionals – particularly when the solutions are relatively complicated operations such as grouting (which applies equally to a stone wall). This is the process of filling the cavities within a wall, either intentional or accidental, by the injection of liquid mortar which consolidates the fabric on setting. For

less comprehensive solutions Timothy Bidwell's authoritative book (see Bibliography) differentiates between cracks where rebuilding is required and those where raking out and filling should suffice. In the first category he places:

(a) fine cracks in dense non-porous brickwork where water penetration is a risk

(b) medium cracks in brickwork built in strong mortar where the cracks follow the joint

(c) medium cracks passing through bricks

(d) all wide cracks

Plugging should be sufficient for

(a) fine cracks in porous brickwork (although these may be best untreated)

(b) medium cracks in brickwork laid in soft lime mortar and

(c) generally all types of cracking in internal walls

Mortaring should always be in lime rather than cement as the former can better accommodate movement and is less liable to attack by sulphates.

Both bellying and cracking can be tackled by the addition of a new internal skin of brick or blockwork to which the damaged historic walling is tied back. It also, like the related bitumen treatments, improves

Thetford, Norfolk. New brickwork inevitably looks raw unless the contrast is reduced by artificial 'soot washing' or some other technique

Hungerford, Berkshire. Mathematical tiles on the first floor. These flanged tiles, of which the earliest dated example is inscribed '1724', are normally red but can be seen with yellow and black glazing. No modern supplier makes such tiles now as a standard item but some brickworks will accept specific commissions. This example is hung on wooden boarding

insulation and is in that respect far preferable to any external rendering, or the addition of water repellents, which although colourless can inhibit 'breathing' and are not permanent in their effectiveness. Any internal skin should not be at the expense of original detailing.

It is often found that the stability of a brick wall (or indeed a stone one) has been impaired by the decay of integral timber members such as lintels, wall plates and bonding timbers. The latter in particular only occur in inner skins and were designed to brace the wall, to assist in the setting of the plaster and like 'wood bricks' to provide a fixing for panelling. Yet many have now rotted, causing the superimposed brick courses to sink. In such cases they can be replaced in brick or concrete.

Where individual bricks have spalled (when the surface flakes), or in some cases disintegrated, they can be cut out and replaced. A more exact match is probably obtained from use of second hand bricks either from elsewhere in the building or from a demolished site, and there is a ready market in this form of recycling. Nevertheless the 30 or so brick companies now produce a great range of bricks and generally welcome demand for 'specials' for particu-

lar requirements. Even those such as the gault brick which have been unobtainable for thirty years are now being produced again in modern form by the London Brick Company (in its Arlesey Range) and in weathered form in Redland's 'Pluckley Sheppey'. Where one long face of the damaged brick is intact it is possible to saw this off as a 'slip' which is then bedded at the face of the wall against lime mortar perhaps with a clip and a backing half brick. 'Slips' in some variety are produced to specially reduced sizes by a number of firms. The infilling of holes by plaster or mortar is rarely successful although the visual contrast can be offset by the addition of brick dust. The insertion of new bricks into uncleaned façades can be disguised by the 'soot washing' of the newcomers or their staining in manure soaked water (not too rich as cow dung has damaging salts). Clearly it also makes sense where elevations have been painted or 'raddled' (reddened) like a doorstep, as was the case in some eighteenth and nineteenth-century façades, for new bricks to be similarly treated. An alternative to dirtying new bricks is to clean the existing ones. Generally speaking bricks can withstand harder treatment than some stone, but again sand-blasting should only be reserved for the more durable brickwork and less important buildings. The removal of paint and render is rarely successful and can lead to the 'blowing' of the faces of the brickwork. This is one reason why the British Standard Code of Practice advises against the painting of brickwork, something which is normally an aesthetic disaster as well.

FURTHER INFORMATION

T.G. Bidwell's *Conservation of Brick Buildings*, Brick Development Association 1977, is now out of print but may soon be reprinted.

The following publications may also prove useful:

Ronald Brunskill and Alec Clifton-Taylor, *English Brickwork*, Ward Lock 1977.

Alan Cox, *Brick Making: History and Gazetteer*, Royal Commission on Historical Monuments and Bedfordshire County Council 1977.

Robert Hayward, *The Brick Book*, Batsford 1978.

Nathaniel Lloyd, *A History of English Brickwork*, 1925, reprinted Antique Collectors' Club 1983.

W.G. Nash, *Brickwork Repair and Restoration*, Attic Books 1985.

Jane Wight, *Brick Building in England from the Middle Ages to 1550*, A & C Black, 1972. (Miss Wight's travelling exhibition *Patterns in Brick* illustrating the history of brickwork is no longer operative but is still available in dismantled form.)

Architects Journal, Masters of Brickwork, Supplement 1984 and 'Products in Practice: Bricks', 1 December 1982 and 27 November 1985

Alec Clifton-Taylor's *The Pattern of English Building* (Faber 1972) pp. 281–6 has been updated in the chapter on Lewes in the same author's *Six More English Towns*.

Ian Ashby's article on mathematical tiles appeared in *Traditional Homes*, April 1985. Maurice Exwood has written on the subject in *Vernacular Architecture*, vol. 12, 1981, and in *Period Home*, vol. 3, no. 6. See also Terence Paul Smith in *Vernacular Architecture*, vol. 10, 1979.

Maurice Exwood can supply copies of the *Notes of a Symposium on Mathematical Tiles* held in 1982, including information on the proposal to establish a register of all examples to be lodged at the Weald and Downland Museum in Sussex. The address to write to is: Mr M. Exwood, 64 The Green, Ewell, Epsom, Surrey KT17 3JJ.

ADDRESSES

The Building Centres at London, Cambridge and Southampton contain Brick Advisory Centres where the great range of present day bricks are on display. The London Centre is in Store Street, off Tottenham Court Road.

The Science Museum has a national brick collection (although it is not on show).

There is a British Brick Society (Archives at County Hall, St Helen's, Ipswich, Suffolk) and a Brick Development Association based at Woodside House, Winkfield, Windsor, Berkshire SL4 2DX. A number of local museums have displays on brick making, for example the Arundel Museum.

For a list of brickmakers making genuine handmade bricks (as opposed to simply finishing by hand) see *Traditional Homes*, May 1986.

---

9 TERRACOTTA

Terracotta means literally 'baked clay' and it indeed possesses the same basic constituency as brick. Its first dated use on an English building is 1502. In the sixteenth century it was almost always unglazed. During its heyday, starting from the 1860s and associated with firms such as Blashfield of Stamford, Doultons of Lambeth and Burmantofts, it was more normally glazed and known as 'faience'. Although it found its most famous expression on buildings like the Natural History Museum and Harrods it appeared on many domestic buildings even if only to provide decorated ridge finials to the roof. The clay employed, the principal sources being Cornwall, Dorset, Northamptonshire, Ruabon in North Wales, Tamworth in Staffordshire and Everton in Surrey, was buff or red in its natural colour. Variations in green, grey, blue, black and mauve were possible with the addition of pigments and coloured slips. The sections, almost always cast in moulds rather than sculpted, were solid if small, hollow if large, the voids generally being filled with crushed terracotta, brick, cement, concrete or even paper. The hollow was cross-chambered for extra strength and rarely had to take loading, the terracotta being a facing to a shell of brick, stone, concrete or steel. The connection was by mortar or cramp.

The claims made for the material a century ago have largely held good. It is more resistant to pollution than most stones, it is lighter but has a high crushing strength and in the glazed form, it can be self-cleaning. Some unforeseen difficulties have arisen. The widespread use of a very hard non-sacrificial mortar forced the evaporation of water through the external glazed surfaces, not the joints. Unfortunately, where the glaze did fail water seeped in to freeze in the cavity and cause fractures. Where the armature rusts or fails it is very difficult to replace it without breaking the facing terracotta. It is possible to repair fractures with epoxy resins and fill cracks with ground terracotta mixed with a bonding agent followed by the application of a water repellent. Where complete sections have failed, only three firms can now provide terracotta replacements. These are:

Shaws of Darwen (Ceramics) Ltd., Waterside, Darwen, Lancs BP3 3NX
Hathernware Ceramics Ltd., Hathern Station Works, Loughborough, Leics. LE12 5EW

Other firms can provide passable replacements in synthetic materials cast in moulds. Real terracotta takes a long time to dry during which time the outer surface may shrink by a factor of a twelfth – and it is harder to fabricate the effects of age and weathering than with stone or brick. Nevertheless the effect of authenticity is highly prized. In the summer of 1984 the Secretary of State upheld the refusal of the GLC to allow the two lost terracotta domes from the famous Hackney Empire of 1901 to be replaced in glass fibre and insisted on the re-use of terracotta.

FURTHER INFORMATION

John Fidler's 'The Conservation of Architectural Terracotta and Faience' was published in the *Transactions*, 1981, of the ASCHB (two articles).

Generally speaking unfired earth was used constructionally in three forms, as cob, clay lump or pisé, in decreasing order of frequency.

Cob is by far the oldest and probably the best known. The word first appeared in 1602 (McCann) although the earliest cob walling to be excavated has been found in Oxfordshire and dates from *c.*1250. The London Assize of 1189 refers to 'mud plasterers and torchers'. The basic constituent is subsoil (topsoil normally possessing too much humus) strengthened by chalk, dung or ash, and aggregates like sand and fibre, or barley straw perhaps now with a small amount of cement or lime as a stabiliser. A section of the field well manured and churned over by the feet of cattle offered earth already well prepared as did mud from the unmacadamed roads. In Cornwall 'clob' (sic) depended on the slivers of broken slate called shilf used to bind road surfaces. After laying a foundation of stone or brick, although this was not a universal prerequisite, the well trodden cob was applied wet in courses or 'lifts' (as in concrete), each layer being superimposed once its predecessor had dried normally in a minimum of a week, a process which was the better for being slow, curing being left ideally to the natural effect of humid weather. The alternative seems to have been unconscionable speed, it being recorded that some clay houses in Cumberland were completed in a day. Shutters of wood could be applied to both sides until the cob had set, in the manner of concrete, although this was not as common as unshuttered or 'free pile' work. A summary of traditional practice compiled in 1848 (in *The Ecclesiologist*) affirmed that the cob wall should project 1½in beyond the face of the stone foundations which should themselves rise at least 2in above the surface. DPCs within this plinth, as long as they went through all the wall, offered further guarantee against the great enemy, damp, as did slate DPCs over windows as in some examples in Cumbria. DPCs where there are no plinths are not recommended as the cob underneath it becomes sodden and can collapse.

Most ancient clay walls are load-bearing although there are examples of concealed timber members designed to consolidate the wall and take some of the weight of the roof. This was ubiquitous in the 'mud and stud' cottages of Lincolnshire. 'Sleeping timbers' placed horizontally within the wall could provide the bearing for any suspended floor. Window apertures, which were apparently either accommodated into the wall as it was 'lifted' or cut out retrospectively could be strengthened and articulated by stone reveals. Although cob could serve for flues and chimneys, brick appeared to offer greater resistance to heat and some gabled walls in cob shells would have been in brick from the start. There are passionate devotees of unrendered cob, but an annual coating of limewash or 'slapdash' (as in Devon) to the outside and perhaps a lime plaster facing to the interior were normal. However, regional variants, be it the 'cob' of Devon and Dorset, the 'mud' of the East Midlands, the clay 'daubins' (one of many names) of Cumbria, the houses in 'puddled clay' of Suffolk, those in 'cat and clay' in Dumfriesshire, the examples in 'chalk mud' in Wiltshire, or those in 'white earth' or 'wichert' in Buckinghamshire; each have their own peculiarities.

Cob is monolithic. Clay lump follows the principle of adobe in Africa and is formed in blocks. This makes them much closer to bricks (which are after all fired as opposed to unfired clay); even more so as they are formed in moulds of wood and laid in courses. They are, however, much larger, normally the size of a stone block. If laid when still slightly tacky it seems that a mortar can be dispensed with although the use of puddled clay in this connection seems to have been more accepted. Once complete the walls were lime rendered, the most distinctive 'casing' being two or three coats of coal tar left exposed to deter cattle licking it in a farmyard but normally sanded when wet and then colour washed on residential properties. As with cob there was a plinth at the base, timber ties to take the floor and perhaps a cavity wall, the inner skin only being in clay lump, the outside in brick. It appears to have been limited to East Anglia and the northern Home Counties and to have been introduced only from the early seventeenth century (Barley, p. 202).

Pisé de terre, meaning simply rammed earth, was introduced from France (and Spain) in the late eighteenth century. It is, like cob, monolithic but the clay differs in being dry or semi-dry on application, in lacking added fibre and in being raised within wooden shuttering or formwork, later re-useable as floorboards attached to the bond timbers. The walls were erected on stone or brick foundations and if necessary timber piles, a recipe of 1848 indicating that the last course between the foundations and the pisé should be in Roman cement, flat squared stones or slate, designed to act as DPCs. Finished walls could be limewashed. Examples of pisé construction are exceptionally rare. In the eighteenth, nineteenth and twentieth centuries its use seems to have been limited to 'model' constructions (e.g. schools at Aston and Walkern, Hertfordshire; see *The Ecclesiologist* 1848, p. 220).

The effect of water on earth walls can be as dramatic as that on the Wicked Witch of the West in the *Wizard of Oz*. Water penetrating from the eaves, the foundations or through cracks in the coat of limewash or chalk slurry (in Wessex) can induce collapse. Hence the constant advocation of proper foundations and overhanging eaves. Cob demands a roof or 'hat' for freestanding garden walls. Hence the importance too of attending to cracks. Lesser examples should be mortared but larger ones can be filled with stone, crushed brick or roofing tiles mixed with, or bedded in, lime mortar and disguised with a lime render. Unfortunately the most obviously invisible method, that of adding new cob, is the least practical for this will shrink on setting and thus crack again. This problem will not arise, however, if the wall is cut through to its full depth and the new cob placed on the old on an even bed. If reclaimed cob is reused it may require mixing with fresh subsoil free from all vegetable matter; it should be mixed dry with alternate layers of earth and straw and then thoroughly trodden with additional straw, if necessary, and gently wetted. In new cob a sample of the earth to be employed should be tested as a soil with more than 35 per cent clay content is unsuitable. Using a 'control' and 'experiment', one sample can be mixed with water which is then poured off until only the sand remains and the proportion of this can be compared with the control. The visible use of materials like brick, tiles, cobbles and stone to build up collapsed sections of walling has been common for years, albeit that the visual contrast is softened by the annual, and very advisable, coat of limewash. Chicken wire has been used as a binder operating in much the same way as expanded metal laths. The addition of buttresses is not uncommon and in a newly discovered refrigerator barn at Cheshunt in Hertfordshire the earth is banked up against the base on the whole perimeter which brings added advantage in throwing off water and protecting the base from physical impact (although in cob the base will tend to be more compacted and therefore stronger than the upper sections of the wall, just as the north wall will be stronger than the south, as it has taken longer to dry out or 'cure' in the comparative absence of the sun).

Damp is as much an enemy to the timber lintels and other inserted wood. Any new timber placed vertically in the walls must be in reverse to its direction of growth to avoid water absorption from the cob, through the end grain.

FURTHER INFORMATION

The following publications contain useful information on earth construction:

R.W. Brunskill, 'The Clay Houses of Cumberland', *AMS Transactions* 1962, pp. 57–80.

Alec Clifton-Taylor, *The Pattern of English Building*, Faber 1972.

J.R. Harrison, *AMS Transactions* 28.

John McCann, *Clay and Cob Buildings*, Shire Publications 1983.

Eric Mercer, *English Vernacular Houses*, HMSO 1975.

J.M. Proctor, *East Anglian Cottages*, Providence Press 1979.

Clough Williams-Ellis and J. Eastwick-Field, 'Cottage Building in Cob, Pisé and Stablized Earth', *Country Life* 1947.

Further reading on building repair includes the Building Research Board's Special Report No. 5, 'Building in Cob and Pisé de Terre', HMSO 1922, and also the SPAB *News* for July 1982.

The SPAB is preparing (1986) Information Sheets on: *The Repair of Cob* by John Deal and *The Repair of Clay Lump* by Michael Wingate. Richard Hughes is carrying out a research programme for ICOMOS on the conservation of soil-constructed buildings.

The primary purpose of a roof is to offer protection from the elements. In foreign climes where the chief enemy is the sun a thick flat roof often without additional covering suffices. In Britain, however, where the greatest threat is from rain and snow, roofs nearly always have to be pitched to throw off water. Prior to the discovery of steel the most flexible material for the construction of pitches was timber, but as this in turn is vulnerable to water an additional roof covering became essential. The choice of covering dictates the thickness of the supporting timbers and the angle of the pitch. Thatch, the thickest but also the lightest, can dispense with timbers altogether, as is evidenced by the few remaining examples of 'solid thatch' roofs, whereas the heaviest stone slabs require framing of very thick scantling or cross-section. The weight of the covering is one of the determinants of the pitch although it is not often the predominant one. Thatch is rarely laid under 50° whilst Welsh slates can be 20° or lower, a decided advantage to Neo-Classical architects who disliked the roof as a challenge to the rectilinear form which they most admired. And yet both these coverings are light. Clearly it is true that the steeper the pitch the greater is the weight on the battens. A material like slate, which is very resistant to water, can risk a lower pitch which in other materials without compensatory overlap would encourage the 'creeping' of water on the underside of the tiles or slates through capillary action. A light covering such as pantile is generally speaking the more protected against wind. Acute pitches tend to provide a greater chance for workable spaces within attics and also offer the air space and possibilities for drying out that are useful in the battle against condensation, heightened by the modern demand for insulation and central heating.

Thatch

Thatch is one of the oldest of all roof coverings and yet one of the least durable. As a result there are far more buildings which were once thatched than now remain so. Telltale signs are the steep pitch, lips running continuously round the base of the chimneys but at a level higher than the present roof covering and three or four courses of stone tiles at the eaves of a now otherwise tiled roof to prevent dislodging of thatch by wind or cattle, although the latter is the least reliable of the clues. And yet there are still some 55 000 thatched buildings in England, the vast majority being in the South and West, although even in East Anglia there are pockets of virtual non-appearance. In Lavenham there is only one surviving example (nos 45–46 Church Street) – a sure sign that thatch had become unfashionable in

This diagram from the catalogue of a Victorian builder in Reading gives the terms applied to the various pitches current in the late nineteenth century

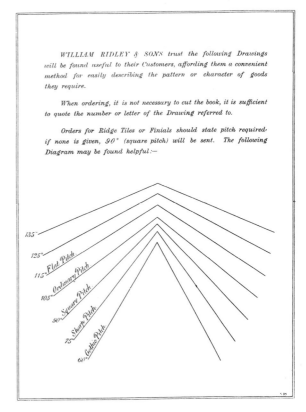

WILLIAM RIDLEY & SONS trust the following Drawings will be found useful to their Customers, affording them a convenient method for easily describing the pattern or character of goods they require.

When ordering, it is not necessary to cut the book, it is sufficient to quote the number or letter of the Drawing referred to.

Orders for Ridge Tiles or Finials should state pitch required; if none is given, 90° (square pitch) will be sent. The following Diagram may be found helpful:—

135°
125°
115° Flat Pitch
105° Ordinary Pitch
90° Square Pitch
75° Sharp Pitch
60° Gothic Pitch

this wealthy wool town. Fashion had become progressively enforced by law, thatch being banned, primarily because of its fire hazard, from London in 1212, Cambridge in 1619 and Wareham and Brechin in 1762. It is now highly likely that the retrenchment has gone as far as it is going to go. The presence of thatch tends to add rather than detract from a building's financial value and most planning authorities take the view that it should only be replaced by other coverings on listed buildings in exceptional cases; some offer grants or loans to ensure that this is the case. Numbers employed in the craft of thatching may now be as high as between 800 and 1000. The Council for Small Industries in Rural Areas, COSIRA, (see Useful Addresses) has regionally-based thatching officers and holds courses to instruct newcomers and encourage apprenticeships (the standard train-

ing period is now four years). There are minor inconveniences, particularly the reconciliation of thatch with soil and vent pipes (which can be solved by the use of disused chimneys) but any extra cost thus incurred is offset by the ability in most cases to do without gutters. There remain however two great disincentives: the cost of rethatching, an operation which has to be faced by each generation, and that of insurance. In areas where thatch is rare and the craft is not practised locally, firms tendering may have to charge board and lodging to house their men near the site. Two-year waiting lists are not uncommon. Insurance premiums can be as high as five times those for a tiled property. Fire has always been the most obvious threat – as long ago as 1212 the London

Great Tew, Oxfordshire. Tiles fitted below dormers or at the eaves assisted in the disposal of water

decree laid down that existing thatch roofs should be limewashed. But fire continues to rank high in the considerations of insurance companies and premiums will be affected by the presence of an open fire and the regularity with which chimneys are swept. Burning of the old thatch on site may not be covered by the thatcher's insurance. A number of companies however are now offering more competitive quotes and are regularly advertising in magazines such as *Traditional Homes* and *Period Home*. The Thatch Owners Protection Scheme, operated by the Thatching Advisory Service (see Notes), to which beneficiaries subscribe on the basis of an annual fee, offers a 24-hour emergency service, an annual roof inspection and advice on seeking suitable firms as well as cheaper insurance. Similar advice can be obtained from the National Society of Master Thatchers, the relevant county-based Thatchers Associations (addresses in *The Care and Repair of Thatched Roofs*, see Further Information) and the two thatching officers of COSIRA. The Protection Scheme can significantly reduce premiums through the installation of a free smoke detector on the main landing. The danger is posed not by spontaneous combustion but by external action, so further preventative measures are always advisable, including the insertion of spark guards or 'arresters' to chimneys, regular sweeping and maintenance of the latter, the laying of sparge pipes from which water can be sprayed onto the thatch, the installation of lightning conductors, the ducting of electric wiring away from the thatch and the removal of any wire netting which would prevent the quick removal during a fire (although where the latter is applied to long straw it is now normally lightly fixed). Chemical formulas have been developed for the coating of straw and reed before the thatching operation begins to improve durability and fire resistance, and there are herbicides to discourage mosses. Re-thatching may provide the opportunity for the addition of fireproof sheeting as an underlay. But a sense of unease can be carried too far. There is after all some implied reassurance in the fact that whereas present day Building Regulations are generally much tougher than those of the Middle Ages, on thatch they are less restrictive. No new thatched building can be constructed less than 12 metres from any point on the boundary if the adjacent roof is inflammable unless a waiver is granted but there is certainly nothing like the total bans mentioned before (although it must be said that these Regulations are primarily based on the risk of spread to other properties rather than damage to one's own). Next to fire, perhaps the worst nuisance is posed by birds. Sparrow pots placed

under the eaves are a traditional method of enticing this particular species away from the straw or reed itself.

There are occasional thatched roofs of heather in Scotland, other examples in sedge (generally used for the ridging of reed roofs) and the very occasional example of 'artificial thatch' (composed of panels of glass fibre coated in coloured polyester resin or bundles of plastic straw). The latter may be fire retardant but is singularly unattractive and unconvincing and can become brittle. There are, after these, two principal thatching materials, each one associated with the vernacular of particular regions. These are the straws, either 'long straw' or, in spite of its name, 'wheat reed' or the water reeds, of which the most celebrated is Norfolk Reed. In the past such products were almost invariably gathered from local fields or marshes. Now much more is being imported even from as far afield as Eastern Europe.

Protagonists of each argue their corner strenuously but statistically it is 'long straw' which is on the retreat, burdened most particularly by the tendency of presently favoured straw species not to grow high enough and the single-mindedness of combine harvesters in going for the grain at the expense of the stalk. 'Long straw' is losing out to 'combed wheat reed' and the marsh or water reed – most particularly the Norfolk Reed.

Availability is certainly not the only difference.

Historic roofs may overlap with neighbours and where these have been demolished odd segments of roofs survive to differing eaves and ridgelines

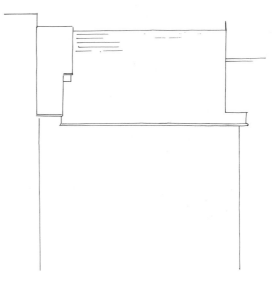

'Long straw' can have a life as brief as twenty years, Norfolk Reed one as long as eighty with 'combed wheat reed' falling in the middle. In the nineteenth century it was accepted that the expectancy of wheat straw was fifteen to twenty years and oat straw, only eight. Nevertheless, replacement is not always wholesale and there are surviving examples of smoke-blackened rye straw undercoats from the Middle Ages. Norfolk Reed may last longer but it is not uncommon to find it half as expensive again as 'long straw'. There is a consensus that Norfolk Reed is the more obstreperous to work with but opinion remains divided on aesthetic appeal. The principal visual difference is that straw is laid lengthwise, and produces more rounded outlines, whereas Norfolk Reed is applied so that the sharp ends of the stalks are exposed. Sedge tends to have the same life as 'long straw', or a few years shorter.

Tiles

Tiles, like bricks, were the subject of regulatory statute in 1477 by which standard dimensions – $10\frac{1}{2}$in length, $6\frac{1}{4}$in width and $\frac{5}{8}$in thickness – were estab-

The unorthodox roof shape should be highly prized. This five-sided pitched roof in Wolseley Road, Ashford, Kent was unfortunately demolished in the early 1980s

lished. The Act was reaffirmed under George II and even today the British Standard is $10\frac{1}{2}$in $\times$ $6\frac{1}{2}$in $\times$ $\frac{3}{8}$in or $\frac{5}{8}$in. Well known regional variants such as the Kentish peg tile hardly differed at 10in $\times$ 6in from the national model. In the middle years of the nineteenth century the smallest tile was $9\frac{1}{2}$in $\times$ $5\frac{3}{4}$in. Further categorization is by 'gauge' which also applies to slates. This normally means the measurement of that section of the upper surface known as the 'lap' running from the base to where the counterpart on the superimposed course overlaps. It has, by extension, been applied to the spacing between the rows of horizontal laths or battens from which the tiles are hung, being either the distance from the top of one lath to the top of one below or that of the next but one. Nowadays, however, the middle and last definitions are less accepted. Alternative words with the same meaning, 'bare' and 'margin', are both now obsolete.

A stone slate roof laid to diminishing courses with a reducing overlap, the higher the course, has no consistent gauge on the one slope. 'Plain tiles' are 'double lapped' in that the 'gauge' represents only a third or less of the upper surface, the remainder being concealed under two overlapping courses. Old tiles are often pleasantly irregular in cross-section. A slight arch or camber secures a more watertight

Ely – a contrast between plain and contoured tile

*A stack of new pantiles showing the nibs and splayed
corners*

lateral joint, as does a counter arching on the other axis in 'double cambered' tiles.

It is the length of firing and clay employed that governs colour, as with bricks, although generally speaking tiles need a better quality clay as they have to be thinner. Shapes peculiar to particular regions make for a rich variety in outlines that can still be respected where the more enterprising tileries and brickyards are able to produce 'specials'.

The most widespread alternative to the 'plain tile' is the 'pantile', the former being flat save for the camber, the latter giving the appearance of frozen waves to a roofslope, through the slight contour on each tile. 'Pantile' should really be 'pentile' for the word is derived from the French 'pente' or bending. They are single lap where plain tiles are double lap. The Dictionary of the Architectural Publications Society (1852–92) reported that the overlap then could be $3\frac{1}{2}$in but in many examples it is minimal – being far less than the side lap where the curved ends of two juxtaposed pantiles interlock. On old and new two of the four corners are cut to a splay to assist in the jointing. As with plain tiles one face of old pantiles has a more agitated surface, deriving from the sand sprinkled on the bottom and sides of the mould to prevent the clay sticking – although unlike plain tiles this sanded surface was generally placed downwards rather that upwards. They differed too in being larger – the British Standard of $13\frac{1}{2} \times 9\frac{1}{2} \times \frac{4}{10}$ in dating back at least to an Act in the reign of George I – but were nevertheless thinner and therefore lighter. This permitted laying to a lower pitch. The reduced overlap and lightness made for greater vulnerability and 'torching' to the underside of the roof (see page 21) or direct bedding on lime mortar was widespread, particularly in East Anglia. Many early examples were imports from Holland, although there do seem to have been home-produced examples in Bristol from as early as 1670. The distinctive black-glazed examples of East Anglia, of which modern versions are still available, also derive from Holland. The earliest recorded example dates from 1771.

The pantile was the most popular contoured tile but others have found intermittent favour including the Marseilles tile, and the Single or Double Roman – the latter being produced from the nineteenth century in Bridgwater, Somerset which was also an early source of pantiles.

All tiles are secured to their battens either by pegs (hence peg tiles) or by nibs. The battens were themselves nailed directly to the rafters, although in modern practice reduced heat loss is assisted by the introduction of an insulating membrane, perhaps of polystyrene foam and improved 'sarking' with untearable felt in place of the earlier torching. Pegs, now normally replaced by copper or other non-ferrous nails, are secured through a hole in the head of the tile (normally tapered in early examples) and hooked over the back of the batten. Two holes were often provided but it is quite common for only one to be pegged. As an alternative, the peg can be gripped between two rows of battens. It has been stated as a rough guide in Kent that the older the tile, the larger the hole. The nib is a semi-circular or square lip formed in the tilery at the back of the head of the tile, which allows it to be hooked over the top of the batten. Examples from the fourteenth century are known but it only became widespread from the nineteenth. There is clearly greater risk in holding and hammering pegs through contoured tiles and the nibs became as common on the pantile as the plain tile. Some examples of the Bridgwater Double Roman and modern tiles have three nibs. The two methods are not mutually exclusive: today tiles and pantiles are produced with both nibs and nail holes allowing the user to decide how they should be fixed. Most present-day manufacturers of clay tiles suggest that each tile in every fifth course should be twice nailed. Tiles at the eaves ridge and verges are also nailed.

Battens are still almost universally made from wood. This is despite the perishability of the material, which so often means that it is the battens rather than the roof covering itself which fails first. Battens in iron were used in 1829–30 at the Pantechnicon near Belgrave Square and the *Practical Mechanics Journal* of 1854 suggested laths of thin strips of slate. Neither example was followed. Early battens in wood (with or without vertical counterbattens running at ninety degrees underneath them) were invariably split or cleft along the natural grain. As a result they were thin (sometimes merely $\frac{1}{2} \times \frac{1}{2}$in as opposed to modern battens of 2×2in) and irregular in profile, thus contributing to the pleasing waywardness of coursing lines on ancient roofs. The grain is better able to withstand weathering when it is not sawn. This was helped by the use of heartwood only, whether of oak, chestnut or fir. Moxon in his *Mechanick Exercises* of 1700, (p. 7) distinguishes between heart of oak laths for outside tiling and plastering, as against those in fir for inside plastering and pantile lathing. Heart of fir laths, particularly from old ships' masts, were recommended in the nineteenth century. Cleft laths are still being produced in small numbers, but as the technique is labour-intensive, they are expensive. Cleft chestnut battens were used in the reconstruction of the medieval hall house from North Cray in Kent at the Weald and Downland Open Air Museum at Singleton, West Sussex. The house required 5000 feet of tiling battens and a further 11 000 for daubing the infill panels between the main structural members (composed of elm). From 1846 almost all tiling battens have been sawn and today they would be in softwood and pressure-impregnated with preservative.

The device of 'torching', by which the heads of tiles were bedded on both sides in lime and hair mortar, or alternatively with clay, moss or straw, provided extra protection against driven rain and the same device is seen in many stone slated roofs. (With stone slates, roofs could also be 'double-torched' at the top and bottom of the laths and 'fully-torched' in all the space between the laths.) Bonnet tiles running along the ridge (of which a surprising number of medieval handmade examples survive in the West Country) had to be mortared into position. On pantiles and other single lap roofs the mortar could be concealed by the addition of tile slips in a process known as galleting (c.f. page 116). As in modern pantile roofs a small square of tile in the middle of the mortar improved adhesion.

Most tiles are now either wire-cut or pressed, but hand-moulded examples are still available from firms like Bulmers and Keymers. Pantiles are being produced in abundance in Yorkshire, Humberside and East Anglia, and there are imports from Holland, Belgium and France. The beauty and variety of variegated clay tile roofs can be approximated in modern colour ranges and historically textured 'sanded' examples are obtainable. Some firms offer metal and concrete coated versions to match the colour and texture of plain and pantiles. It is possible to simulate the effect of age through a spray of chicken-dung. There is a ready market in second-hand recycled tiles, although any temptation to use those which are heavily laden with moss or lichens should be avoided as these absorb water and therefore render the tile peculiarly vulnerable to frost. Moss generates acid which can attack lead guttering and flashings (although water running off from copper undercloaks is said to inhibit the growth of lichen). Any resort to artificial substances should also bear in mind disparities in weight. Concrete tiles, for examples, are much heavier than slates.

Slates

Natural slates are normally considered as a relatively modern roofing material because of the association with the Welsh slate industry and the great boom it enjoyed from the mid eighteenth century. Many of

Water running from copper, in this case from a ventilating cupola, deters lichen growth on stone slates

the products of the Principality were of a uniformly dull dark blue that made slate cheap in price and cheap in appearance. This is, however, unfair. Welsh slates range from dark to light blue and rare examples are described as Red or Green. Unlike tiles they could come in massive sizes, compensating for characterless colour by drama of scale. The largest ever, sent to the 1862 International Exhibition, was 20 feet long, 10 feet wide and weighed 4½ tons. Other slates are noticeably more attractive and some like the 'scantle' slates of the South West are particularly small. Although the last quarry producing examples at Swithland in Leicestershire was closed in 1887 there is still a ready supply of recycled examples (except for those of the largest size). Delabole slates from Cornwall, available at least since the sixteenth century, are still in production despite a hiccup in 1977 when the firm producing them went into liquidation. Their good fortune was matched by the well-known Honister Pass quarries, producing Westmoreland Green, worked since 1643 by the Buttermere and Westmoreland Green Slate Company which laid off its last workers in October 1984 but is now once again in production. Devonshire slates, associated particularly with the Mill Hill Quarry near Tavistock, are still being produced in small numbers.

The extensive grants programme for the rehabilitation of nineteenth-century housing stock has led to a re-invigoration of the industry in Wales, although demand is also drawing in competition from foreign natural slates, particularly from France. The two main domestic rivals, Westmoreland Green slate and Delabole, are protected in their geographical strongholds, Cumbria and the South West respectively, by the conservation policies of planning authorities who have rallied to the defence of vernacular roofing materials. The great attraction of both, the first in variegated light green and capable of being laid in diminishing courses, and the second, normally in grey or blue with veins of green, has gained clients throughout Britain. The fact that Westmoreland can cost three times that of Welsh slate remains a strong financial barrier to wider use. The famous quarry of Burlington (Blue) Slate at Coniston, Cumbria is presently enjoying a boost in demand both at home and abroad. All natural slate is in competition with artificial slate, but it can better these rivals in durability whilst Welsh slate remains competitive in price. The natural product enjoys a wide range of subsidiary applications and has in the last two hundred years been used to provide window sills, copings, damp-proof courses, shelving, flooring and gravestones. It is light, colourfast, non-combustible, highly resistant to rain and frost and polluted atmosphere, and Welsh slate is economic in use with the 20 per cent minimum overlap that is generally stipulated. In modern practice Welsh slates are secured by nails (in aluminium alloy, copper, silicon bronze or stainless steel) rather than the oak pegs in use until c. 1830 or are alternatively held in position by tabs, tingles, hooks or clips. Individual slates may have two or even three holes and occasionally one at the head and one nicked out of one side ('Cheek nailed'). The nails are normally secured on laths over boarding laid on the rafters. James Wyatt did invent a Patent Slating with no boarding and no battens where the slates were screwed to the rafters themselves, narrow slate strips bedded in putty being applied over the joists, but this alternative did not catch on. Tabs are far more often seen where individual slates have had to be pushed back into position. As they grip the centre of the base of the slate they have the clear disadvantage of being visible. They are normally now in stainless steel, as copper and lead display a tendency to open up and rise away from the slate, thus facilitating slippage. Clips are being used more frequently to secure the asbestos slates which have been in production since the early twentieth century. Largely invisible tabs fixed to undersides are available, although the lack of a camber on a slate (the principal difference in section from a tile) is a mixed blessing in this respect (also see p. 76).

Stone slates

Whereas the quarrying of natural slates is continuing, the production of the so-called 'stone slates', either in limestone or sandstone, is now very rare. Although second-hand examples can be recycled, a famous quarry, such as Stonesfield in Oxfordshire, a principal source of Cotswold stone, has been unproductive since 1909. The Purbeck quarries did not survive the Second World War. Flags are still obtainable in Ham Hill stone in Somerset, parts of West Yorkshire and Hexham and two small quarries for the production of Cotswold stone re-opened in 1981 and 1982 at Brockhill near Guiting Power, Gloucestershire and Filkins, Oxfordshire. Nevertheless, where sizeable new quantities of stone slates are required for works of repair, difficult decisions have to be taken. The dilemma is whether to raid an existing building for re-used slates (or, less painfully, resort to a materials bank) or to use artificial substitutes. Perhaps one of the bravest experiments to encourage the use of the natural product is taking place in Northamptonshire, at Collyweston. Slates produced from a number of quarries at this village were used widely from the eighteenth century to roof many traditional properties, particularly in Northamptonshire and Cambridgeshire. They are one of the stone slates produced by the natural action of frost which splits the stone 'logs' produced from the quarries along the bedding plane – a process last recorded in Rutland in 1611. However the mining ceased in the early 1960s and a sequence of mild winters (save for those of 1981–82 and 1985–86) have precluded delamination by the traditional methods. This deficiency prompted the organization known as 'Men of the Stones' (see Useful Addresses) to establish the Collyweston Stone Slaters' Trust, which was registered as a charity in October 1982. The trust is experimenting with artificial refrigeration, and the long-term aim is the continuous production of slates on a commercial basis. The Trust acknowledges that Collywestons will never be financially competitive with mass production concrete tiles and slates; but it is hoped that the preservation of traditional appearance, the considerable durability which such slates can offer and their relative lightness in comparison to some artificial substitutes will count in their favour. Where an existing roof is to be recycled it should be remembered that it was traditional for Collywestons to be bedded in mortar as well as nailed, whereas many Cotswold stones were laid dry. The mortar employed was normally of a fairly weak mix and dismantling need not therefore lead to damage. Resetting of stone slates is now nearly always by nails driven into single, or less commonly, clasped between double battens, the traditional use of riven oak pegs or sheep bones hung from battens posing too many long-term problems. Hanging the pegs would tear the felt on most present-day roofs unless greater depth is obtained through raising the battens with counterbattens underneath.

In the absence of widely available natural stone slates the field has been open for 'reconstructed' or 'artificial' stone. Perhaps the leading firms in this field are Hardrow ARC and Bradstone Traditional Roofing. The latter introduced reconstructed Cotswold slates in 1970 and the Moordale slate for use in the North in 1980. Nibbed versions of both are available. Although Collywestons are lighter than some artificial slates that relationship is normally reversed, as for example with Filkins slates. Sufficient time has now elapsed to show that some Bradstone roofs weather well, but the effect of a gently rippling lichen-covered real stone roof is hard to capture, and the saw-cut edges can look more mechanical, further exaggerating the differences in colour and texture. As the acid test remains the willingness of the planners to accept it, the Public Inquiry on the reroofing of the Old Hall at Bradford-on-Avon, Wiltshire in 1980 proved a milestone. The Secretary of State permitted the use of Bradstone on this Grade I building, swayed no doubt by the support for the product presented in writing by Mr Alec Clifton-Taylor. But in August 1985 the Department prohibited the replacement of natural stone slates by 'artificial' substitutes on four listed inter-war council houses in Saxon Close at Filkins, the Oxfordshire village which houses the newly opened quarry. Cotswold District Council has no set policy on the use of artificial stone slates but there are certain highly sensitive areas, for example Northleach, where it insists on the use of recycled authentic slates.

Shingles

Few roofing materials have fallen so dramatically out of favour as wooden tiles, or shingles. Salisbury Cathedral was first roofed in this manner but it is now hard to name one major building that is still so covered. The vulnerability to fire, heat and rain is obvious. The susceptibility of iron nails to the attack of tannic acid where the shingles are in oak lead to the occasional use, as with stone slates, of sheep bones. Such a problem can in any case be alleviated through the burning of the nail holes with a hot iron, or more easily, by the use of oak pins. In fact, good quality oak shingles can enjoy a life of sixty to seventy years, on northern and eastern slopes, rivalling that of the most durable thatch. Longer life is promised for modern versions by pressure impregnation with preservative and regular recoating, for example with tar resin. But sawn cedar shingles, primarily from North America, have displaced almost completely the traditional cleft English oak. The red cedar weathers to an attractive silvery grey, but the individual units are larger and the saw gives a mechanical edge. The cleft sweet chestnut shingles, also used in America, and imported from South-West France by W.H. Colt Limited, the principal importers of cedar shingles, are widely considered to offer a more plausible substitute for oak. As with thatch, building regulations preclude the use of shingle on roofs less than 12 metres from a side boundary on a new property and like the straw and reed of thatch, shingles enjoy a peculiar attraction for birds such as woodpeckers. The use of zinc sheets as an underlay is one safeguard against such an attack. Shingles can be used for covering walls as well as roofs, in the manner of tile hanging.

Lead

Lead appears more often on domestic historic properties as protective 'flashings' to door surrounds and chimney bases and as rainwater goods, although it has the ability shared by other metals to cover flat roofs (remembering that the so-called 'flats' on a house were never absolutely flat, each area requiring a slight fall towards a gutter). Lead is either cast in craft workshops, run in molten form over a bed of sand, or milled in rolling mills. The first and traditional method, almost universal until the end of the seventeenth century, is still practised by some specialist leadworking firms, particularly for ornamental work and is greatly valued for its appearance. The casting would normally have been carried out by the plumber. The belvedere on the roof of the Manor House at Wareham in Dorset is inscribed 'This platform was cast by James Gaylord, Plumber, for Mr George Gould 1712'. Most lead in the last century and a half is the product of rolling mills although, in the words of the Lead Development Association, 'Apart from surface texture and less accuracy in consistency of thickness, there are, for all practical purposes when the composition of the metal is similar, no significant differences between the properties and working of cast lead sheet and of milled lead sheet'. To resist its inherent tendency to 'creep' the medieval preference for small sheets is still followed; indeed it is even more important as present day lead sheeting is thinner. So is the similar custom of laying in 'herringbone' fashion – that is with raised joints at alternate diagonals, although the joints are now generally in the form of upstanding welts rather than circular rolls (either hollow or wrapped around wooden rods). 'Creeping' is more likely on a south-facing slope and slippage into the gutter may have to be trimmed back. As well as being light, malleable and longlasting (with an accepted life of some two hundred years) lead has the further advantage of being recycleable. It can, with the addition of a small portion of new lead, be melted down and re-used, although this is clearly a course of action only to be followed at historic properties with a great deal of caution. It is not just initials which might be lost but evidence of the curious habit of cutting footprints into lead roofs as at Melbury House, Dorset. King Christian IV of Denmark had the outline of his foot cast into the lead roof at St Paul's Cathedral. As always, there are disadvantages – it does wear thin through the process of oxidization and it was early understood that even tiny pinpricks in cast lead would let in water through capillary suction. It cannot be laid directly on to oak or cement

and reacts unfavourably with creosote. It is nowadays expensive and because of its high scrap value it is the only roofing where theft remains a real danger. This has been increasingly overcome by the use of lead clad steel, which as well as being of no value to thieves is also highly resistant to vandalism. Ternecoated stainless steel, introduced into Britain in 1982, is the equivalent of fools' gold to lead thieves. It has been used in the repair of Albert Docks, Liverpool and lead and tin-coated stainless steel replaced the lead roof of the 1754 Temple at Hagley Hall near Birmingham in 1984. This substitute, however, is not particularly cheaper than lead and has no scrap value which can be set against the cost of a new roof. Moreover, there have been cases where angry thieves, having struggled to the rooftop to find that the lead was of no use, have vandalized it in frustration. Modern lead is categorized into codes, defined by thickness, drawn up by the Lead Development Association. Broadly speaking Codes 3 to 8 are suitable for external work. The LDA can supply a list of specialist leadworking contractors (34 Berkeley Square, London W1X 6AJ, tel. (01) 499-8422).

There is a permanent exhibition on lead in building arranged by the Worshipful Company of Plumbers at the Weald and Downland Museum, Singleton, West Sussex.

The other roofing metals are principally copper, zinc and aluminium. Copper, by far the oldest of the three, is considered lighter and stronger than lead and produces salts which boring insects and organic growth find off-putting. But it does transfer noise fairly easily and the green colour to which it turns in the space of a decade (from an initial rich yellow and a secondary lightish black) can be run on to adjacent parapets and decorative features by rain. As with lead there is a specific Development Association (at Orchard House, Mutton Lane, Potters Bar, Herts EN6, 3AP, tel. 50711).

Zinc was first produced commercially in this country in Bristol in 1740 and that city and Swansea, where the zinc works were first opened in 1836, remain the centres for smelting. As with lead and copper it is equally used for rainwater goods and flashings and as a protective coating for steel. It is only about a third of the price of lead but the Technical Panel of the SPAB considers that is is not so durable. Aluminium was put into commercial use from 1877. By that time the roofing material which has given metal its worst reputation, corrugated iron, was in fairly widespread industrial use, the earliest examples dating from the mid nineteenth century. Felt roofs were in use in the west of Scotland in the eighteenth century. The ever resourceful nineteenth century produced other ideas too. The great architectural publicist, Mr J.C. Loudon, gave an account in 1811 of the 'paper roof' used at Tew Lodge, Oxfordshire. There may yet be surviving examples waiting to be found. Stout paper was dipped into tar and pitch, dried, laid on a roof in a manner of slates and then tarred again *in situ*. Loudon favoured further applications of powdered chalk, coal or brickdust.

Roof failure

The failure of a slate or tile roof is more normally that of the battens or nails rather than the covering itself. As battens are still always in wood, there is an ever present danger of rot. Where batten failure and what is still picturesquely termed 'nail sickness' affects more than a third of the roof piecemeal repair is generally to no avail. However, if the problem can be diagnosed early on, a number of alternatives to stripping and relaying are available.

Two in particular require access to the underside of the roof. A number of firms specialize in the application of an adhesive foam plastic which reinforces the fixing of tiles and slates on to their battens as well as improving insulation. Although the principle is much the same as the more traditional 'parging' or 'torching' of the underside of tiles with lime mortar there is a risk of impeding ventilation to the roof space. The now standard application of a roofing felt under the battens, with or without the traditional boarding, further reduces the entry of air. Compensatory ventilation can be introduced through 'whistle vents', by allowing air to pass at felt laps, by air bricks and apertures within eaves and gables, by the use of ventilating slates or tiles now produced by a number of firms or by 'open tiling' or 'open slating' – a less common, and older, name for single lap roofing. Protective measures against the entry of birds and insects might be advisable. The second alternative has been christened 'Roof Bond' and was patented by a Hampshire firm in 1973, although it is now offered

The addition of skins to the external surfaces of roof covering, as in this example in Yorkshire, is ugly, prevents the re-use of tiles or slates and impedes ventilation

by a number of builders. This involves attaching each slate on the underside to its batten by a fire-retardant polyurethane block glued with polyester resin. It is clearly dependent upon the continued serviceability of the battens but it is highly competitive compared with the cost of complete recovering so has been used on a number of outstanding historic buildings. There is normally a 20 or 25 year guarantee. As the blocks can be cut through with a sharp tool the slates so fixed can be reused.

The third option approaches the roof from the topside and involves the addition of a black compound skin of bitumen and hessian. Although the primary purpose is to increase weatherproofing it consolidates a roof where failure of battens, nails and individuals slates or tiles threatens.

The process was first used in America in 1897. There are precedents in traditional practice, particularly in the slurrying or 'grouting' of roofs as far afield as Cornwall and Yorkshire. However, the process is certainly not to be used on attractive historic roofs. The visual effects are obvious; it can trap moisture and merely puts off the day when the complete recovering has to be faced, a process which it renders more difficult by making all existing tiles or slates unreuseable. Such a process is used a great deal in industrial building, particularly those with flat roofs, and that is the market for which it is intended. The traditional application of tar to weatherboarding falls into much the same category; it impedes the entry of moisture, inhibits its release and makes all the boarding unreuseable.

Where individual tiles or slates have failed, localized repairs are possible. Cracks in stone slates can be repaired *in situ* and it might be possible to 'turn' selective examples on relaying. The repair of a cracked Welsh slate is not worth the effort and it is best removed by a long tool known as a slate ripper, which normally has a cranked handle and heart-shaped head and is slipped under the broken slate in order to pull out the nail. Because access to the batten is still concealed by the overlap the new slate has to be secured by a clip, tab or 'tingle' in wire or strip metal which is hooked over or nailed to the batten. The proliferation of such clips, also used on single lap tiles, is not advisable and where failure has reached that degree complete stripping should be entertained. Where amateurs, or indeed professionals, are seeking to replace individual units, sacks of straw or

hay laid beneath the ladder reduce the risk of shattering the tiles or slates beneath.

Where complete stripping is unavoidable the chance is normally taken to replace nails and battens, particularly as both these have to be removed to fix the roofing felt. The British Standard recommends aluminium, copper or silicon bronze nails. In exceptional cases where the nails only have failed it might be possible to avoid the wholesale stripping of slate roofs by opening up a slanting 'ladder', moving progressively across the slope and running down the roof. Slates are stripped off in a vertical band to help keep off the weather during the relaying. Stripped tiles must be checked for damage and normally cleaned before re-use. If only a certain proportion prove suitable the most appropriate can be rationed to the prominent slope. The Victorians took advantage of the discrepancy between old and replacement tiles by banding them in deliberate contrasts of colour and texture. Where new tiles of differing colour are to be introduced, the planning authority will require an application for listed building consent. The introduction of any new roof lights or solar panels also requires explicit permission.

Any recovering of the roof must precede a careful examination of the roof timbers to ensure their capacity to take the loading not just of the new materials but of the operatives clambering about on them. The desire of some thatchers to remove ancient roof trusses as it is easier to drive spikes into softwood must be resisted. Dips and sags are obvious signs of distress, yet some ancient roofs were designed to be hogbacked with a hump in the middle and cocked up with the ridgeline rising towards lateral chimneys on gable ends. A slight upturn at 'sprocketed' eaves was similarly intended. There is great attraction in the wavy line caused by the gentle warping of green timber over the centuries and generally speaking these should be braced and consolidated by the careful addition of new timbers or mild steel angles rather than ironed out. Problems of infestation are dealt with elsewhere (chapter 20). The removal of roof coverings offers an important occasion for the careful archaeological examination of the roof timbers themselves, particularly, on medieval properties, for any soot blackening caused by a former central hearth – and on these and later buildings, transverse timbers indicative of louvres and belvederes (viewing platforms).

FURTHER INFORMATION

The following publications contain useful information on roof covering:

Michael Billet, *Thatching and Thatched Buildings*, Robert Hale 1979.

Peter Brockett and Adela Wright, *The Care and Repair of Thatched Roofs*, SPAB and COSIRA 1986.

R.A. Cordingley, 'British Historical Rooftypes and their Members: A Classification', reprinted from *Transactions of the Ancient Monuments Society*, vol 9, 1961.

Keith Darby 'Thatch as a Modern Building Material', *Architects Journal*, 3 September 1986.

Derbyshire County Council, 'Stone Roofing Slates', 1977 (draft).

J. Miller, *Slating and Tiling*, 1937.

ADDRESSES

Thatching Advisory Service Ltd., Rose Tree Farm, 29 Nine Mile Ride, Finchampstead, Wokingham, Berkshire RG11 4QD, tel. (0734) 734203. This company publishes a number of useful leaflets.

Guild of Master Craftsmen Ltd., 170 High Street, Lewes, East Sussex. A good source of information on thatchers. There are a number of regionally based Master Thatchers Associations. COSIRA (see Useful Addresses) can also advise on thatchers.

The National Master Tile Fixers Association, Fairfax House, Fulwood Place, London WC1V 6DW, tel. (01) 405-8422.

The Clay Roofing Tile Association, Federation House, Station Road, Stoke-on-Trent ST4 2TJ, tel. (0782) 416256. This organization has seven member companies. There are also companies such as Swallows, which produce handmade tiles but are not members.

The North Wales Slate Quarries Association, Bryn Llanllechial, Bangor, Gwynedd, N. Wales.

Ashurst and Dimes (see p. 43) give out a list of quarries supplying stone slates.

---

12 WINDOWS

Elevations without windows are described as 'blind'. Sometimes it seems aptly romantic, too, as one sees houses disfigured by the black patches of infilled openings and new off-the-peg windows lacking all the 'life' and character of the original.

The derivation is a useful reminder that the first domestic as opposed to ecclesiastical windows in the present millennium lacked glazing. Glass first appeared in houses in the thirteenth century – although it only became expected in houses of any pretension from the beginning of the sixteenth century. The cost precluded window glass in some humbler rural homes even into the Georgian period.

Security was offered by horizontal saddlebars and vertical mullions normally squared off but set obliquely in diamond section. Protective skins of horn, pierced wood, waxed paper or oilcoth, if necessary stiffened by a wooden frame or by diagonal lattice work, offered some protection in inclement weather. It seems likely that the same lattice frames were retained when glass was introduced to offer external protection to the highly valued new amenity. Where shutters for unglazed openings have been found these are normally internal and formed of ledged and battened boards that slide into place in grooves housed in horizontal beams and secured by

The Marlborough Head Public House, Dedham, Essex. An early lead ventilator, now glazed. (Courtesy, National Monuments Record)

Wilberforce House, Hull, East Yorkshire. Only one casement (second from right on third floor) remains on this famous building of the seventeenth century, all the rest having been replaced by sashes. Even this apparent survivor was inserted by the first curator of the museum now housed there

pegs. Reconstructed examples can be seen at the Weald and Downland Museum at Singleton and in the tower of Mundon church, Essex owned by the Friends of Friendless Churches. In the more ornate medieval window the upper sections of the tracery could be left unglazed and unshuttered for ease of ventilation.

Where unglazed windows have survived, this is nearly always as a consequence of an originally external wall being incorporated within an interior through extension and retained as an opening, very often to introduce 'borrowed light'. The presence of mullions without a glazing rebate is an obvious clue but not an infallible one. The earliest casements were simply attached to the mullions by wire, being regarded as moveable items that would not remain on a change of ownership. Framed oilcloths referred to before sometimes required a rebate. Housings for shutters are similarly inconclusive for these were very common in glazed openings as well.

The two great historic forms of window frames are the casement, first mentioned in the thirteenth century, and the sash, introduced *c.*1670 into England and 1715 into Wales and now confirmed by a South African scholar (H.J. Louw SAHGB 26 1983 pp. 49–72) as a product of English inventive genius.

The casement is side-hung and opens in and out, although some early examples did not open at all and it remained common in a window of, say, four lights for only one to be hinged. The introduction of a pierced lead ventilator could offer some compensation on hot days. There was never an occasion when the casement passed entirely out of use, although it did become unfashionable in the eighteenth century. Perhaps the most attractive examples are the 'leaded lights' where panes or quarries are contained by lead cames laid either to form squares, or more commonly diamonds – and many inventive configurations besides. A certain Walter Gedde published a book of over one hundred designs for glaziers in 1613.

In some cases small casements opened in individual lights of upper or lower sashes. But the more obvious intermediate form was the horizontally sliding window known as the Yorkshire sash. This originated in the eighteenth century in the county of its name but soon became nationally based. These generally operate by sliding along a waxed oak bead set behind the fixed light(s).

The sash, which like the casement, could be in metal (normally wrought or cast iron, occasionally copper and bronze) as well as wood (oak, mahogany etc.) opened up and down rather than in or out. It was operated on a system, concealed in sash boxes set into the reveal, or side, of the window, composed of

Variations on the horizontal sliding sash at Leighton
Buzzard and Abingdon

pulleys and weights suspended on a sash line of hemp or flax, replaced in later examples by braided copper wire or leather strips and later still by copper chains. Some simple examples, of which more survive in Ireland than on the mainland, relied on pegs rather than weights. Arkwrights cottages at Cromford, Derbyshire retain pegged vertically-sliding sashes of *c*.1780. The first sashes were normally single-hung, the lower light only operating by sashcord, the upper relying simply on catches or pegs. If the window was rendered double-hung, as later examples almost invariably were, the box would have to be deepened.

When sashes were first introduced, glazing bars or 'astragals' were thick with a tendency to flatter, unmoulded surfaces – and panes were squarer in proportion. Generally, despite a confusing revival in their use at the beginning of the twentieth century, these passed out of favour in the second half of the eighteenth century to be replaced by thinner and more elegant examples, facilitated in part by the new material, cast iron, which was capable of such attenuation.

The first sash windows also tended to be flush to the façade but the degree of recession into the aperture was progressively controlled in London by the great Acts of 1707 (which required the frame to be set four inches back) and that of 1774 (which enforced recession behind the brickwork itself). Compliance was not strict and at a time when there were no national building regulations London's example was not necessarily followed. Moreover, such regulations hardly affected rural areas, the purpose of the control being very largely to prevent the spread of disastrous fires in built-up areas.

If the recession of window frames is to be treated with great caution as a guide to dating, this applies even more to the number of panes. Six over six or four over four were perhaps the most favoured in the Georgian period but there are early and late examples where the total is 30 or more.

The notorious Window Tax enforced under varying terms between 1694 and 1851 cast its pernicious effect on all windows regardless of form. Great ingenuity was shown in its evasion, as with all taxes. The owner of the early-nineteenth-century Ashmans Hall near Beccles in Suffolk introduced thin sheets of slate, painted white, instead of the glass between the glazing bars in those courtyard windows he chose to take out of commission to reduce the taxman's burden.

By the mid nineteenth century development largely centred on the increased use of plate glass.

Elegant catches on eighteenth-century casements

Plate is distinguished from sheet and crown glass, both of which have been in production since the thirteenth century, by, generally speaking, being cast, the latter two being blown. It was first devised in France in 1688, first manufactured in a works in Britain (at Ravenshead) in 1773 and was first available commercially in this country from 1838. As panes became larger, glazing bars became less and less necessary and from the mid and late nineteenth century many sashes had none at all. The increased fashion for glazing bars in upper sashes only to define margin lights demonstrated how their effect had become purely decorative. Moulded triangular 'lugs' or 'horns' normally below, but occasionally above, the bottom rail of the light testified to the greater weight of plate glass, although as they are first noted c.1820 their introduction seems to have had a great deal to do with changes in the nature of the joints. Extra catches offered further support to the lug when the upper light was in the lowered position. Whereas the lugs themselves must post-date 1820 and normally 1850, the window itself may be older and reconstructed to take plate glass.

Plate glass was far more of a rival to crown than it was to sheet which also witnessed considerable technical advance in the 1830s. The retreat of crown has been widely bemoaned as its manufacture by spinning into discs rather than casting in a plate gave it the brilliancy and the more resonant 'ring' that comes from uneven surface, varying thickness and centrifugal 'waves'. Surviving early examples of crown demand the greatest care – although dating is rarely as easy as in Cootes Farm, Steeple Bumpstead, Essex where the obliging glazier has incribed 'John Choat 24th February 1778' on the outside of the pane. (Incidentally inscriptions have been found on a number of occasions on one of the faces of the control bar of the H section of leaded lights.) Crown was still the commonest form of glass in the mid nineteenth century and its grading into best, second, etc. down to the coarsest produced at the bottom end of the market – a glass so green that it impaired visibility. Nineteenth-century sheet glazing was described by the contempoary encyclopaedist Gwilt as 'wavy and undulating'. Crown glass is no longer made. Its name is used by modern manufacturers but such substitutes may not be the best replacements. 'Greenhouse' glass may persuade from a distance, particularly where original and replacement panes are mixed irregularly, but on a prominent elevation it might be worth asking a specialist glazier for hand-

Totnes, Devon. Surviving examples of the earlier thicker glazing bars in use until the mid eighteenth century

'Blind' sashes in Glasgow, known in Scotland as 'dummies', included a transverse change of plane to echo the bottom rail of the upper light on the functioning neighbours

Eighteenth-century external shutters in Shrewsbury. Note the stays at the base and the holes for ventilation, and to allow the night watchman to spot any fire. Internal shutters could slide up from the panelling below in the manner of a sash window

made replacements or simply tolerating the crack if necessary after bonding with a patent sealant.

When one recalls that sashes with thick glazing bars on early-eighteenth-century properties are likely to be original it follows that surviving examples, and there are a surprising number, must be at least 220 years old. Almost all the components of a timber sash or casement are infinitely renewable and capable of 'overhaul', whether this be the timber lengths, the putty, the panes, the sash cord or the lead caming.

Because the frame of a four-square window would be very difficult to make other than with four joints at the angles the principal members can be replaced independently from each other, though dismantling may require not just the unpicking of the joint but the removal of overlays of paint and the steaming off of any reinforcing glue.

However, the timber may well be capable of retention. There are a number of proprietary products or 'plastic wood' available for the patching of fissures and depressions; a common filler is sawdust and Unibond mix. One Repair System involves the cutting back of the rotten wood to a sound surface and the addition of a hardener and filler prior to repainting with a primer and final coat. The recurrence of wet rot is prevented by the insertion of small plugs or tablets into predrilled holes (Ronseal Wood Repair System, Sterling, Roncraft, Freepost, E. Moseley, Surrey KT8 8BR). Such plugs tend to be

Internal hinged pelmet in mid-nineteenth-century property that lifts to permit the raising of a very early example of internal roller shutter

more efficient in the injection of fungicide than simple brushing. It was traditional practice to dress superficially decayed sills with painted lead, but this solution has many critics (SPAB News, Vol. 1, No. 3 July 1980). Even where the sill is not to be replaced it might be worthwhile having a look underneath as it was the custom in places as far apart as Bristol and Warwickshire to place a coin thereunder during the construction process. In later buildings the presence of a groove underneath the sill, known as the throat, encourages water to fall to the ground and it is wise to ensure that this is not blocked by any external ducting of wires. A slight fall to the top of the sill further assists the disposal of water but a slope as pronounced as that on 15 St Cuthbert Street, Bedford is rare. Where a glazing bar or astragal requires replacement any competent joiner should be able to take a profile from an unpainted equivalent elsewhere on the window and provide an exact match. Except in the particular case of crown glass or early sheet referred to before, panes are the easiest of all to replace, although even a slight variation in weight can upset the counterbalance mechanism by which a sash is opened – albeit that this can be

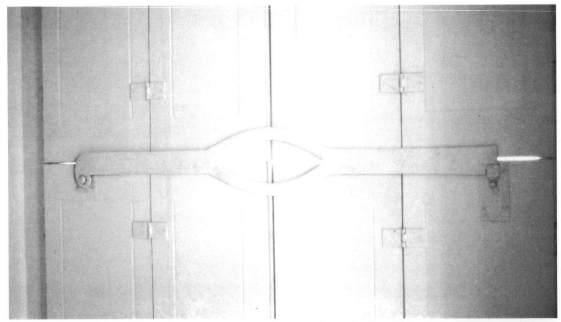

Internal stay bar with central hand hold to secure internal shutters; an alternative to the pullbar pushed into holes at the side, lined in wood. (In The Grange, White Hart Lane, Tottenham, North London)

adjusted. L-shaped angles, now normally in steel, countersunk into the surface of the wood, provide a traditional method of bracing joints that are working loose. Modern sashes can dispense altogether with sash boxes by the use of spiral or spring tape balances set into the top of the window jamb or even into the side (the stile). Where the more traditional weight and pulley have survived there are strong practical and historical reasons for their retention. There may be more elements, but modern nylon sash cord is very cheap and the pulleys and weights can provide more exact clues to the date of the house than almost anything else.

Once the window has been repaired it can be repainted, although this is inadvisable in foggy or inclement weather. The removal of old paint with pumice stone or glass paper can allow earlier paint surfaces to survive for future archaeological investigation and offers less danger than burning off. Sash boxes were notorious for their tendency to fire, the tall oxygen filled sash box acting as the perfect flue. The majority of country house fires probably started this way. The newly developed microporous and 'breather' paints do not impede the evaporation of moisture and thus reduce the risk of rot.

Where complete windows are beyond repair it might be possible to take the chance to reinstate earlier forms. In eighteenth-century buildings the

15 St Cuthbert Street, Bedford. Window sills normally slope only on part of their upper surface to throw off the rain, the section beneath the bottom light known as the 'stoop', being flat. Here the slope is unusually pronounced

replacement of lost glazing bars will nearly always be an improvement. In Bath the Preservation Trust is actively encouraging owners throughout the City to reinstate on eighteenth-century properties through a system of grants. It should however be an authentic reinstatement. The attaching of moulded strips to nineteenth-century plate glass – introducing a sham sub-division into panes – fools nobody.

Sometimes the tensions displayed in window frames are more apparent than real. It was quite common in the eighteenth century for large shop windows to be constructed to the profile of a barrel. Where such bellying is distorted and less rounded it may well be a useful indication of an overloaded lintel, or other structural faults. This might have to be reconciled by the introduction of steel or rein-forced concrete joists behind the original flat arch or window head, involving the removal of an earlier wooden lintel. Even where pressures have distorted the frame, original windows can be accommodated to the idiosyncratic shape by the planing down of top or bottom rails and specially shaped weather stripping.

Under the Building Regulations a minimum size is set for the admission of light and ventilation through windows. Nevertheless it is important to repeat that such regulations do not generally apply to existing properties.

The repair of metal frames is more of a specialist matter. The enemy primarily is rust rather than rot. Small smithies or foundries should be able to attend to cracking. If a window is beyond recall injection

Segmental or flat arches over window heads usually conceal a timber member now sometimes replaced in concrete or metal to take the loading, with the outer surface reinstated

moulded plastic replacements identical in everything except weight have been developed of late, particu-larly for warehouse conversions. Leaded lights can distort through contortion of the lead itself, failure of the soldered joints or of the wire ties that secure the light to the mullions and the equivalent border ties.

Most modern windows, almost always bringing with them the advantage of double glazing, are now in wood, aluminium, (first introduced in the late 1930s), steel (first used in Britain in 1884), UPVC or a mixture of these materials. Double glazing need not of itself be inconsistent with historic character. 'Double windows', normally casements in front of sashes to exclude noise and retain warmth, were in domestic use in the mid nineteenth century before it became standard in conservatories from 1884. More-over the word is often used imprecisely. The introduction of a single new skin of glass, sash for sashes, casement for casements, to the interior which keeps the existing window and is known strictly speaking as 'secondary glazing' can avoid all external change other than on reflections. It is normally cheaper, and can be inserted without the presence of a professional. It is however incompatible with the retention of shutters; which are, in any case, equally effective as a skin of glass. Simple weather stripping

Ellesmere, Shropshire. 'The Laurels', Scotland Street (demolished). A fine house of c.1820 disfigured by metal windows in widened openings

of junctions, costing a few pounds, will have a marginal effect on noise but a marked one on draughts.

The danger comes from the threat of wholesale refenestration. Aggressive marketing campaigns often make it difficult to examine the rivals dispassionately. A very useful technical appraisal published in the Architects Journal in April 1985 compared the four basic materials outlined above and found that timber windows properly maintained (including redecoration every three to five years) had a proven expectation of 30 to 40 years, and up to 60 in high performance. (A conservative judgement when one remembers the life of older timber windows and a clear indication of the much reduced life of modern timber windows often employing poorly seasoned softwoods as opposed to old ones.) They were relatively cheap, enjoyed unlimited colours, had a good U value (i.e. were a good insulator), were not dependent upon regular cleaning, were renewable and could be safeguarded by readily available maintenance skills. Aluminium and UPVC windows were much more expensive. UPVC is given a life of 30 to 40 years and may need repolishing after 15 to 20 years. In both cases damaged surfaces were difficult to repair successfully; regular cleaning was required and the colours on offer were limited. Steel rusts, plastic discolours and aluminium oxidizes.

Clearly it is absurdly reactionary to complain against technological advance. New window forms have an important role in new building. Yet by the same token they can look painfully out of place in historic structures. It is not just the shiny hard material that stands out but the form of these off-the-peg units. Particularly misleading is the type which is marketed as being suitable for historic buildings because it possesses glazing bars. Very often these are no more than unmoulded plastic strips pressed within the double glazing and clearly visible close to as shams. They do not frame the glass but are contained by it and they offer no relief to the surface of completely flat, dead glass. The situation is even worse where the frames are flush to the surface rather than recessed and where there is no difference in plane between the 'upper' and 'lower' lights as would of course be the case in a true sash window. With timbered windows the material alone is no guarantee of acceptability. Varnished hardwoods are rarely appropriate. The form is vital. Many local authorities are hostile to top-hung 'night vents' in listed buildings and the pivot-hung window introduced from Scandinavia, known as the 'tilt and turn'. Bottle glass is also inappropriate. Such spun glass is meant to represent the centre of the disc from which crown glass is cut, but these 'bullions' were traditionally discarded or used in secondary positions.

Refenestration in other than facsimile requires listed building consent. Some authorities, for example Calderdale in West Yorkshire, have taken a very hard stand particularly against UPVC and have pursued enforcement action where new standard double glazed units have been inserted without authorization.

FURTHER INFORMATION

A History of the Window is being written by Henti Louw and Robert Crayford. Consult also *Traditional Homes*, October–November 1984, 'Sash windows', and *Period Home*, vol. 3 no. 3, 'Cast Iron Windows and Fanlights' by John McCann.

ADDRESSES

Glass and Glazing Federation, 6 Mount Row WIY 6DY, tel. (01) 409–0545.

Floors are either 'suspended' or 'solid'. The differentiation is twofold, the former being upper floors spanning between walls, as well as ground floors that do not rest directly on the earth but have an intervening air space. In best practice, this is ventilated through air bricks with the boards supported on honeycombed sleeper walls. The earliest ground floors were solid. So indeed are the most modern in view of the difficulty in preventing rot and rising damp – albeit that they assume a much more sophisticated multi-layered form. A standard present-day sandwich has the screed and floor finish over a layer of concrete, over a damp-proof membrane, over a blinding of rolled dry sand – the whole being bedded if necessary on an expanse of consolidated hardcore.

Such sophistication born of empirical experiment seems light years away from the early floors composed simply of the earth on which the dwelling was constructed, rammed to a flat surface; the ramming in Ireland, Cumbria and Britanny being assisted by the neighbours called in to celebrate the completion of the house in a dance where stomping was compulsory. The use of earth was not as primitive as it sounds. Its ability to take a polish made it suitable as a final layer and its great strength when compacted led to its choice even into the years of the Industrial Revolution in workshops. Binding was assisted by the addition of ox blood, bone, ashes and hydrated lime (see p. 113) and, in floors without a clay content, by pozzolanic cement (also see p. 113). (Ashurst *Mortars, Renders and Plasters* p. 34) A layer of rushes offered further protection to the surface. Lime, river sand, gundust or anvil dust from the forge was a mixture used in nineteenth-century maltings. Such traditional treatments continue to be valid provided the dreaded enemy of damp is kept at bay. The curiously named 'grip' (plaster) floor, composed of lime ash (the residue on the floor of the lime kiln left after burning) bonded with reeds and straw or laths with an optional admixture of sifted coal ashes, clay and horse dung and normally laid on joists, can have an equally long life. Medieval mortar floors have been excavated and examples in plaster,

both in lime and gypsum, are common in some areas up to the nineteenth century and still prized for their durability and incombustibility. The earliest documentary reference, to Chatsworth, dates from 1556 and there was clearly a prestige attached to their use. Lord Burlington employed them coloured in imitation of marble at Old House, Chiswick. Plaster floors of lime and coal ashes were made in Bath in 1788 at 9d per yard. They have the great advantage of being recycleable, and there are a number of recorded instances of their being sold for reburning and relaying. The construction of a plaster floor has been opened up for display at Gainsborough Old Hall, Lincs, showing the finish of gypsum over two skins of lime ash.

Floor surfaces in brick, in pamments (unglazed clay tiles) and stone paviors could be laid directly on the earth or with an intervening bed of sand or ash. Such surfaces can have an indefinite life and have the virtue of looking more attractive the more worn they become. Even where the surface becomes too eroded, individual bricks or flags can be taken out and turned over, an operation much the easier where traditional lime mortar rather than cement has been employed. Complete relaying is probably best, carried over a layer of concrete and a DPM. Where laying a membrane, however, it is important to ensure that the surrounding walls also possess DPMs. Where water cannot enter through the floor it will seek out the walls and rise there instead. No system can guarantee the complete eradication of damp and surfaces should not be sealed to prevent the evaporation of moisture. Wax polishing proceeded by a lustre coat of linseed oil is widely recommended, and modern research has yet to debunk the age old method of cleaning and glossing flagstones with soured milk (first noted by Addy in the late nineteenth century in the Wakefield area). If nineteenth-century decorative tiles require replacement joints are best sawn, always remembering that some were offset and not straight-jointed. Modern silk-screen tiles should be avoided. Cracks are best plugged with inert fillers. There are still firms specializing in terrazzo tiling and one of the most famous of all nineteenth-century firms, Mintons, survives as Minton Hollis. Over-enthusiastic scrubbing with soapy water can be inadvisable, not just in the impact on surfaces, but in the case of floors incorporating new wood there is a slight risk of reactivating dote (a heart rot) that affects living trees. Where 'pugging' (see p. 91) has been in sand wetting can increase its weight and encourage rot. This is not quite the licence for the lazy it sounds, and the best rule is to ensure that where water is applied in abundance it is washed off rather than allowed to seep through.

Leaving aside the fireproof arches in iron and concrete floors developed from the late eighteenth century and mid nineteenth century primarily for commercial architecture, virtually all suspended flooring is in wood. C.F. Innocent writing in 1916 found early floors in the Sheffield area composed of floorboards alone but the most common examples are the Single, the Double and the Double-Framed. In some rare examples the boards run parallel to, rather than across or 'athwart' the joists the top of the latter, thus serving in effect as boards. Speaking very generally, the older the property, the thicker and perhaps shallower the joists and the less planed or wrought. Cecil Hewett has stated that joists deeper than they were wide first appeared in 1528 in the Queen's House, Tower of London.

The floorboards themselves were laid either square-edged or butt jointed, were tongued and grooved (or 'ploughed'), rebated, secret-nailed or dowelled, although these methods of jointing need not be mutually exclusive. Joints were rendered watertight by 'caulking' through forcing in hemp or yarn, which might be pitched on the lower surface. Further security was afforded by wooden or iron nails or 'brads', askew nailing being less visible. It was and is still possible to disguise nail heads when they are countersunk by the addition of putty stained to the colour of the floor. Evelyn recommended that the boards be tacked only for the first year and then nailed to accommodate any 'creep'. Generally the inside of a plank was turned to the joists to counteract the natural tendency of the edges to twist, and to secure further solidity; the central two out of every four in a 'folded' floor could be rammed home by workmen jumping on them. In 'folded' as opposed to 'straight joint' boarding the boards are not continuous in their edging, the divisions or 'heading joints' also being square-splayed (to allow one nail to secure both adjacent boards), or tongue and grooved. The joints are staggered to prevent continuous lines of weakness. In some early properties floorboards are found laid without either nailing or other security.

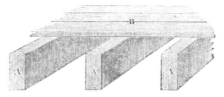

Single Floor

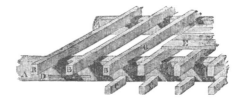

Double Floor

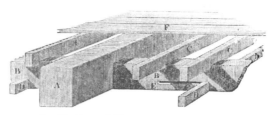

Double Framed Floor

The Single Floor, Double Floor and Double Framed Floor as illustrated in Gwilt's Encyclopaedia, a standard work of reference in the nineteenth century

This is partly because, much like panelling, they were regarded as moveable fixtures following the householder from home to home – but also because it was much easier to haul furniture through widely spaced joists than up narrow winder stairs. In parts of Hereford and Worcester sections of the first floor at the front of the house contain 'coffin holes' to allow dead bodies to be conveyed easily to the front door and to burial. In the same area the 'treading hole' was a circular hole for the hop pocket or sack.

The more decorative timber floors include those in parquet, which was introduced from France in the early seventeenth century, and is generally composed of hardwoods, now normally laid on a thin veneer of plywood; the earlier marquetry floor with inlays of different coloured woods and the wood block floor (laid on a bed of concrete and/or pitch and most common in the kitchen) was invented *c.*1856 by William White. Another favourite of the kitchen, the cork floor, was introduced slightly later. The polishing of wood floors is a fairly recent innovation, acquiring social fashion when it became easier

Denny Abbey, Cambs. Massive early joists with softwood outer edges removed

Boughton House, Northants. The interior of an unfinished late-seventeenth-century wing shows the spandrel pieces designed to take a cove

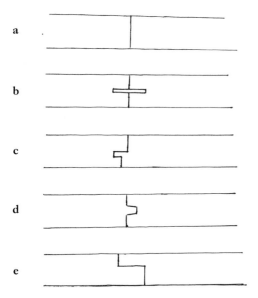

Floorboard joints

a *Square-edged*
b *Dowelled; cross-tongue or 'mid feather' (Scot.), normally in iron*
c *Tongue and groove. On more modern examples the tongue is not placed centrally. Certainly in use from the mid 1820s. In some joints the dowel is dovetailed*
d *Secret-nailed. Nail (omitted from drawing) is driven through the tongue into the joist*
e *Rebated. Certainly in use from the late Middle Ages*

through the introduction of polishing machines. In the eighteenth century wooden floors and stairs were almost always dusted using damp sand, followed occasionally by the strewing of herbs such as mint. Hannah Glass in the Servants' Directory of 1760 specifically denounces soap. Dry scrubbing with white sand was an alternative.

In timber-framed buildings the wood employed is normally oak, although it seems to have been far more usual to use it after seasoning for the boards, rather than green as was the case for the principal members of the frame itself. Elm later became very common and in the eighteenth and nineteenth centuries the foreign softwoods, particularly deal and pitch pine, came to predominate.

The airspace, particularly in double-framed floors, as well as being essential for the purposes of ventilation, has proved a blessing for the heating engineer who can house heating systems there rather than have to disfigure historic spaces by radiators. It is also a convenient route for much service ducting, pipes being fixed to the side of the joist. Nevertheless it is important that if joists have to be notched and cut to take pipes and cables that this is done at the centre, which involves less weakening and reduces the likelihood of the cables being pierced by a nail. Electric power points within the floor under hinged flaps avoid sockets disrupting the continuous line of skirting or panelling. It must not be supposed however that joists are always continuous in their span. In a good many floors the joists are placed at curious angles or are divided into almost maze-like configurations. Where timbers were not long enough there was no alternative to the use of jointed or angled joists and intermediate 'trimmers'. Nor does it follow that the air space will be empty. To reduce sound transference and increase insulation 'pugging' was inserted, whether chaff, chopped straw, sand or silk-waste as in Spitalfields. Shells were used at Hampton Court. Lime and ash 'deafening' is still standard in the Georgian New Town in Edinburgh, new fly ash being obtained from the National Coal Board. Modern insulation board has the obvious advantage of being far less weighty and bothersome but is perhaps less effective. Single floors or open ceilings were normally pugged by the addition of lime and hair plaster or reeds in plaster to the underside of the floorboards between the joists.

When taking up floorboards, particularly where later 'casing' is suspected, the archaeological eye should be alert: for an original lower floor, the stones of a former central hearth, trimmers (shorter joists trimmed around openings) within upper floors indicating the head of lost staircases or the remains of ceiling pieces and moulds. A long diagonal beam running towards an external angle, known as a dragon beam, is a clear indication that a property which might now boast an eighteenth-century elevation originally had timber framed jetties on both principal facades. The boards themselves may be splashed with paint from earlier lost colour schemes.

Apart from rot at the beam ends traditionally anticipated by pitching, setting in loam, wrapping in metal or engineering an enveloping air space, the chief danger facing the suspended timber flooring is central deflection with or without pronounced and picturesque lists. And this is despite the fact that it seems to have been standard practice, at least in the nineteenth century, for floorboards (when first laid) to be kept $\frac{1}{2}-\frac{3}{4}$in higher in the middle of the room to compensate for the subsequent natural shrinking and settlement. Nevertheless the warping is as often explained by the movement of the whole building as by that of the floor alone. In isolated cases floors might actually have been designed with a slight fall. This is certainly true of many external verandahs. The topmost floor at the Queen Elizabeth Hunting Lodge at Chingford in Essex slopes towards the outer wall as the room was once open as a belvedere and the fall encouraged rainwater to the edge. The practice of adding firring (or 'furring') pieces underneath the depressed stretches of boards to raise them to a level height has been standard for centuries and the word was certainly known in the sixteenth

The principal floor from Wollaton Hall, Nottingham. Many a historic floor has discontinuous joists and trimmers where single timbers have proved too short to bridge the suspended area

century. It presumably came from the use of fir for the practice. Where there has been lateral deflection, the introduction of herringbone struts shaped like a St Andrew Cross between the joists also has a long history.

Failure of the joists themselves is a much more serious matter. It can be tackled by introducing extra joists or inserting a new post in the room below at the point of failure, but the latter in particular can be

Wisbech, Cambridgeshire; 12 North Street. A recently discovered example of a painted floor of the eighteenth century. Only two others are known at Crowcombe Court, Somerset and Belton House, Lincolnshire. There is evidence that floorboards in medieval Sussex were whitewashed. (Photo, C. Godfrey)

disruptive in appearance. The SPAB gives a number of methods of strengthening timber floors in its Technical Pamphlet 2. These for the most part involve girding timber by the addition of metal plates, either slotted into the centre of the beam (the flitch plate), attached to it as straps and stirrups, or introducing rods and cables. Where joists are seated in damp walls the sockets can be treated with zinc oxychloride paint, be supported on a corbel with a DPC or enclosed in a steel shoe.

The capacity or 'loading' of a floor is dictated as much by use as by condition. The Building Regulations of a century ago directed that the loading capacity of floors in heavy goods warehouses should be much more than double those of domestic dwellings. Similar regulations apply nowadays where a house is to be converted to offices. Even where partitions are added to suspended floors the joists may need doubling up at that spot to form trimmers – where the partitions in question run parallel to the direction of the joist span. There is a similar doubling-up under the string of any new

staircase. The vibration caused by the 'live load' of walking feet can be reduced by a deep underlay under the carpet and the 'dead loads' imposed by furniture have less potential to damage if they are spread rather than concentrated, with appropriate respect for areas of bad deflection or weak beam ends. Having said that, a certain springiness in the floor is a sign of healthy wood.

Ceilings

'Open ceilings' are in effect the exposed undersides of floors left without the 'underdrawing' in plaster normally understood by the word 'ceiling'. In the 'camp ceiling' in attic rooms the plaster is placed under the rafters and quilted or bowed in profile. Original examples are now rare, for it is difficult to insert the 100mm quilt required by the Building Regulations without battening out the rafters to achieve the required depth. It may be necessary to reduce the depth of the spaces between the joists of the horizontal open ceiling by the addition of plasterboard or fibreglass, but the original ceiling board or fresh plaster can still disguise them. Clearly great caution must be exercised where there is any suspicion of original painted decoration or mouldings on the joists. This is obviously even more the case where it is tempting to strip later staining.

The very word 'ceiling' with its earlier more general application to any second skin such as panelling that insulates a principal structural component, makes 'open ceiling' appear a contradiction in terms. 'Ceiling' normally denotes plaster. The introduction of lining paper in the nineteenth century, and particularly the dominance of plasterboard and skim before and since the War have made life much easier. Nevertheless the traditional practice of three successive layers of plaster, the lathing or scratch coat, the floating or straightening coat and the setting or finishing coat, largely composed of gypsum, each keyed to the other and the first 'pricked up' between the laths to form hooks remains the most advisable way of guaranteeing historic character, both where ceilings require complete replacement or partial renewal. Two coats sufficed in inferior rooms. Each layer differed in consistency, but the standard ingredients were lime, common sand and animal hair. Plaster of Paris (sulphate of lime) or cement could accelerate the set. Laths designed to increase the coherence of the ceiling during setting and reduce the likelihood of a failure of the bond have been standard practice at least since the sixteenth century. Reeds performed the same function. Until the patenting of metal laths in 1841 by Leconte they were invariably in wood, the first ones riven rather than sawn, and nailed in separate lengths between the joists spaced normally at between $\frac{1}{4}$in and $\frac{3}{8}$in, the optimum width to squeeze the neck of the plaster 'hooks'. Counter lathing could be required where laths nailed directly to the underside of joists prevented formation of hooks. Nails in oak ran the risk of attack from tannic acid and as early as 1700 Moxon in *Mechanik Exercizes* (p. 7) declared a preference for fir for use in ceilings. Where wooden lathing is used nowadays it should be pressure impregnated with preservative and the nails galvanized.

Laying the flat 'bed' of a ceiling could be merely the first stage followed by the addition of ornamentation in relief, whether in the form of compartments, cornices, central 'roses' or comprehensive patterns. Basil Champneys, writing in the late nineteenth century, (see Bibliography) laid down the three 'principal modes of executing plaster ceilings'. In the first, ornament was modelled *in situ* on the flat ceiling. In the second the entire ceiling was cast in sections formed in moulds and pressed home with nails on a layer of wet lime. One of the most famous firms associated with this method, George Jackson and Sons, jointly founded by Jackson and the Adam brothers in 1780, is still using some of the original eighteenth-century moulds in boxwood, although there were moulds in other woods, iron, wax and, from the 1840s, gelatine.

The modern preference is for vinyl. The most common form of casting today is fibrous plaster traditionally known as 'rag and stick', which is hollow and strengthened by canvas, wood and/or metal mesh. It was patented in England in 1856 by Desashy, having originated in France. The various sections are screwed home. A number of firms specialize in the field (see Alan Johnson in General Bibliography). Champneys's third method was the moulding of the ornament by hand whilst the plaster was still soft and manageable, known appropriately as 'finger and thumb work' although nevertheless reliant on a large number of tools (Beard, p. 15, see General Bibliography). Where the work was in high relief the use of internal armatures was unavoidable. The over-quick setting of plaster was a great menace and additives like treacle, sugar or milk helped to keep it soft for many days. Champneys's assumption that historic work was normally a combination of his last two options seems to have been borne out by subsequent research. In the New Town, Edinburgh cornices were cast *in situ* profiled by a metal template run along the cornice rod, extra enrichments being cast separately with projecting nails and adhered using the latter and wet stucco. Drury (p. 70) found

Canons Ashby, Northamptonshire. The mid-eighteenth-century ceiling in the Spenser Room dismantled prior to repair. The individual decorative sections were found to be in papier mâché and are here shown laid on the floor prior to conservation

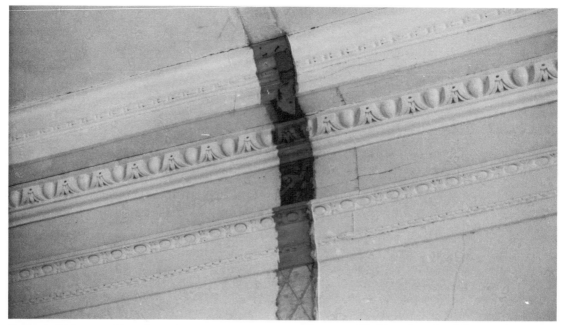

Removal of a later partition of an otherwise wholly whitewashed room has revealed a section of the original painted and (marbled) colour scheme

that the dentils or teeth so common on Classical cornices were cast in lengths and cut to size, the small additional ornamentation like rosettes being fixed with lugs, nails, pegs or scored bases. Solid, and cheaper, plaster cornices were preferred in the late seventeenth century at Flatt Hall, Cumbria (AMS *Transactions* 28, p. 81) because hollow wooden 'corniches' 'afforded a great home to rats and mice', a bother to which no doubt coves were equally susceptible, as their curved profile made the use of wood other than to form bracketed armatures highly problematic. Advantage could be taken of the hollow core to fret the cornice or cove so as to allow colouring previously applied to the wall behind to offer an ingenious form of silhouetting. The grilles around nineteenth-century 'roses' were to ventilate gas lighting. Modern smoke detectors can be concealed in the centre of existing 'roses'.

Not everything in relief on a ceiling is necessarily plaster. Gesso (linseed oil, melted animal glue and whiting) normally on a softwood beading, was common. The mid-eighteenth-century ceiling in the Spencer Room at Canons Ashby in Northamptonshire looks deceptively like plaster but in the recent restoration carried out by the National Trust the various emblems of the ceiling were taken down and found to be in papier mâché (or 'carton pierre') secured by nails. Ceiling paper in high relief rejoicing

under names like 'Anaglypta' or 'Lincrusta' invented in 1860 enjoyed a great vogue in the nineteenth century. It obviously follows that where paper rather than plaster is suspected the use of hot soapy water and a brush can be disastrous.

The question of paint is largely a matter of interior decor and therefore beyond the concern of this book (see General Bibliography). Nevertheless, two points are worth making. Firstly, there are now increasingly sophisticated techniques (other than 'scrapes' or 'cross sections') for ascertaining original colour schemes. Perhaps the most famous practitioner in this field is Ian C. Bristow, ARIBA, whose authoritative book on the subject is eagerly awaited. Occasionally this adventure into the past may be made easier. The removal of an ugly later partition from a room otherwise completely whitewashed can reveal the original colour scheme to the cornice and the original wallpaper. Secondly, there are strong arguments for the continued use of water-based paints or distemper as opposed to the emulsions that were invented in the late thirties. It is true that emulsions can be watered down and that some can be applied over washable distempers. Nevertheless the advantage of distemper to be set against its tendency to dirty quickly is in its chalky finish, its ability to allow the wall to breathe (as do the new microporous paints) and the fact that it can be removed easily, preventing detailing becoming clogged by successive layers of repainting. Emulsion may require methylated spirits or steam for removal. Walpamur distemper can be ordered through the SPAB.

*Baynards Park, Cranleigh, Surrey (demolished). The
circular supports to an earlier ceiling revealed by the
collapse of its successor*

*Burton Agnes, Humberside. The ceiling of the
reconstructed Long Gallery recreated under the supervision
of Mr Francis Johnson, RIBA, in 1974*

Donington Hall, Castle Donington, Leicestershire. The late-eighteenth-century chapel. The effect of water penetration on plaster work. The interior is now largely lost. (Large photo, Christopher Dalton)

Redecoration should post-date repair and not vice-versa. Cracking, bulging and discoloration from damp are obvious signs of distress requiring careful examination from above and below. On plain ceilings differential discoloration is quite common. Those areas without joists immediately above grow markedly dirtier than those immediately below the timbers. This is apparently simply because the passage of dirt is easier at these points and is not of itself alarming. Indeed, the prolonged abstinence from repainting may eventually allow earlier ceiling configurations to leave their trace on later surfaces. Unfortunately the collapse of a ceiling does not always have such clear markers and it is well worthwhile arranging for regular professional assessments, where there has been a recent water pipe burst or the property suffers from the vibrations of heavy traffic. Once opened up the suspect ceiling may show the failure of the laths and battens, their nails, a loss of key or, far more seriously, the failure of the supporting joists. It is surprising, however, how much can be retrieved even from apparently alarming situations.

Starting from the less serious, where the key is sound, crazing on undecorated 'beds' or plain ceilings can be closed with lime putty or powder filler or lining paper or a covering of fine jute scrim or muslin with flour paste and glue. This can be followed by a coat of flat white limewash, or painting. Again, where the ceiling is otherwise sound, cracks can be widened to where the plaster is firmly attached, the edges undercut, the area wetted and then replastered normally with superfine plaster of Paris (its setting time retarded if necessary). A coat of thin Shellac in methylated spirits helps in the words of J.F.S. Jack 'to bind looseness in the old plaster but not to destroy the key offered by its rough surface'. Plaster 'bridges' can substitute for intermittent broken laths and those too closely spaced. The application of a completely new plaster layer over wire netting or open copper mesh (formerly canvas) can remedy more comprehensive failure. Needless to say both operations are carried out from above and the latter adds both water and weight. Resins and glassfibre add neither. Bulges within the ceiling can either be consolidated and braced by the use of cradling pieces between the joists, or pulled back to the horizontal and screwed to the joists using brass metal discs countersunk into the ceiling with a system of double washers. The whole can then be plugged with plaster of Paris – although, sadly, patches can be visible despite being bonded, skimmed on the underside, primed and painted as recommended. Screwing is far less risky to fragile ceilings than hammering nails or brads. Where a plain section of the ceiling has collapsed and timber laths are found to be damaged, a new key will need to be provided before replastering if not with wooden laths then with expanded metal lathing or some crumpled thickish paper wetted and soaked in the plaster. Where an ornamental section has fallen and remained undamaged, re-application using wet plaster or screws with countersunk heads would be well worth attempting. Always try to avoid replacing in plasterboard.

There are certainly firms able to remould lost sections and to remove and resite complete ceilings. The most difficult, and sometimes fearfully expensive, option is called for when the joists themselves have failed. Even where they do not have to be renewed, the splicing in of new beam ends, and the strapping of 'shakes' or splits can dictate that the weight of the ceiling itself has to be taken on steel hangers, rising through one storey or more to be suspended from the nearest available sturdy hori-zontal member, whether that be in the floor above or in the roof. Even where the use of epoxy resin avoids the need to saw through defective timber great care needs to be taken to avoid staining the (normally white) ceilings. Once it has set, epoxy resin is almost impossible to remove. The most intractable problem of all involves the decay of the armatures within the depth of the ceiling. Nowhere is the dilemma more acutely seen than in the once gorgeous late-eight-eenth-century chapel at Donington Hall, Castle Donington, Leicestershire where the wooden supports around which the plaster is moulded suffered a comprehensive dry rot attack.

Ceilings may have to be upgraded as well as repaired to comply with building and fire regulations, particularly on a change of use – something on which your professional adviser can help. In complicated floor structures, particularly those carrying service ducting or those below an attic, he may also care to advise on the introduction of hatches.

FURTHER INFORMATION

The following are useful general studies:

John Ashurst, *Mortars, Renders and Plasters* EASA 1983.

James Ayres, *The Shell Book of the House in Britain*, Phaidon 1975.

Geoffrey Beard, *Decorative Plasterwork in Great Britain*, Phaidon 1975.

Ronald Brunskill, *Timber Building in Britain*, 1985 (section on floors).

Basil Champneys, RIBA *Transactions* 1889, pp. 123–136.

Paul Drury, *The Antiquaries Journal*, 1984.

John Fidler, 'Save the Ceiling', *Traditional Homes*, March 1986 concludes with a list of Master Plasterers and Fibrous Plaster Manufacturers.

J.F.S. Jack, RIBA *Journal* 1950 pp. 416–419.

W.D. Stagg and Ronald Masters, *Decorative Plasterwork, Its Repair and Restoration*, Orion Books 1983.

SPAB Technical Pamphlet No. 2, *Strengthening Timber Floors*.

A book dealing with floors is in preparation as part of the Temple Newsam *Country House Studies* series.

ADDRESSES

Tiles and Architectural Ceramics Society, Institute of Industrial Archaeology, Ironbridge Gorge Museum, Telford, Shropshire TF8 7AW.

It has been calculated that a middle-sized country house (60 × 70 feet) in the north-east has to dispose of 70 000 gallons of rainfall a year. Whereas in the simple thatched cottage the pitched roof and the overhanging or 'dripping' eaves is sufficient to project the water to earth, in taller more sophisticated properties an independent system of rainwater disposal is essential. The water gliding down the roofslope is first gathered in gutters at eaves level that disgorge into spouts or, more commonly, into hoppers and downpipes that channel it directly to a gulley and drain. This necessity was clearly understood: a bye-law of 1763 in York made the introduction of gutters and downpipes compulsory.

Some of the very earliest rainwater furniture is in wood. Although wood remained common into the nineteenth century and was even favoured for the gutters on Paxton's revolutionary Crystal Palace, otherwise all in iron and glass. The wood, normally oak and less commonly teak, was nearly always treated on its internal face. In the earliest examples the original treatment would have been in pitch but later examples have linings or relinings in zinc, lead and asphalt. Wooden gutter sections are still obtainable, for example in Sheffield and Derbyshire, as a standard product. A lining for gutters formed as stone channels at the head of a wall was normal, although certainly not universal. Gutters in metal, whether copper, lead (certainly in use from the fourteenth century), cast iron or zinc (both in use in the late eighteenth century) were only very rarely reliant upon a reinforcing lining. The ever experimental nineteenth century attempted complete gutters in asphalt, concrete and tiles but none became popular.

The variety of materials now on offer where downpipes and gutters, or indeed soil and vent pipes, require replacement is much greater. These newcomers include asbestos cement, cast or cold formed aluminium, plastic GRP (fibreglass) and UPVC. Where the surface can be disguised by painting, and the prices are competitive, it is tempting to go for substitutes. Indeed fibreglass has been used in the present repair programme at Westminster Abbey and Barlaston Hall, Staffordshire. UPVC is accepted in Edinburgh New Town and has the great attraction of cheapness, lightness and not requiring paint (it generally comes in white, black or light grey). Nevertheless it has been criticized where paint is necessary for the sake of blending with a wall surface; this is made more difficult through the marked tendency of fibreglass to expand at high temperatures. Purely utilitarian arguments can be treacherous. Throughout its period of use lead which could on occasion be painted has been employed to imaginative decorative effect particularly on the hoppers and 'ears'. Even in the downpipes the peculiar attraction of the gently serpentine outline of ancient lead cannot be repeated in any other material. Lead's toxic quality persuaded the government in 1982 to extend the Home Improvements and Repair Grants system to cover the removal of lead pipes supplying domestic drinking water but the only possible hazard offered by rainwater pipes is where these disgorge into butts collecting water for domestic use. Lead's unfavourable chemical reaction with oak (through tannic acid), with mortar (either Portland cement or lime) or with rainwater running off a roof covering with significant lichen growth can be countered by its easy workability, its generally long life and the ease of repair through redressing, burning or recasting. In some cases a generously-sized circumference has allowed faulty lead pipes to be lined with slightly smaller plastic counterparts. This cannot be recommended in abstract but it is clearly preferable to removal. Cast iron pipes differ from lead both in their peculiar susceptibility to rust and the consequent need for frequent repainting. Nevertheless they too can be of considerable importance to the character of an historic house and as with some examples in lead, dates and monograms on the hoppers provide irreplaceable clues to the building's construction. For these reasons many planning authorities will resist the introduction of standard units in inappropriate materials. Most historic building grants will normally insist on cast iron.

As virtually all historic gutters and pipes, whatever the material, are made in sections, the joints

A decorative lead 'ear' at Rodmarton, Gloucestershire, an outstanding Arts and Crafts house of the late nineteenth century

being protected by gutter clamps or what are now called union clips, replacement of badly rusted runs is possible without total substitution, although modern profiles often differ slightly from old ones in cast iron. In early arris box gutters each section will be composed of nailed planks. Where cracking, particularly in cast iron guttering, is not advanced, the fissures can be filled with red or white lead putty preceding two coats of bitumastic paint. This paint, generally best applied in the spring, is also used in protecting gutters in stone and lead. Bitumen paint can arrest the attack of dilute organic acids that come from lichen and mosses on tiles and slates on non-ferrous metals. It may be more advisable particularly with cast iron to dismantle the whole system, clean the pieces, treat with a rust inhibitor, prime, repaint and the refix. Whilst for visual reasons conservation efforts should be concentrated on decorative hoppers, where these have decayed beyond recall and cast replacements are considered too expensive, some firms produce substitutes, for example in GRP that could be taken for cast iron at a distance. Any attempt at facsimile reproduction of existing guttering would also need to follow existing profiles

Grantham, Lincolnshire. The sunken downpipe and hopper of 1792, less vulnerable to impact and extremes of weather

and sections (and reincorporate any brackets cupping the gutters, nailed or screwed either to a fascia board or sometimes to the rafters).

It is sometimes tempting to 'internalize' ugly external pipes and by so doing add protection from the extremes of weather. Nevertheless a pipe burst is far more distressing to occupants when it takes place inside rather than outside.

Moreover, there are certainly cases where rainwater pipes were carefully disposed by the original designer to enhance the balance of a facade.

Rainwater disposal systems should not be replaced or altered other than with the advice of a professional for effectiveness can be impaired or improved by the subtlest of changes whether to the shape of the cross section or the length and fall of the gutter. Melville and Gordon point out (see General Bibliography) that 'a level of 36 feet (11 metres) length of $4\frac{1}{2}$in (114mm) half-round gutter can dispose of 15 gallons (68 litres) per minute; when laid to a slope of 1 in 216 however it can dispose of 26 gallons (118 litres) per minute'. Adjustments may be required where the fall becomes newly exposed to

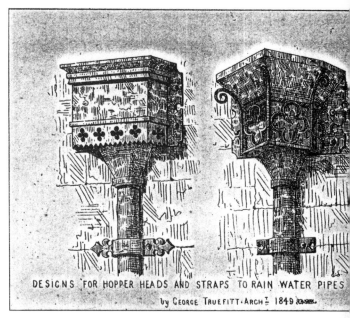

'Gothic' hoppers of 1849 designed by George Truefitt, as illustrated in The Ecclesiologist

Market Weighton, East Yorkshire. Downpipes and hoppers used on an eighteenth-century house to accentuate the symmetry

strong winds or where the original designer, probably for visual rather than practical reasons, fixed neighbouring gutter sections to slope both ways to a downpipe in the middle so that the fall was not continuous and therefore less conspicuous. The householder can be a very useful vigilante. He should be on the look out especially for cracks that might shoot water on to vulnerable walling, for trees shedding their leaves into guttering, particularly during the autumn, and for debris blocking the top and bottom of pipes. If bottom sections of piping do not ring hollow when tapped a blockage can be suspected. The curved section of the pipe known as the 'shoe' which disgorges into the gulley is, like its equivalent or 'swan-neck' at the head of the pipe peculiarly susceptible to fallen birds nests and the like and it was for this reason that later pipes very often have 'rodding eyes' incorporated to allow cleaning by rod. It clearly makes sense to catch the debris at the base of the pipe rather than allow it to further block the drain. 'Balloons' or other perforated covers at the head of the pipes reduce the danger of the debris getting in in the first place. Square piping, which can be important architecturally, can rust on its flat face placed against the wall. A strip of DPC behind may help. Blockages behind cast-iron pipes which can have 'ears' but normally stand proud of a wall secured by 'holder bats' or bobbins round the (larger) screws so that they can be painted on all sides, are more easily spotted and removed. The problem does not arise with lead pipes which are fixed by 'ears' without the intervening air gap,

although they can still split down the back.

The more complicated the roof system the more tortuous the rainwater disposal. Some householders will even find internal gutters running in front of the sill or dormer windows which spill over in a storm into internal spaces. In houses of a depth too great to allow the span to be bridged by single timbers parallel pitch roofs became inevitable. They joined at a 'valley gutter' in the centre. These can be far more disastrous than gutters on the edge of a building, when they develop faults, as water can easily seep through into vulnerable roof spaces. As with eaves guttering there should be a gentle fall formed with steps if in lead to encourage the water to the nearest roof edge. When a gutter is completely invisible and no archaeological damage would result the temptation to fill in the valley with a higher flat roof can prove very tempting. Tracer-electric wires have been used in valley and ordinary gutters to assist in the early melting of frozen water.

Once the water has reached the ground it can still prove a menace, creeping up the wall this time in a reverse direction as rising damp. However, the question of soakaways is a technical one beyond the competence of the amateur and the issue of damp-proof courses is treated elsewhere (chapter 19).

Note on nomenclature: eaves gutters are known in Scotland as 'rhones', in Derbyshire as 'launders', and in Norfolk as 'troughs' (pronounced 'trows').

Internal gutters, running, as here, in front of window sills can be preserved for historic interest even if the water is diverted elsewhere

The chimney has a visible function in providing a channel for the emission of smoke and an invisible one in inducing a draught of air to draw the fire. Even in the event of disuse of this, its primary function, it can still serve to ventilate internal spaces, add drama to a romantic skyline and accentuate the symmetry in a balanced composition. Where natural fuels have been abandoned, retention of the chimney is an intelligent hedge against the day when they may return to fashion. Disused flues can help to direct and conceal vents for a central heating system and channel those for a drainage system.

In the Middle Ages chimneys were generally reserved for 'polite' buildings. In vernacular structures, particularly in the earlier 'open halls' which lacked suspended flooring, the smoke was allowed to seep through the roof. Even where full height smoke bays were provided, the fumes were not channelled in their passage to the roof and generally exited through a hole in the gable or through a system of louvres and funnels.

The chimney became more general from the fifteenth and sixteenth centuries, facilitated by the reintroduction of brick – which was more heat resistant than its rivals, either plaster, bottomless wicker baskets, stone or indeed timber, a material occasionally used with a skin of wattle daub and in the form of bottomless barrels but expressly forbidden in London in the fourteenth century. The chimney accompanied the drive for greater comfort and the introduction of floored dwellings, both of which made it undesirable for smoke to continue to be emitted randomly. It was understood early that high chimneys rising above the level of the roof were less prone to downdraughts, being freer of the contradictory air currents induced by pitched roofs, and that these lofty features would be the more stable, and indeed less prone to downdraught, for being clustered (with more than one flue). There are early medieval examples of polygonal stacks, but perhaps the most memorable results were the enormous brick chimneys that punctuated the East Anglian skyline from the sixteenth century. The number of chimneys, being a direct expression of the number of fireplaces, was a highly visible symbol of social status. To the classical designer concerned with purity of form and outline, chimneys could be a nuisance. At Mereworth in Kent, based on Palladio's Villa Rotunda, Colen Campbell converted the ribs of the dome into flues to prevent the arbitrary punctuation of chimneys. The Neo-Classical designer in his preference for rectilinear forms found them even more a nuisance and it was not until the Gothic Revival of the nineteenth century that their Romantic impact was rediscovered. The consecutive revivals of that century continued the loyalty to traditional materials and it is ironic that chimneys in concrete blocks, which were introduced in the second quarter of the century, are as likely to be seen on the unfashionable vernacular property as on the constructional pioneers.

Chimney pots, referred to in Scotland and the north as 'cans', became widespread from the eighteenth century, although medieval examples in stone or clay are recorded in the south from the thirteenth century. These are normally unglazed, characterized on the external surface by pinpricks and stabmarks designed to minimize the danger of cracking during the firing process and, less frequently, to encourage the draw of air. Some were in the form of crudely modelled human heads – looking much like gargoyles – and these and other examples seem to have been fitted directly to the roofline and not necessarily on the stack. Such pots, and the later rotating cowls, are designed to accentuate the function of the chimney in preventing a downdraught and promoting an updraught. The medieval tradition of the human head continued in some eighteenth-century examples (see Robert Clevering's 'Essay on Chimneys' 1779) and under Victoria some 500 variants were commercially available, the names sometimes evoking their shape – 'Lobsterback', 'H cowl', 'Tallboy', 'Rooks' and 'Bishops' (the last costing 1/6 to buy and erect, in 1880). The range is so great that it was possible to open a museum in 1981 specifically dedicated to the chimney pot. This is based at No 8 Percy Gardens, Blandford, Dorset DT11 7PN (0258) 52290 and is run by the Revd. Valentine Fletcher

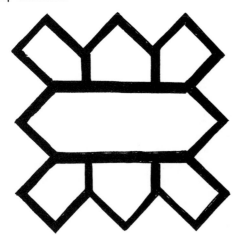

Cross section of a cluster chimney of the sixteenth century in Shropshire showing the walls or 'withs' dividing the flues

(see Bibliography). Admission, by appointment only, is 50p (children and OAPs 25p). The earliest examples have the attractive texture that comes from having been turned on a potter's wheel. In Edinburgh the New Town Conservation Committee has had a stock of new fireclay pots copied from the originals by the Redbank Manufacturing Company of Measham, Burton-on-Trent, one of the oldest, and still one of the leading firms in the field. The same firm promises that it can reproduce any damaged terracotta pot. The habit of dating pots can offer further scraps of information, by which to build up the history of a house. Nevertheless the chimneypot has its detractors, and it is true that some examples are certainly inelegant, while others actually impede the drawing power of the chimney. As it seems to be the reduction in the width of the flue occasioned by the pot rather than the height which offers most inducement to the drawing of the smoke,

Leamington Spa, Warwickshire. The Kingsley School. Chimneys demolished in 1976

No. 96 High Street, Stevenage, Hertfordshire. Following refusal of permission to demolish the central cluster of three chimneys on this sixteenth-century property it has now been rebuilt

by the eighteenth century pots rising only a few inches had been introduced. (Although many eighteenth-century prints show pots on the same stack each rising to a different height.) There have been traditional alternatives. The 'table top', a slab supported at the corner on four brick or stone piers, the 'tent' used in the Lake District where two slabs lean against each other forming a pyramid and the 'whale's teeth', in effect upended slates or tiles mortared into the top of the stack often with raking sides, all have their modern counterparts. The SPAB suggests that any new 'table top' should be in stone or cast concrete and that the top of the stack should be coped with two courses of slates laid to a slight fall outwards and bedded with a lap joint. In the 'tent' they advocate the bedding of the slabs in mortar with upper edges pegged with non-ferrous dowels, each open end being protected against birds by galvanized mesh guards. Both these options fulfil rather more adequately than the pot its secondary function of preventing or decreasing the ingress of rainwater.

There are more applications each year to demolish chimneys than any other single feature in historic buildings. Their loftiness and location make them peculiarly vulnerable to wind and rain, internal acid attack and violent contrast between internal and external temperatures. The leaning chimney, bowing as a result of differential erosion and condensation on the weather side and the uneven decay of the flue lining principally through sulphate attack, is a frequent sight. Some comfort can be derived from the supposition that where the lean is away from the

prevailing rain-laden winds the chimney may have been built out of plumb in compensation for the anticipated effects of the elements. It is certainly the case that some stacks were deliberately built to a crooked outline as this was held to offer some relief from smoking fires. Problems posed by age are of course exacerbated where the stacks are disused – although planning authorities can insist on the retention of chimneys even where they are out of commission. An application in 1983 to demolish the large and mostly original sixteenth-century chimney on No. 96 High Street, Stevenage, Hertfordshire was refused in emphatic terms (there had been a previous offer of a grant towards the cost of repair). Other cases are less straightforward. Where a roof covering has been changed a chimney can be more elongated than originally intended. This is particularly the case where it is thatch which has been lost, the lower pitch of replacement tiles or slates exposing an extra one or two feet of the base of the stack. Rebuilding the stack to the lower height corrects the proportions but removes archaeological evidence.

If the decision is taken that the retention of the chimney is important aesthetically, either with or without continued practical application, the owner should keep a watchful eye against signs of decay. Leans, cracks and the spalling of brickwork are obvious. Less so is the failure of mortar listings, lead flashing or slate and tiles all at the base of the stack and the mortar flaunching in which the base of the pots are embedded. Field glasses help. Lead or copper flashing are normally stepped, the ends tucked into the mortar joints.

The failure of any DPC (for example a lead tray or two courses of slates at the base), and the fracturing of an internal lining is only appreciable at close quarters. Even before lining became essential with new heating systems, 'parging' of the internal surface was common. The use of cow dung as a constituent of the parge continued to be in favour well into the nineteenth century. Deficient linings are doubly serious where a casual approach to fire danger persuaded some early builders to carry flues dangerously close to floor timbers, especially as some flue walls may only be half a brick thick. It is obviously easier to spot flaws after the chimney has been swept. Cracks can then be detected if not by the human eye then by sophisticated machinery like fibrescopes or by a smoke pellet test, or simply putting wet newspaper on the fire to make it smoke.

By far the best summary on repair is that offered in the SPAB's Technical Pamphlet no. 3 (see Bibliography). The most useful guidelines given therein (with ancillary thoughts in parenthesis) are:

1 Where the chimney is reasonably plumb and the erosion is not more than 25 per cent of the thickness of the chimney flue wall, it can be left for the time being. Where this percentage is exceeded individual bricks or stones should be carefully cut out and replaced.

2 Where the mortar has failed, this should be carefully raked out to a depth of at least ¾in or twice the height of the joint – whichever is the greater – and repointed in a mix of 1 : 1 : 6 mortar in sympathy with the adjacent pointing and slightly recessed from the surface. The precise mix must be dependent upon the degree of exposure to the extremes of weather. (The inference is that where the failure of the mortaring has led to a lean this should be contained rather than reversed.)

3 Where the flue is not being used the chimney can be stabilized by the insertion of a reinforced concrete core. However, this can cause problems of weathering and differential expansion.

4 Where the flue has to remain in use an asbestos pipe can be inserted, although a minimum of 4in should be left between the outer face of the pipe and the inner face of the flue.

5 Where the top courses of a smaller chimney need to be remortared a non-ferrous wire tie should be inserted in each joint before repointing.

6 If a flue is to serve an oil or gas fired boiler it should be lined, the simplest method being through a flexible stainless steel flue liner. (This is also the cheapest method). Socketed clay flue liners or lining in concrete using a removeable inflated tube or most of the other alternatives advocated in the Building Regulations tend to be considerably more expensive. Choosing the lining must be a matter for professional judgement, not just financial considerations. (It may be that existing clay pots will have to be replaced with louvred terminals but these can be set inside the top of the existing pot, and some are designed in terracotta to look like a pot).

7 Where a flue is disused it still has value in ventilating the room which it serves and to allow this but at the same time prevent the ingress of water the top of the chimney should be capped. This can be done in a number of ways, for example in lead with eyebrow slots and half-round clay tiles arched over the flue with ventilation allowed through the open ends. Airbricks in the side of the stack, the top being solidly capped, can be unsightly. Capping presupposes the loss of pots, but these can be retained and drilled.

Where the lean of a chimney is physically precarious or aesthetically unfortunate, it is possible to hinge the stack back to the vertical in some circumstances – although in others rebuilding may be unavoidable, particularly where hinging back might damage the flue lining. There are many hazards in the traditional but essentially expedient solution of clasping a leaning chimney around its midriff with a steel tie strapped back to the roof or parapet. It does not prevent decay, it can damage mortar joints and profiles and creates rather than solves problems if the roof timbers or parapet begin to move.

Rather more makeshift solutions for bracing damaged pots bring less attendant problems. One leading architect has found that fissures can be stopped by the use of car body repair filler combined with the more usual device of a circle of non-ferrous, normally copper, wire around the neck. Epoxy resins would be more orthodox.

FURTHER INFORMATION

The following publications include useful advice on chimneys:

Rev. Valentine Fletcher, *Chimneypots and Stacks*, Centaur Press 1968.

SPAB Technical Pamphlet No. 3, 'Chimneys in Old Buildings'.

Traditional Homes, December 1985, article by Peter Mytton Davies.

16 Stairs

The earliest stairs were noticeably economical of space, whether they were vertical ladders hooked to the ceiling or wall when not in use, or external stone steps (known in Scotland as forestairs). Nevertheless the increasing concern for comfort meant that, despite partial enclosure by a pentice (or lean-to) roof, the external steps, a common feature of the medieval 'first floor hall' fell victim to increasing intolerance towards the British weather, surviving only in the farmyard, particularly for the hayloft placed over the cart stall. There was a brief revival this century for the two superimposed maisonettes. Similarly the ladder remained in attics but was soon abandoned elsewhere because of its awkwardness and danger as the principal means of circulation in houses with any pretension to display.

If internal space has to be sacrificed, one of the least demanding is the spiral or turnpike stair where steps of triangular plan taper towards, and wind around, a central newel post or pole – these principal components being in wood, stone or a mixture of both. The pole or winder stairs survived in many humbler dwellings well into the nineteenth century, sometimes so cramped and concealed by a door that it was known as the cupboard stair. Less pokey and in a higher social level was the bracket staircase, which rose not as a corkscrew but by a series of superimposed inclined flights each cantilevered from the side wall of a stair hall or stair well and the top of one connected with the bottom of the other by winders or flat landings. Where there is no 'open well' between the flights the form is known as 'dog-leg'. In the earliest timber examples, up to the sixteenth century, the steps were normally solid but subsequently timber was spared by the substitution of two planks, the horizontal 'tread' and the vertical 'riser' jointed together or connected by a moulding. In cellar steps, where resistance to damp was essential, brick or stone were usual.

You could fall down spiral stairs but you could not fall off them. In straight flights other than those rising around a solid core this was, however, a real danger and necessity mothered a new art form, that of the balustrade, the preserve of the joiner or more

accurately the 'turner'. Probably for reasons of lightness such balustrading or bannisters were normally composed of freestanding balusters, rather than panels (as was almost invariably the case on chapel gallery fronts), despite the latter being continuous, as they were safer and less liable to damage. Panels, nearly always moveable, did become more common in the late nineteenth century, but balusters in all their wonderful variety were even then generally more popular. Some known as 'splats' were flat like planks with matching, often serpentine, edges but almost invariably from the eighteenth century, and on the better stairs, they were in the round, the profile being tooled as the timber revolved at high speed on a lathe (the same principle employed by the chair bodger for furniture legs). At their head balusters are dovetailed, nailed or glued into the

Part of the collection of eighteenth-century balusters maintained by the GLC Historic Buildings Division (now part of the HBMC). Note how only one is tenoned at its base, the rest being butt-jointed and secured by nails

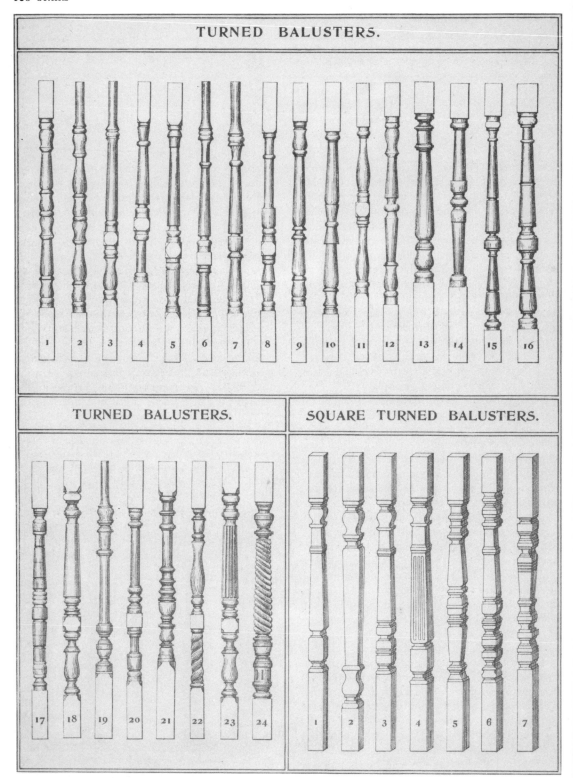

Selection from a builder's catalogue of the 1880s showing the variety of balusters available

handrail – which in the better houses was normally in mahogany from the 1720s. Steam or dry heating enabled the rail to follow the line of the circle of balusters formed for beauty and strength at the base of eighteenth-century staircases on the 'curtail step'. The summit of achievement is the wreath which is curved both in plan and section. It was hard, however, to avoid visible jointing in any superimposed veneer on the utmost surface of the rail. The treads themselves were housed into bearers or strings, although on the near side they were often bracketed or cantilevered from the wall. The area between the treads and the height of the handrail could be reflected particularly on eighteenth-century examples by dado panelling, often echoing the ramped swan neck of the handrail as it swoops to join the newel post, the latter being echoed by an applied pilaster. The strings were either 'closed', rising in a continuous raking line, or 'open', being stepped to follow the profile of the treads and risers. In open string stairs as the base of the balusters meet a flat plain they could more easily be housed in sockets, or sometimes continuous grooves, where their equivalents on closed strings cannot avoid a splayed base and are therefore nailed home. The junction with the handrail is always raked, so oblique double nailing from one side is common. The open string gave the joiner further scope for exuberance in the great variety of tread ends which are normally scroll or console shaped like the base of the stair. Iron balustrading in use from the late seventeenth century

Glentworth Hall, Lincolnshire. Eighteenth-century staircase (now destroyed by vandals). Inset shows how 'carriage' negotiated the landing halfway up the first flight (main photograph, courtesy National Monuments Record)

was normally housed into sockets run with lead to avoid rusting or small blocks of wood or plaster.

Repairs

There are tried and trusted methods in the repairing and strengthening of stairs. The underside is very often braced from the first by one or more counter-parts to the outer and inner string. This is generally known as a 'carriage', although it also goes under the more colourful term of 'stairhorse'. The photos of the staircase at Glentworth Hall, Lincolnshire show how such carriages could negotiate a landing. They also offered the incidental advantage of providing an intermediate fixing for any lath or plaster on the underside or soffit. In at least one case, a spectacular 'flying' example at Woodbrook in Ireland, the stone staircase is supported (invisibly) by a chain following its dip from top to bottom.

It is of course possible to add new carriages. Melville and Gordon (p. 721) suggest that one carriage is sufficient where the staircase is three feet wide, an additional one being advisable for every extra fifteen inches in width. Where the junctions of treads and risers are suspect, these can be reinforced by triangular blocks or blocking pieces nailed to the angle and by wedges following the line of the riser and tread and tapering towards the junction. It is possible to contain any lateral spread of the treads by the insertion of mild steel rods, provided the stair is freestanding, and to brace a sagging cantilever by the addition of columns – but not of course if this threatens the proportions, the visual appeal and historical integrity of the stair. More subtle bracings, doubling as decorative embellishments, practised in the eighteenth and nineteenth centuries, included the addition of staybars and brackets projecting into open wells and the substitution of the occasional wooden baluster, normally every fifth one, by an example in cast iron (detectable as such through its greater flexibility, coolness to the touch and probably a screw fixing). This of course was only possible on stairs with stick balusters. In some staircases every baluster was shaped like a staybar with a central or lower belly. On formal stairs this allowed ladies with crinolines and on service stairs maids with slop buckets to pass each other without bumping. The loss of individual balusters is quite common but there is normally little trouble in using neighbours as a model for the carving of substitutes, although it can be bothersome to clean off all the paint from the exemplar in order to return it to the original profile. Tread ends which were very often formed independently from the tread itself are even more susceptible to theft. However, the example in The Grange, Tottenham, shows that replacements formed entirely from beeswax can appear remarkably authentic. Replacements in wood must remain the first option.

An eighteenth-century 'tread end' on an open string staircase renewed entirely in beeswax as part of a repair programme completed in 1985

Worn treads can at once be a picturesque evocation of use over the centuries – and highly dangerous, especially if the indentations are uneven. Stair carpets in use since the early nineteenth century (preceded by cloth for that purpose at least from the seventeenth century) especially where there is protective underlay can greatly reduce the erosion. They can however endow the simple vernacular stair with too much of a 'polite' feel. In renewing a carpet do watch out for the carpet runners; the earliest machine-made examples date from the mid nineteenth century. Where the damage has been done the surface of the treads and their projection over the risers, known as 'nosings', can be replaced. It may be wiser to build up stone steps using plastic repairs (see 'Stone') and use plastic padding on wooden stairs rather than remove too much original material. New stone, bedded in epoxy resin, may be the only answer where the treads are cracked as well as indented. There are eighteenth- and nineteenth-century precedents for the substitution of slate or lead nosings or edgings in brass on stone stairs in public buildings. Stone steps should be cleaned with a damp but not wet mop without the use of soap. In wooden stairs any cupboards formed underneath flights should be kept free from damp and should not be used for the storage of inflammable material. It can take just a few minutes for a fire to destroy the staircase – and with it the principal means of escape for those on the upper floors.

The current Building Regulations, revised in 1985, say a great deal about the design of bespoke staircases in new structures, and mass produced examples. They govern everything from the pitch, the height of the handrail and the gap between balusters – dictating in particular that all treads and all risers should be equal. Fire regulations have led to appalling disfigurements with the insertion of fire screens into stair halls and the boxing in of balustrades, so it is worth repeating that they do not apply to existing buildings except where new works are to be carried out or there is to be a change of use – and where they do, waivers can be sought if inflexible compliance would lead to the unacceptable loss of features of architectural importance. There is nothing in law to say that the offer of a grant under the Housing Act must be dependent upon the eradication of features such as winder stairs which do not comply with the present Building Regulations, and it is in any case always useful to keep such stairs even when generally not in use to serve as an invaluable alternative means of escape in the event of fire. The Regulations can be met almost invisibly by the use of a fan pumping air into the stairwell so that the air pressure is maintained to a higher level than those of the spaces opening into it.

FURTHER INFORMATION

There is an unpublished thesis by J.P. Colclough, RIBA entitled *The Staircase in Irish Georgian Architecture: A Conservation Study*, 1981.

Other useful publications include:

George Ellis, *Modern Practical Stair Building and Handrailing*, B.T. Batsford.

Walter Godfrey, *The English Staircase*, B.T. Batsford 1911.

Traditional Homes, illustrated articles June-July 1985.

There were a number of treatises on staircases written in the eighteenth century, most of which can be found in the RIBA library. A leading example is Abraham Swan's *The British Architect: or the Builder's Treasury of Staircases*, first issued 1738.

There are two distinct operations in the mortaring of a wall. Firstly the bricks or stones are 'bedded' during the construction of the shell. Secondly, on completion of the structural work, the wall is 'pointed' on its external face, for the better protection and the better appearance of the joint. The division between the two operations became much clearer in the eighteenth century although in a good many historic buildings the work was carried out at one go in a united process termed 'common pointing'. As mortar joints normally fail on their outer face repair generally amounts to no more than 'repointing'.

There are two basic constituents apart from sand in mortar, lime or cement. The latter is now in universal use for new construction, but until the early twentieth century it was lime mortar which predominated and it is still almost universal in the repair of historic structures. The two are not entirely mutually exclusive; a small proportion of cement is used to gauge (assist in the hardening of) non-hydraulic lime mixes and hydraulic cement mortar can be used, for example, in very damp areas in a building where the remainder of mortaring is in lime. Rich lime, moreover, can be actively harmful to sandstone. Nevertheless, whereas there are some sceptics on the merits of lime as a preservative applied to exteriors in the form of limewash, there are no dissenting voices on the general suitability of lime mortar. In modern structures the function of mortar is to bind the wall, but in old buildings it also has to provide an alternative to the stones or bricks for the evaporation of moisture and salts and to accommodate the compressive movement and the slight settlement which is common in such buildings.

Mortar is not indispensable in historic construction. Dry stone walling where mortar is omitted (except sometimes for the securing of the coping stone and the consolidation of the 'heart') is proof of that and indicative too of its limitations. Such walling is normally self-buttressing, both the inner and outer faces leaning slightly towards each other in a 'batter'. To build higher, and to build as part of a shell, mortar becomes almost universal. There are, however, drystone single-storey houses in Wensleydale and Scotland and even in the nineteenth century there are two-storey working class terraces in Cumbria without any mortar, the granite and slate stones being laid so that all joints slope towards the outside to assist in the disposal of water.

Cement mortars are the least suitable in historic buildings. Portland cement not only shrinks on setting but becomes so hard that it inhibits the 'breathing' of the wall and can force downward pressure to bypass the joints and pass through, and therefore, crack the bricks and stones themselves. Its strength means that when it fails it might not merely crumble in small particles but become detached in large sections. Moreover, without the addition of pigments the colour of Portland is generally a dispiriting grey (except for 'white' Portland) compared to the off-white of lime (except of course when it is dirty). Differentiation other than by colour can be difficult. If necessary a small piece of the mortar can be placed in a container of dilute muriatic acid (available from hardware stores), sealed tightly and shaken. If the sample dissolves then it is lime.

Limes can be differentiated into the non-hydraulic, the semi-hydraulic and the hydraulic, the hydraulicity being the capacity to set underneath water. In this sense hydraulic limes used by the Romans but not subsequently until the eighteenth century are natural cements. The three are further differentiated by colour – non-hydraulic which is purer in limestone being white, hydraulic generally being greyer or browner. Non-hydraulic remains soft indefinitely under appropriate conditions, whilst hydraulic has to be used within four hours of mixing. The main difference is simply one of availability. Natural hydraulic limes used to be produced in Britain from places as far afield as Keynsham, Warwickshire, Lyme Regis, Dorking, Guildford, Downham Market and Swindon. Now, however, there are none. The sole present day source is French lime, available, in the south, through the Chichester Cathedral Works Organization (Terminus Road, Chichester), in the north, from William

Anelay Limited (Murton Way, Osbaldwick, York, YO1 3UW), and in Scotland, from the Edinburgh New Town Conservation Committee. The setting of limes is speeded by the addition of so-called pozzolanic additives such as brick dust, wood, coal ash and nowadays pulverized fuel ash (and cement). All lime is produced from limestone burnt in kilns to form quicklime (calcium oxide). In Scotland the cheaper source was the burning of the cockle shells of the edible sea mollusc. The oxide is then slaked or hydrated by water to calcium hydroxide in a violent reaction that produces a considerable amount of gas and heat. The result is lime putty (which can be stored for years but improves little after the first two weeks). Nowadays, however, the spectacular, and dangerous, process of slaking on site is normally bypassed by the purchase of hydrated, powdered, lime mixed with water and then dried out. This has been produced commercially since around 1920. Such lime is added to water (not the other way round) and mixed to a putty and left for twenty four hours before use. Lime putty too is purchased in bags. Normal 'bag lime' from builders' merchants is not recommended.

It is the sand or other aggregates (the 'fillers') that predominated in volume in mortar but the presence of lime or cement (the 'binders') that gives it its primary quality. Most lime mortars are categorized in ratios of three (cement: lime: sand), if cement is added as it normally is with non-hydraulic and semi-hydraulic or two if cement is not present. Sometimes the addition of cement as a strengthener will be so nominal as to be omitted from the ratio. Portland cement need not be added for the pointing of limestones. A much favoured lime mortar is measured in the proportion $1:1:6$, where the wall in question is neither below ground nor particularly exposed nor where the mortar is being applied in harsh weather. Sand and lime mortars can be purchased already bagged but in many DIY stores the mortar for sale is far too hard. Although it is the lime which gives the basic character, it is the sand and certainly the cement (which is normally applied last to the mixed lime and aggregate known as the 'coarse stuff') which provides the degree of strength. It is the sand which decides the colour of the mortar, although it is not the only aggregrate: the Town Schemes run in Bath specify a mortar mix of four parts Bath stone dust to one part lime, with a sprinkling of Portland cement. Similarly mortar can be made to blend with brickwork by the addition of brick dust or where the pointing needs to marry with existing examples by the mixing in of crushed old mortar (provided this is free from contamination by salts and ash, etc.). It is however unwise to try and blend the mortar with dirty brick or stone for this will stand out after cleaning of the shell. The proportions are worked out either by weight or by volume with the use of gauging boxes. By tradition the ratios never mention water although this is essential in converting hydrated lime to lime putty and may be required to help in 'knocking up' surplus 'coarse stuff'. In the past limewater, hot water or water charged with iron have been employed. The amount of water used in the general mixing process is normally very small. The plasticity or the ease of spreading of a mortar (its degree of 'fatness') is generally dependent upon the amount of lime, although some stranger additives such as malt, beer, wine, milk and eggs were used for that purpose and to make a mortar harder on setting. It remains the golden rule that mortar should never be stronger than the wall materials it is bonding so as to provide a sacrificial channel for the evaporation of moisture. There are always exceptions. A particularly intriguing one is Margam Park, a substantial Romantic early-nineteenth-century mansion near Port Talbot where the finely laid joints are faced in lead, one of the most impervious of all materials. This impeded evaporation through the joints, but by the same token also helped to prevent the entry of water in the first place. Lead has been employed in the jointing of tracery and the bedding of columns.

Considerable circumspection is necessary before any decision is taken to repoint. Even though a hard cement render may be ugly and may be perceptibly damaging the wall, its removal could make matters worse, with a very clear risk of damage to the edge or arrises of the blocks. Even where lime mortar is crumbling through the action of mortar or frost or the inadequate preparation of the lime, repointing may be inadvisable unless there is a clear penetration of water or the danger of bricks and flints coming loose. Regular holes in a mortar joint could indicate the securing of a lost creeper by nails. There are obvious dangers of a patchy appearance through selective repointing. Once the decision has been taken to go ahead the joints should be raked out – ideally with a flat-bladed, pointed 'quirk' or a plugging chisel – until hard mortar is reached. This will almost always be more than the height of the joint, if not twice so, particularly in stonework. Loose mortar may yield to a hacksaw blade. Obviously great care should be taken in those rare cases where the outer skin of brick only extends to 3in.

The joints are then washed out with clean water and new lime mortar pushed or 'tamped' home using traditional metal tools (the new devices of caulking guns are not recommended). A hypodermic may be

of use with the very thin joints of 'rubbed' brick. The addition of sacking and/or irregular wetting prevents the pointing drying out too quickly and facilitates the removal of 'buttered' mortar. Once set the surface should be lightly brushed or sprayed to remove the 'laitence' and prevent too smooth a finish. The most common joint in historic buildings is one brought flush to the surface although that with a slightly sunk or recessed face known as 'hungry' or 'hollow key' was also common. An alternative description is 'bucket-handled' after the habit of forming the recess by drawing the handle across the face. Where arrises have been damaged flush joints are obviously inappropriate, as they create water ledges and emphasize the damage – joints 'struck' to an angle might then be used, but only then.

The finer the joint the greater the risk of the mortar smudging or 'buttering' on to the wall itself. It is possible in such cases to apply lime putty into the joint against two sheets of greased paper which are then carefully withdrawn, the putty being held in place by a pointing iron. Where 'buttering' has occurred the mortar can be brushed off the next day. The mortaring should always work from the top of a

A bad example of 'buttering'

The harsh effect of ribbon or strap pointing (Courtesy National Monument Record)

wall down and should not be undertaken in very cold conditions.

Apart from 'buttering', one of the biggest dangers is posed by the habit particularly prevalent in the north of ribbon or strap pointing where the joints in a hard cement are flattened at the edges to a rectilinear section and stand proud of the wall. The effect is ugly and counter-productive, for once again water's passage down the wall to the ground is repeatedly interrupted by ledges on which it sits and seeps in. This is a risk attaching to all pointing that projects beyond the face of the wall although it was certainly used, particularly in the nineteenth century, and the effect was partly obviated by the introduction of raking lines top and bottom and is surprisingly common on the Continent. Some courses were made to project to act as a key for a render which might have been lost in the interim.

Even 'buttering' was normal in the vernacular of some counties like Rutland. Vernacular variants should always be respected. In Cardiganshire and in the Pennines, for example, there was a tradition of painting joints white. Similarly decorative devices

Repointng can appear stark in contrast with untreated neighbours

Tuck pointing where thin lines of white lime are drawn along the centre of the mortar joints

should be respected; such as 'tuck pointing', developed from the early eighteenth century where thin lines of white lime putty are scored into the centre of the mortar and galletting or cherrycocking (Scot.), where, in the first case, flints and, in the second, stones or bits of slate are pressed into the pointing.

The treatment of ashlar joints should nearly always be a matter for professional opinion. This is not just because the joints are very often very fine but because they could, as for example in Edinburgh, disguise V-shaped bedding joints of a much greater width and therefore vulnerability.

FURTHER INFORMATION

John Ashurst's *Mortars, Plasters and Renders in Conservation*, The Ecclesiastical Architects and Surveyors Association 1983, is the key book for professionals.

It may be useful also to consult John Fidler's *The Art of Repointing*, and 'Lime Mortar' in *Traditional Homes*, June 1985 and *Lime Mortar*, October 1985.

Burnley Borough Council published a pamphlet entitled 'Are you Thinking of Repointing Your Building? Beware' in 1982. There is also a Derbyshire County Council publication, 'The Repointing of Brick and Stonework', (1982).

An international perspective can be gained from the ICCROM publication *Mortars, Cements and Grouts used in the Conservation of Historic Buildings*, Rome 1981.

The SPAB Technical Pamphlet No. 5 is entitled 'Pointing Stone and Brick Walling'.

18 EXTERNAL RENDER

External skins of mortar, or render, were primarily designed to offer protection from the elements. Hence the isolated rendering of walls facing north, of plinths, chimneys and the outer faces of parapets. A secondary purpose, particularly with the 'stucco' common in the eighteenth and nineteenth centuries, was to feign the use of more fashionable but more expensive building materials such as stone, a deceit made only slightly more convincing by the introduction of scored lines in imitation of courses of dressed ashlar.

In historic renders the predominant characteristics derive from the use of lime, gypsum and cement or a selective mixture of the three. Lime and natural cements were both known to the Romans, although gypsum renders do not appear until the mid thirteenth century and artificial cements until the late eighteenth and early nineteenth centuries.

For historic buildings lime render is by far the most appropriate. This is principally because of its 'weakness', which allows the wall in question to breathe, is more tolerant of movement and appears less 'hard' on the surface and rectilinear at the edges. It can be time-consuming in application and generally benefits from a slow set, during which process, unlike gypsum, it is prone to shrinkage and consequent cracking or crazing. Nevertheless these are minor inconveniences to pay. The proportions of the mix normally with cement and sand (see 'Mortaring') will depend upon the location within the building and normally vary between the first, second and third coats (see 'Floors and Ceilings').

Among the hydraulic cements the most famous 'natural' is Roman Cement, given that name in 1796, and among the 'artificials' Portland Cement, patented in 1824 but not in widespread use until the later years of the century. Both tend to be far too 'strong' for historic buildings, although there is certainly attraction in the pinkish colour of Roman. Whilst the latter is no longer produced, the popularity of Portland Cement has grown to the point where it dominates the field. A further product of the

Internal plaster on laths and 'grounds'

eighteenth century, the so-called oil mastic, represented particularly by Liardet's Cement (patented in 1773 and valued for its water-repellent properties) was last used in documented repair work in 1854 (Melville & Gordon, p. 175).

Gypsum, a natural product burnt in a kiln like lime, is the basis for many present day patent plasters and as Plaster of Paris (burnt gypsum) it has been in widespread use. It can be used to gauge a lime render to improve early setting and strength, although when it predominates it can, like cement, develop a hardness which can be quite inappropriate in a historic building, especially as it is susceptible to disintegration in very damp conditions.

Rather more surprising natural products could be added to lime plaster/render to improve workability, be it cheese, cow dung or road scrapings (also see 'Mortaring', chapter 17). Strands of animal hair and particles of saw dust added to the undercoat improved cohesion, whilst internal frames of interwoven reeds or twigs and wooden laths could provide reinforcement and backing. Laths in wood seem to have been introduced in the late Middle Ages, the first examples being cleft. Production by saw developed from the late eighteenth century. The earliest examples were in oak although softwoods came to predominate, as they do now, from the last century. The first use of wire lathing in 1841 paved the way for the expanded metal mesh in 1890 which is now standard in aluminium. Where render is over mouldings an additional base can be provided by

brick externally and softwood beading internally. Coves are normally suspended from curved wooden brackets.

Reinforcement internal to the render has to be coupled almost invariably with the creation of a 'key' on the surface to be covered. This was generally achieved mechanically by raking out the mortar joints and scoring or holing the bricks for the undercoat. This is particularly necessary where the surface has had a distemper or a water repellent oil mastic applied. The first spatterdash coat, thrown not brushed on to the surface, assists in this as does the process of 'dubbing out' voids and cracks with bits of stone or slate, tarred twine or quick setting plaster of Paris. The scoring can be carried out by a wood float with a protruding nail tip.

Other than providing a key the prerequisities to the application of the render are mundane but essential; the surface should be clean and it should be damp. In some early works a single coat 'daub' suffices and some recent inventions have included one coat patent plasters. Nevertheless, most renders have more than one coat, three being standard for exposed spots. If one discounts the initital dubbing out coat or splatterdash, the first is known as the render coat, the second the floating or backing coat and the third the setting, finishing or skimming coat. The successive coats should be thinner and usually less rich in cement than the predecessor, the first being combed or scoured to provide an additional key. A minimum of two days in the summer and seven in the winter should pass before the undercoats are covered and work should not be undertaken in extremes of weather unless precautionary measures are adopted. Anti-freezing additives are available but there are drawbacks to their use. When the work is almost dry a light brush can take off the surface laitence.

External surfaces on historic buildings are generally finished by a wood float which gives a flat, sand-faced texture which is both more resistant to weather and less monotonous than the steel float finishes which are more appropriate for internal surfaces. So-called tyrolean renders, now so common in East Anglia, are too smooth and too manicured compared with the gentle bumps and contours of an old-fashioned lime mortar, and alien too in the common use of projecting 'bells' over DPCs or the heads of openings. Sometimes 'texture' is deliberately contrived by drawing a sackcloth across the surface or using a toothed tool known as a 'drag' which emphasizes the aggregate in the resultant 'scraped' surface. The alternative to these plain renders is the 'dashed', either pebbledash (dry dash) where small particles of stone or pebble are thrown at a wet render coat or 'butter coat', or roughcasting (wet dash). Where the final coat with the predominant aggregate

Sgraffito work on the former St Paul's Choir School, City of London, 1875

is thrown at the surface these 'dashed' surfaces can discolour dismally but there is no doubt that they are a traditional form of render, particularly in Scotland where roughcasting is known as harling. The dullness of the finish persuaded some sixteenth-century designers to include fragments of glass in the aggregate 'which made a brilliant display when the sun shone and even by moonlight', and, in later years, colours from the ochre range, with attractive weathering qualities, became more common. They also appear more resistant to water penetration (provided the undercoats are waterproofed) and to cracking. They are however heavy and demand a secure backing. It is clear from eighteenth-century recipes for the rendering of 'polite' buildings that although roughcasting created too disturbed a surface, the throwing of sand on to painted surfaces, in the process confusingly also known as harling, was much more common than hitherto suspected. The slow setting of lime mortar precipitated the development in the fourteenth century with an apogee in the seventeenth of the craft of decorative external plasterwork known as pargetting, which flourished particularly in East Anglia. This relied on patterns in relief either cast in beeswax moulds, modelled around armatures or incised by the use of combs and scratches. Original colour rarely survives and the patterns are normally protected like the rest of the render by a limewash, the repeated application of which inevitably dulls the outline. Repairs should

always be in lime rather than cement to maintain physical compatibility. The only printed guide to pargetting, published by Essex County Council (obtainable at 80p from County Hall, Chelmsford) recommends that undercoats should be the same mix as the top coat to offer further guarantee of consistent movement characteristics. The recommended mix is 1 : 6 : 9. The use of hair in undercoats is recommended, although not more than two inches long, well teased, and in the proportion of one pound to every three cubic feet of mix. Hand-carved stamps will prevent too mechanical an edge. Too rapid a drying out of the mortar can be prevented by keeping work damp in the summer through a cover of wet hessian.

The pleasing imprecision of outline of ancient pargetting should not lead to the automatic rejection of the more regular work used on many Victorian properties mostly produced by the use of stamps. The late nineteenth century also saw the revival in England of a technique of incised decoration in plaster often using coats of different colour known as sgraffito.

Faults in renders range from cracking or crazing on the surface, 'popping' and delamination due to the efflorescence of salts and frost, to the moving of the plaster away from its backing. Voids can be detected simply by tapping the surface. In many parts of Europe partial loss of render or skim is broadly acceptable but in Britain where the cold weather is more aggressive more practical considerations often push themselves forward. As plaster is a film selective patching is less advisable than is the individual replacement of failed stones or bricks. It is often very difficult to get an exact match in colour or texture and the new and old are likely in any case to weather differentially. Nevertheless a junction between the two can be disguised by the natural break of a window or door or the incisions in a scheme of sham ashlar. The failed render is normally cut back to the laths – if there are any – and certainly to a straight edge with an undercut profile. An amoebic outline invariably continues to look like a blob. However, patching can sometimes be avoided. 'Bellies' can be screwed back to the wall surface following the injection by hypodermic syringe of lime putty grout (Ashurst p. 53). Cracks need not necessarily of themselves be alarming. Small examples can be stopped with a resin or latex based filler and the larger examples with building mastic which will continue to allow them to serve as a useful monitor of any underlying structural movement. At the other extreme some cracks, particularly those curled at the edges, are found only to be as deep as the paint. Clearly the application of one of the proprietary transparent water-repellent liquids can be negated by excessive cracking. It may be advisable to delay

Nos. 4–14, Sutton Stop, Longford, Coventry, Warwickshire. The local authority refused an application to render the terrace in 1980

New renders may blend with the existing over time, but others remain clearly obvious

the application of a limewash or a paint for up to a year to allow drying out.

The repair of existing renders is only half the story. There may be cases where walls in stone or brick are so damaged or so porous that the stark alternatives are refacing or rendering. In some cases it may be clear that an early render has been lost. This is suggested by an irregular white patina, quoins projecting beyond the surface of the shell (intended to stand proud of a plaster finish) and the scoring, particularly in the case of brickwork, of the outer wall surface. Such apparently vandalistic hacking can only indicate the introduction of a key. Nevertheless even here the render may have been removed for perfectly justifiable reasons. It is in any case technically most inadvisable to render a wall not merely pointed but bedded in ordinary Portland cement, just as a render of Portland cement should not be applied on bricks with soluble salts (Melville and Gordon, p. 165). The aesthetic arguments against a render which obscures subtly variegated masonry walls or disrupts an otherwise unrendered terrace are obvious. (Once the damage has been done and a render applied removal may 'blow' the surface of the stone blocks or bricks, particularly where the render is in cement and the wall in question faces south, and the sun, rather than north.) The obverse argument can apply equally strongly. There is a growing and tendentious fashion in stripping off

ancient undulating lime renders to expose random rubble elevations that were never meant to be seen.

A transparent water sealant may offer some protection against water penetration, but such liquids do require regular renewal. If the wall is altogether too important to be rendered the problem can be tackled from the inside. 'Dry lining' using

Morton, Lincolnshire. 3 Trentside. White patina points to a lost render (Photo courtesy, National Monuments Record)

plasterboard or 'wet lining' with plaster provides a second insulatory skin rather on the same principle as panelling and indeed wallpaper placed on wooden grounds. The nineteenth century in particular devel-

Lime putty and horsehair prior to use on the building site

External covering may, as here at Trowbridge, Wilts, be a trellis for the trailing of a creeper

oped the idea of battening out on laths or 'hessian paper' and plaster to create an air gap which was felt to inhibit both the loss of heat and the entry of water and also, in public buildings, to improve acoustics. On renovation, however, this air space is now almost always abandoned. Great care should of course be taken to avoid the loss of internal finishings of interest during such work.

19 DAMP

In the parlance of structural decay damp is either 'penetrating' (driven rain entering via the roof or walls) or 'rising' (water driven from the earth on which the building sits through the process of capillary suction, whether that water be rain, the effluent of blocked drains or spillage from water butts). The simplest solution to the immediate problem is to encourage evaporation, which depends in turn upon adequate ventilation. To prevent its occurrence the structural flaws need to be tackled. Deficiences in roofs and wall surfaces are dealt with elsewhere, but the problem of rising damp in particular has promoted a complete new branch of the building industry specializing in the insertion of damp-proof courses (DPCs) and damp-proof membranes (DPMs). DPM is a more general term covering the addition of a water repellent surface to the inner or outer face or into the cavity of any architectural element. DPCs are placed either horizontally or vertically but only across rather than on the outside of a wall. The phrase is most generally used for a course placed around the base of the shell of the building but smaller DPCs are commonly inserted for the protection of windows, doors, parapets and chimneys. DPCs to the shell of buildings were stipulated under local building byelaws from *c*.1870, although they did not become widespread until after World War I. They are now very often essential before a local authority will consider a grant under the Housing Act or a building society, a mortgage (both of which are also likely to specify which sort of DPC should be used).

There is no doubting the damage which excess damp stimulates in the form of rot, in the discolouration of plaster and wallpaper and the efflorescence and subflorescence of salts on the surface or within the depth of a wall. In addition, there is a proven risk to human health. Nevertheless a moisture content of 5 per cent in brick and even as high as 16 per cent for timber is considered to be healthy and the complete drying out of a building, particularly through constant high heating without ventilation creates its own problems. Cob is a good example of a building material where some moisture is essential to maintain strength and where DPCs are generally not advisable (see chapter 10). There is a small school of thought which believes that DPCs are superfluous in timber-framed buildings but their desirability in brick and stone constructions is hardly challenged at all.

It would be quite incorrect to assume that damp-proofing only post-dates the 1870s. DPCs in lead and oyster shells are recorded in the Middle Ages and although it is true that medieval man was sufficiently untroubled to gird the better buildings with water filled moats he also appeared to understand the benefit of dry moats. External evaporation ditches surrounding a house and given a base of gravel are still used particularly where the floor is below the ground level. Surface water is carried away to a soakaway or ditch by pipes set beneath the gravel. The latter inhibits damp rising from below by capillary action. The enveloping gravel based ditch remains a standard device for the protection of medieval churches. If the setting of a house precludes a ditch, it is possible to backfill once the base of the wall has been waterproofed, although this should not be above the level of the DPC.

DPCs are divided into the mechanical or chemical and the flexible and the rigid, the latter generally being less advisable in walls more susceptible to movement, such as parapets and chimneys. The flexible include copper, which can lead to unpleasant green staining, heavy duty felt, lead, usually coated in bitumen to protect it from the damaging effects of water, and bitumen itself which can visibly extrude under the superimposed pressure, although rarely to the detriment of its efficiency (this is also true of mastic asphalt). The rigid include vitrified stoneware, dense brick (semi-engineering or en-

gineering) generally laid in two courses and slates also generally laid double (or triple), overlapping and normally in cement rather than lime mortar, and cement itself laid as a continuous bed joint. Other techniques make use of porous siphon tubes to evaporate the water (on much the same principle as the weepholes used in new construction to prevent water from travelling down the walls to sit on the DPC) and electro-osmosis designed to counteract the electrical charge associated with capillary action. Both these, however, have their detractors. Another 'non-traditional' technique introduced just after World War II has found very considerable favour. This involves the infusion or injection of water repellent substances through holes into the wall which set and form what is generally called a chemical DPC. They are particularly useful in very thick or less stable walls and are generally cheaper than the alternatives. They are for the most part the preserve of specialist firms which normally offer a guarantee of between 15 and 35 years (for a small extra payment the Guarantee Treatments Protection Trust offers a full guarantee, should the firm in question go bankrupt).

Horizontal DPCs are inserted at least six inches above the ground level (above the area likely to be splashed by water) and must follow a continuous line both through the wall and around the building. Traditional methods are inserted either by the removal of two courses of brick either side of the selected bed joint, one section at a time to avoid settlement, or by sawing through the mortar joint. Insertion is followed by reinstatement although, as stated, with compressible DPCs such as bitumen the material extends slightly beyond the face of the wall. Chemical DPCs are inserted through holes cut either into the mortar or the masonry. Some firms may insist on the removal not only of immediately adjacent plaster and jointing but of creepers and plants impeding the complete circuit of the building at its base. Walls greater than 460mm (18½in) thick are normally injected from both sides. Where a building is terraced, clearly horizontal DPCs on their own may need to be combined with vertical DPCs rising through party walls and indeed at the junction with boundary walls and garages, especially as the latter are exempt from the statutory requirement that DPCs be installed. Neighbours should be forewarned before any sawing takes place. Similarly, DPCs installed at the ground floor level offer no protection to subterranean basements or crypts. Such spaces can be comprehensively treated through a process known as 'tanking' which normally involves lining with bitumen or asphalt and a superimposed DPC.

This is however criticized by Andrew Thomas in SPAB Technical Pamphlet 8 (see Bibliography). At the other extreme basements were regarded as sacrificial spaces where rising damp was encouraged to evaporate through generous ventilation before it reached the ground floor. This had positive advantage in wine cellars.

Even after the insertion of a DPC the affected walls may take months or years to dry out, roughly at the rate of 1in per month, during which time crystallizing salts may appear (and require removal by poulticing or simple washing). It makes sense to leave the holes open and the old plaster on the walls during the drying out period so that hygroscopic or deliquescent salts (which extract moisture from the air) can be concentrated and taken off with the plaster. Once the wall has dried out replastering (perhaps using a salt inhibitor) can take place. To be on the safe side it should be taken some distance above the tidemark indicating the visible height to which the rising damp had previously reached. It must also be in accordance with the specialist contractor's recommendations, otherwise his guarantee will be null and void. If the intention is to repaint and there is doubt about the dryness of the walls (and moisture meters are not always reliable) a water-based emulsion is preferable to an oil-based.

Distemper or limewash allow the wall to 'breathe' better. It is important that the render or plaster is not taken down over either the internal or external line of the DPC, otherwise the latter will be 'bridged' and water will by-pass it by rising through the render. The piling of earth or firewood or other such material against the external wall has the same effect, providing easy channels for the water over the DPC.

Condensation either on the surface or interstitial (that is within the depth of the wall) is, like damp, an inducement to decay. Generally speaking it is caused when warm air meets a cold surface, especially those facing north or east. Water is condensed once the 'dewpoint' of the air has been passed. It can be easier to control than damp. There are some easily obeyed do's and don'ts. Among the former, keep bathroom and kitchen doors shut and windows open for ventilation during use. Don't overheat the house; a continuous low level of heating is the best. Remember that flueless heaters require extra ventilation. Don't dry clothes on radiators and don't allow a kettle to overboil. Mouldicidal anti-condensation paints are available for use in kitchens and bathrooms. And remember too that limewash has the great advantage of holding condensation until it can be evaporated through a change in temperature.

FURTHER INFORMATION

The following publications are useful:

C.R. Coggins, *The Decay of Timber in Buildings*, Rentokil 1980.

John Fidler, 'Damp Down Below', *Traditional Homes* September 1985.

Andrew Thomas, 'The Treatment of Damp in Old Buildings' SPAB Technical Pamphlet No. 8.

'Condensation and Mould Growth in Your Home' Department of the Environment Information Sheet, 1982.

Wood is organic and therefore subject, naturally and inevitably, to decay. The users of timber thus have to be on constant guard against its degradation. The risk is not evenly spread – softwoods (mostly evergreen) are more vulnerable than hardwoods (normally deciduous) as is the (outer) sapwood compared with the (inner) heartwood of all trees (hence the common practice of chamfering or moulding the edge of timbers, particularly those quarter-sawn, or 'converted' from the outer rings so as to remove the vulnerable sapwood). Differentiation need not be easy. That most robust of woods, the pitch pine, is a biological softwood, whilst balsa is a hardwood. And there are surprising geographical differences in the prevalence of decay – it seems that dry rot is most common in the west and the north, a survey of 1972 showing Wales, Scotland, Northern Ireland and London to be peculiarly susceptible. Surrey, Kent and Sussex escape lightly as does Scotland from the wet rots although these flourish in London, most of East Anglia and the north-west.

The fungus truly gothic in its horror among the 90 000 that exist is dry rot. It may not occur as frequently as the wet rots but it is far more destructive and persistent. Known technically in its true form as Merulius (or Serpula) Lacrymans, it thrives best despite its name (explained by the effect it has on the surface of wood) in damp unventilated conditions and where it can find cellulose to feed on, be it timber, paper or food. Wood must have a moisture content of over 20 or 25 per cent to be susceptible (the optimum being between 30 and 40 per cent) and as most timber in old houses has a minimum of 12 per cent it is clear how easily they can move into the danger zone. The optimum temperature is 22° centigrade, though the growth of Serpula ceases at around 26°; it can grow in lower temperatures but dislikes great heat. The rot is no respecter of the young, and new properties can be attacked as much as old.

Dry rot begins from spores shed from a Mother outbreak, or is brought in on animals, clothing or coal. Having infected the wood it throws out strands or hyphae which compose themselves into a goss-like mycelium, rather like flattened candyfloss that is white but discolours over time. This in turn sends out 'rhizomorphs' which hone in on the unaffected wood softened by the 'tears' which give the rot its misleadingly romantic adjective (lacrymans, weeping). These feelers spread through, although they do not infect, brick, stone, and even concrete. The cycle is completed by the development in the autumn of pancake-like fruiting bodies or sporophores which generate millions more spores. These spread the infection and can pose a health risk. The tenacity of the cycle is legendary - it can rise from a cellar to a roof in days and even more easily from one terraced house to another. In an important legal judgement in 1983, an owner who allowed her semi-detached house to become so infected with dry rot (among other dilapidations) that it had to be demolished was held liable for the rot that had spread to her neighbour's property. Insurance against infestation is rare in ordinary household policies, although in some foreign countries such cover is compulsory. Empty houses without ventilation and heating are particularly vulnerable.

Although the later manifestations are only too obvious the early stages can be secret as it develops behind panelling or under floors. Telltale signs apart from the spores themselves, which are like red dust, are the cracking and bulging of paintwork and the loss of nature in the wood which becomes darker, is easily penetrated by a screwdriver or gimlet and offers a 'dead' noise when tapped.

In the wet rots the wood almost always separates along the grain. Dry rot stimulates cracking both horizontal and vertical, breaking the surface up into eerily neat squares. This is accompanied by a smell often compared in its incipient growth to the subtle odour of mushrooms. The infection should be tackled immediately it is suspected. Having sprayed the fruiting bodies with fungicides, the area should be opened up beyond the surface visibly attacked so

The fruiting body of dry rot in full outbreak

that the exent of the rhizomorphs' system can be gauged. The general advice is to be ruthless. It is urged that renders, even mortar joints, should be removed and affected timbers taken out and burnt. This can be far too demanding for historic buildings and it is possible to impregnate thoroughly valuable timbers or even to take them out, sterilize them in a kiln and return them to the original position. New techniques, developed particularly in repairs at Brighton Pavilion are laying less stress on chemicals and much more on improved ventilation. There are obvious risks in the established technique of burning affected surfaces with a blowlamp, particularly if combined with the application of preservatives which can be inflammable.

There are many fungicides on the market. These are generally brushed on, applied as a paste, sprayed or impregnated (vacuum impregnation was first used as long ago as 1831). Most of the companies offer a warranty of up to thirty years and to cover themselves will treat adjacent timbers presently immune from attack. Important painted surfaces should only be treated with the advice of a conservation architect. Fluid should not be used near insulation material which will absorb the vapour and become a fire hazard. Paste may be wiser in those circumstances.

Once the affected area has dried out and once the house has been thoroughly checked and every effort made to improve ventilation and reduce dampness, reinstatement can take place. The reintroduction of decorative finishes followed by a further outbreak of dry rot remains the owner and the architect's nightmare. New timbers should also be impregnated.

Clearly historic panelling should be retained but it can be refixed with plastic rather than wooden plugs. About the only materials resistant to dry rot are zinc or magnesium oxychloride and their use on the replastered or repainted surface can be often recommended.

Wet Rots

Wet rot is a generic and less precise term. Unlike dry rot it does not spread to sound wood or hardwood and the heartwood is generally immune (although Phellinus megaloporus, oak fungus, does attack hardwoods like oak and chestnut). Like dry rot it is activated by poor ventilation and damp. The most common of the wet rots is Cellar fungus (Coniophora cerebella), which is most active at a moisture content and temperature greater than that which suits dry rot. This must be over 25 per cent and generally between 40 and 50 per cent whilst the optimum temperature is 23° centigrade. Like so many of the colloquial names the title is inadequate, as the fungus can break out in roof spaces as much as in cellars. Unlike dry rot outbreaks can be localized and pockets of decay, for example in window joints, are common. It shares the same cycle of hyphae, mycelium and fruiting bodies but it is quite possible to suffer attacks without progress through this full spectrum. There is in fact rather more than in dry rot a tendency for the surface to belie the outbreak underneath which tends to deepen the colour of the wood and make it brittle. The cure is less drastic than that required for dry rot and normally involves the removal of the decayed timber and treatment with fungicide, although the latter is not always required. It should be stressed that when the cause has been removed (for example, the damp penetration stopped) then the outbreak stops. Only timbers which are rotten need to be replaced.

Beetles

Wood is also attractive to a great variety of beetles, some of which are harmless, others not. They nearly all follow a cycle of eggs laid on the surface, or more commonly in joints and cracks, which hatch into larvae or grubs that burrow through the wood creating a webb of galleries. These metamorphose into pupae and adult beetles which emerge through flight holes in the upper or lower surfaces. The

Death Watch
Beetle
(Xestobium
rufovillosum)

Common Furniture
Beetle
(Anobium
punctatum)

House
Longhorn
Beetle
(Hylotrupes
bajulus)

Dry rot (left), wet rot and beetles (courtesy, Renofoes Ltd)

beetles are generally differentiated by the species of timber attacked, the size and shape of their flight holes and the nature of the 'frass' or dust created by the burrowing. The same damp, unventilated conditions that can induce fungi are likewise attractive to beetles.

By far the most widespread is the Common Furniture Beetle (Anobium punctatum, known as woodworm) which is responsible for some three-quarters of attacks in the United Kingdom and is especially predominant in the South-West. Its name is, like so many, inadequate as it is just as much at home in buildings as in furniture, and in both hard and softwoods including the heartwood (except fortunately that of the oak). It has been known for woodworm to penetrate plastic watertanks. The beetle, usually $\frac{1}{12}$ in long and yellow or red in colour, lays up to 60 eggs, the grubs from which can tunnel within the wood for up to three or four years before turning into pupae and emerging as adult beetles between June and August through round flight holes normally $\frac{1}{16}$ in across. The frass is fairly light in colour and gritty to the touch.

The most sinister name undoubtedly belongs to the Death Watch Beetle (Xestobium rufovillosum), named after the tapping of the head of both the male and the female against the surface of the wood during the mating ritual. It is generally limited to old hardwoods, usually oak, already under fungal attack and will destroy the capacity of heartwood as well as softwood, thus precipitating the sudden collapse of roof timbers. It is virtually unknown in Scotland and Northern Ireland. The flight holes, which are $\frac{1}{8}$in in diameter, can be the end result of a life cycle as long as ten or twenty years. The beetles emerge between April and June and the frass is formed of circular coarse pellets.

The House Longhorn (Hylotrupes bajulus) is at present very limited geographically – to parts of Surrey, Berkshire and Hampshire. Generally only sapwood or softwoods are attacked, albeit destructively. It is not to be confused with the Longhorn (Phymatodes testaceus), which is a bark-borer found generally in timber yards and of little danger to buildings.

Many other insects occur in buildings but without damaging consequences. Most damage by the Lyctus or powderpost beetle, for example, in ancient timbers, is normally inert and has long ceased. Its attack is in any case limited to the sapwood of all hardwoods. Wasps and bees (particularly masonry bees or Osmia rufa) can be a nuisance not least for the noise which is generated by their frenetic activity, but they rarely affect structural stability. The Forest Products Research Laboratory at Princes Risborough in Buckinghamshire will help identify mysterious insects, and the British Pest Control Association (see Useful Addresses) publishes a very handy 'A to Z of Household Pests'.

Whenever insect attacks are suspected professional advice should be sought. There are a number of specialist firms in the field. The British Pest Control Association and the British Wood Preserving Association (see Useful Addresses) are able to supply a list. Manufacturers of famous products like Wykamol and Cuprinol can supply lists of accredited users. Most firms will, as with fungus attacks, offer 20 or 30 year guarantees, or more accurately warranties, which run parallel to the ordinary Common Law rights of the client. Unfortunately, in order to cover themselves, firms may feel obliged to remove only mildly suspect wood, particularly as building societies are generally insistent on a guarantee before offering a mortgage. The Environmental Health Departments of local authorities will usually tackle rodents in houses at no charge but insect control and work in commercial premises normally attracts a fee.

It may be that no action at all is required if the

attack has ceased and has not destroyed the structural capacity of the timber. This is generally the case if the heartwood remains sound and even numerous flight holes in the sapwood need not be alarming if these are clearly old. Some beetles will only attack bark and the first layers of sapwood underneath, and thus offer no structural threat. If treatment is advised the affected area is cleaned, and may have to be stripped (as the treatment of varnished and painted surfaces is difficult), cavities are filled and then insecticide applied. During this process there should certainly be no smoking, and if the application is taking place in a roof space water cisterns should be covered to prevent contamination.

Any incidental hazard is not just posed to humans.

The Nature Conservancy Council is becoming increasingly concerned at the lethal affects on bats. In its report 'Focus on bats; their conservation and the law' (see Bibliography) it points out that 'remedial timber treatment is probably the greatest threat to the species' which so often relies on roost sites in roofspaces. In 1984, in the first prosecution of its kind, a timber treatment firm was fined £1000 for damaging the roost of a colony of whiskered bats and as it is an offence not merely to kill or injure a bat but even to handle one in the wild, more legal action may be anticipated. The National Trust is presently engaged in research into ways of tackling infestation without risking the welfare of bats.

FURTHER INFORMATION

The following publications are useful:

R. Coggins, *The Decay of Timber in Buildings. Dry Rot, Wet Rot and Other Fungi*, Rentokil.

Alan C. Oliver, *Wood Worm, Dry Rot and Rising Damp*, Sovereign Chemical Industries, 1985.

Stanley Richardson, *Protecting Buildings, How to Combat Dry Rot, Wood Worm and Damp*, David and Charles, 1977.

The Ministry of Agriculture, Fisheries and Foods Infestation Control Laboratory at Slough issues, through HMSO, advisory leaflets on particular pests. The Nature Conservancy Council, 19-20 Belgrave Square London SW1 has published a report entitled 'Focus on Bats: their conservation and the law' and a guide entitled 'Bats in Roofs'.

ADDRESSES

The British Pest Control Association, Alembic House, 93 Albert Embankment, London SE1.

The British Wood Preserving Association, 150 Southampton Row, Londong WC1B, tel. (01) 837-8217.

---

21 IRONWORK

Historic ironwork in this country is either wrought, cast or in the form of steel. The first has been in use for 4000 years, the second for 400 and the last for just over a hundred (although fireplaces in steel appeared in the eighteenth century). The adjective in the first two cases implies that the difference is purely one of preparation, the first being hammered, stretched, rolled or twisted into shape, the second formed in moulds. This is true, but not the whole story. They differ also in carbon content, cast iron possessing the most (up to five per cent). The principal purpose of the hammering is to reduce the percentage of carbon. The process of smelting iron ore to form 'pig iron' is common to both. Cast iron is pig which has been remelted and given its form in sand moulds or trays. Wrought iron is pig or 'scrap' cast iron melted with iron oxide and cleansed of impurities, particularly carbon, and then hammered at the forge and rolled at the mill. The hammering is not to be confused with the action of the blacksmith who receives the iron in the form of a 'bloom' from the smelting forge which he then pummels into shape. This hammering can be carried out either hot or cold, in which latter state the iron can also be sawn. There are several hundred grades of quality in wrought, the traditional but rather imprecise grading being indicated by the multiplication of the superlative adjective into, for example, 'best, best, best iron'. Wrought is far better than cast in accommodating tensile pressures, and is employed for roof girders where the brittleness of cast would be a liability. The latter is however good in compression, so was used in abundance to take loadings through columns. Differentiating between the two is difficult, particularly as most examples are painted and both form a protective surface skin to resist rusting. Hollow members can be either wrought or cast. A poor casting can produce a pock marked surface whilst an irregular hammering leads to telltale undulation. Where there is an appearance of oozing as the result of a junction of two moulds the iron has clearly been cast, although this would normally have been filed down. Lamination in section is indicative of wrought iron. Where the metal was laid in sheets in the nineteenth century wrought iron tended to be in smaller pieces. It is of course more difficult for the blacksmith to repeat outlines exactly in repetition than it would be for a founder dealing with identical moulds; so that where repetition of balusters, for example, is irregular they would have been wrought rather than cast.

The structural use of iron from the late eighteenth century was limited almost entirely to industrial and commercial buildings. Residential examples are few and far between. Ironwork in houses was generally limited to railings, porches, balconies, windows and door furniture like locks, fingerplates, footscrapers, knockers and fanlights (although the latter were equally in lead or wood). Iron fireplaces were unknown before the nineteenth century but firebacks and grates always had to be in that material. The growth of fashion by pattern book from the eighteenth century favoured the exact repetition possible with cast iron which thus established an authority in the field, that endured throughout most of the eighteenth and nineteenth centuries. The revival of interest in decorative ironwork in the late nineteenth century associated particularly with the Birmingham School was a rediscovery of the possibilitites of wrought iron.

The decorative display offered by railing off gardens or 'areas' of Georgian terraces brought ironwork to its apogee, not just in the overthrows, porch snuffers known as 'link horns' and lampholders, but in the range of railing heads, many of them variations on the standard spears and *fleur de lys*. Many fine examples were lost as the result of the order given in Autumn 1941 by Lord Beaverbrook as Minister of Supply that they should be recycled for the war effort. But fortunately the round-up was not nearly as complete as originally intended. They can suffer, like all external ironwork, from the effect of rust and impact. In some circumstances the member will have disintegrated entirely, but where the surface only has been damaged the rust and old paintwork can be removed either by dryblasting, a chemical stripper or by wire brushing. The latter, although time-consuming, can have the advantage of allowing some examination of underlayers – the presently ubiquitous black was rivalled in the Georgian period by blue, green and white (in Dublin). The combination of chemical stripper and burning off paint by gas must be out of the question. Stripping down to the iron through all the paint layers, as well as increasing the eradication of rust, also returns the railings and particularly its decorative elements to their original profile, so often obscured by the repainting. The application of red lead (now in disfavour), one or preferably two coats of metal primer, plus one or more undercoats and the surface coat, should all be to manufacturer's instructions – although the presence of a rust inhibiting factor within the paint is advisable as is a surface coat of a gloss rather than matt finish. The concensus that repainting should take place every five years contains sound advice, although it may be less so if the present tendency among paint manufacturers to offer longer periods of guarantee, including some of twenty years, develops. Where the requirement is repair rather than recoating, welding of fractures is possible on both wrought and cast iron. Cracks in members not taking loading can be stopped with epoxy resins. Nevertheless it is still found that where such a welded fracture is subjected to pressure, as on a grille, the break may re-open. This is less of a danger if mild steel plates are strapped either side of the break. This can, of course, be visually unacceptable. There are a number of firms specializing in the repair of historic railings who can provide uprights, back stays and rail heads from stock. Some firms recommend that the upright and head should be cast in one but it is possible for the latter to be screwed on. To prevent the tip of the upright rusting, the mortices, into which they are fitted, within the stone or concrete coping at the base and where the railings

The range of railing heads available from the leading Scottish ironfounders, Ballantyne & Sons in their present catalogue (Courtesy, Ballantyne & Sons)

return into the wall, are 'run' or 'plugged' in the traditional manner with lead (although Portland cement is used in very damp conditions). Lead caulking can also safeguard the intersection of the vertical bar and horizontal rail. The Edinburgh guide advises a teaspoon of powdered resin to prevent a blow out of the molten lead following the nineteenth-century advice to add a pinch of salt. In very important work the ends of the rail can be tipped with stainless steel or bronze. Where the coping at the base is in concrete it is likely cracks will develop on shrinking and these can be filled with a mastic. Throughout works of repair keep an eagle eye for stamps or indents indicative of the manufacturer.

Some obliging craftsmen such as the outstanding seventeenth-century master Robert Bakewell were known to sign their work 'R.B.'.

The repair of external ironwork such as balconies and railings can attract grants, particularly where the buildings lie within Conservation Areas. The Ironmongers Company and a number of charitable trusts have contributed towards the repair of outstanding examples.

Whereas patterns can be taken from damaged cast iron features and exact replacements moulded, the would-be repairer of wrought iron faces the apparently insuperable problem that no wrought iron has been produced commercially in Britain or indeed the world since the last firm to do so, Walmesley of Bolton, closed in the early 1970s. As a result renewal is normally in mild steel (which is stronger but not so long lasting) or stainless steel for structural members. It is very hard indeed to tell the difference once paint has been applied. Moreover existing wrought iron can be remelted and rerolled. Walmesleys, before their closure, survived for a number of years on the wrought iron plates from the fire damaged Menai Bridge purchased from British Rail. The danger of robbing Peter to pay Paul prompted the enterprising Ironbridge Gorge Museum into one of its most ambitious projects in the 1980s. Having acquired the equipment from Walmesleys and re-erected an important early iron-framed building of 1813 from the Royal Dockyard of Woolwich designed by John Rennie at the Museum site, the intention is to recommence the commercial production of wrought iron. This should prove a practical extension to the existing Museum of Iron already established at Coalbrookdale.

FURTHER INFORMATION

See Dorothy Bosomworth's article 'Railings Revived' in *Traditional Homes*, May 1985. This contains a useful list of suppliers and a fuller bibliography. Other publications to consult include:

W.K.V. Gale, 'Iron and Steel', Ironbridge Gorge Museum, Booklet No. 20.04.

John Gay, *Cast Iron*, Thames and Hudson, 1985. Mainly photographic.

John Harris, *English Decorative Ironwork*, Academy Editions.

John Seymour Lindsay, *An Anatomy of English Wrought Iron 1000–1800 AD*, Alec Tiranti, 1964. Excellent drawings.

Raymond Lister, *Decorative Wrought Ironwork in Great Britain*, G. Bell & Sons, 1957.

Raymond Lister, *The Craftsman in Metal*, G. Bell & Sons.

22 DOORS

The door excludes people and draughts and the front door announces social status. For the humble home, the medieval formula of planks strengthened on the inner face by horizontal ledges and/or diagonal braces, the latter possibly secured by clearly visible studs, and with a clamp board at the base, continued centuries beyond the Middle Ages. The joints might be covered by the addition of raised strips to the front ('single batten') and also to the back ('double batten') and the whole might be better insulated by the nailing on of an animal skin. Double thickness with vertical and horizontal boarding laid back to back and, on the grander houses, sturdy and elaborate hinges, gave greater strength. Status in general and ownership, a wedding or a birth in particular were proclaimed on the monogrammed board-heads or lintels specially seen in Wales, Scotland, Cumbria and Yorkshire. Carved spandrels in front of the door and chamfers and chamfer stops at the side and base added to the display.

Inside the medieval house internal social hierarchy is revealed through the doors, or lack of them. Although the absence of a rebate or what in Scotland is termed a giblet check to arrest the swing does not necessarily mean that there was never a door in position, doors upstairs were rare, for example in the Sussex Wealden house. Downstairs the entrance into the parlour from the hall would be announced by an

Unusual recessed Georgian doors in Worcester

arch-head whilst the extra wide external door of five feet or more indicated use for the passage of merchandise as well as people. Somerset and Avon has a number of examples of door architraves deliberately indented to allow the passage of barrels.

For the 'polite' house from the eighteenth century the panelled door became standard. Although a development from those ledged doors which had been framed by vertical 'stiles' and horizontal 'rails', it relied almost exclusively for its strength on this framing, the infill panels being lighter and thinner and especially in the eighteenth century proportioned to echo that of the fenestration, the topmost panels being the smallest. By being set into grooves rather than nailed, panels were less prone to cracking. They could be 'upright' with their longer sides vertical, 'square' or 'lying' with their longer sides horizontal. The variety of appearances was enormous. Speaking very generally, three was the favourite number of panels in the early Georgian period, six in the mid- and late and four in the nineteenth century. Extra framing could be provided by transverse railings top and bottom with one above waistline known as the cock and frieze rail. Any central stile was known as the 'muntin'. The most popular panel particularly in the eighteenth century was plateau shaped or 'fielded', its centre rising flush to the line of the stiles but cambered at its edges. Some panels were completely flush either on the

whole of the door or just the lowest pair, the better to withstand wear and tear. The inner faces of doors were far more normally flush particularly as front doors might be given extra boarding or metal stripping for strength and inner doors in the nineteenth century and before facing with baize or cloth (as well as curtains on rails known as portieres). In the latter case the joints would often be covered with slips of canvas and glued paper. The moulded edges to the panels could be 'stuck', integral to the wood or 'planted', separately cut and attached by glue or pins, the latter likely to be of more recent date. White lead applied to the joints assisted in weatherproofing. Solid doors obviously made it difficult to draw light into the hall. In 'polite' properties the problem was partly offset by the introduction of glazed fanlights over the doors moulded in wood, lead or iron, their capacity to light occasionally improved by the introduction within them of an inwardly and outwardly projecting lantern. The variety of designs was legion. Later still, from the mid nineteenth century, the topmost panels of the door itself or sidelights could be glazed with rippled or stained glass.

If plank and panelled doors were the mainstay, demands of function and the breadth of imagination produced many variants. There was the swept or curved door, the jib door concealed in panelling, the

PLATE X.

ARCHITECTURE.

JOINERY.

Fig. 1.

Fig. 2.

Fig. 3.

Fig. 4.

Fig. 5.

Fig. 6.

Fig. 7.

Fig. 8.

Fig. 9.

Fig. 10.

Fig. 11.

Published as the Act directs, 1810, by Longman, Hurst, Rees & Orme, Paternoster Row.

Engraved by Wilson Lowry.

An encyclopaedia of 1819 shows the variety of doors then available

swing door first introduced in the early nineteenth century, the sliding door mentioned by Isaac Ware in the *Complete Body of Architecture* of 1767 as being new and the wicket, the small door within a larger door as at Oxbridge colleges for the late admission of undergraduates, and in houses from the mid nineteenth century for the safe admission of pets. The half or hatch door, known as a heck in Yorkshire, impeded entry but allowed in fresh air. Vertical half-doors folding in the middle had a long history in domestic use before they became standard in schools and were mentioned by Neve in the 1730s. The earliest doors were in oak, the better quality from the eighteenth century in mahogany (including less commonly the surround) with softwoods as elsewhere in use from the sixteenth or seventeenth century and establishing a commanding position from the nineteenth. At Sherborne Park, Gloucestershire the panels of the inner doors are in yew. Not even wood was universal. Where extra security was required, slate and iron were in use from the mid nineteenth century.

The earliest doors seem to have been completely demountable. The first fixed within the aperture swung on harrs (known in Scotland as 'thirl-pins') which projected top and bottom of the door into holes. A number of harr(e) farmgates survive and there are barn doors so fixed at Field Broughton, Lincs. A more sophisticated harr hinge could be used to fix eighteenth-century doors. The introduction of hinges at the side, firstly in iron and later in better quality houses in brass, gave greater strength and also precipitated the introduction of the doorframe to which the hinge might be attached. At the great Neo-Classical house in Hampshire known as 'The Grange' William Wilkins designed doors that opened upwards and were counterhung on weights just like a sash window.

Where the door is the chief guard against intruders security has always been important. Drawbeams or drawbars, referred to as a 'catband' in the North, have been in continuous use since time out of mind. However, they are only suitable for use at night as they have the obvious disadvantage of preventing legitimate entry when the household is at bed. Locks operated by keys personal to a limited number of individuals have also been known for thousands of years and there are many medieval examples. Nevertheless the first patent was not granted until 1774 and the first detector lock able to identify the use of the wrong key was not invented by Jeremiah Chubb until 1818. Although mortise locks were developed from the 1770s they did not become widespread for a century, security normally being provided by the more visible rimlock. Yale cylinder locks came in in the 1860s. Early locks should always be respected in all their detail, from the escutcheons keeping the wind out of the keyhole to the decorated front or lock plate. So many patents were issued, no less than seventy in the first fifty years of the nineteenth century, that registration and patent numbers can provide indications of dating. There are very useful displays of locks and keys in the Science Museum, the V & A, the Bilston Museum in the West Midlands and J.H. Blakey & Sons, Church Street, Brierfield near Nelson in Lancashire. The centre of the English lock-making industry remains in Willenhall in West Staffordshire where it has been located since the sixteenth century. The town's Lock Museum in Walsall Street (to be rehoused at 54 New Road) is well worth a visit. Once the door was unlocked entry was very often by means of a latch, of which the most famous is undoubtedly the Suffolk Latch.

Nearly all the other door furniture dates from the eighteenth century or later, including the knocker, the bell pull, the door handle and, on inner doors, the finger plate. The nineteenth-century metalworkers, Hart and Son, employed well known architects like J.P. Seddon to design their doorknockers. Letter plates post-date the introduction of the modern postal system in 1840 – and engraved numerals the introduction of lettering in the streets, from the early nineteenth century. Early medieval shoe scrapers in

Shoescraper in Clarendon Square, Leamington Spa (Photo, courtesy Dr R.F.Y. Randall)

Barton-on-Humber, Humberside. This doorcase was originally part of Hawksmoor's projected run of gallieries in Beverley Minster (Information, Dr Ivan Hall). Most Georgian doorcases were hollow and protected at the top by lead flashings

stone survive but by far the majority of examples are in iron and date from the eighteenth and nineteenth centuries. Carron & Company provided many Georgian examples and the firms of William Bullock and Company and Archibald Kenrick & Sons, founded in 1791 and still going strong, both of West Bromwich, were pre-eminent in the nineteenth century.

The most common attention required by doors, particularly those in softwood, is simply repainting (or the application of beeswax and turpentine where they are unpainted). In Edinburgh New Town they have to be repainted every five years. Loyalty to original intentions is probably the safest course of action, even though a surprising number of eighteenth-century doors were often painted a very serious black. Paint strippers should be preferred to caustic baths, and steel wool to scrapers. If door furniture is not removed it can be protected by cardboard templates.

Even where the door becomes disused for purposes of circulation the complete eradication of the opening can be avoided. A doorway between two rooms can be sealed only on one side and converted into a cupboard. If an external door is no longer required and has to be blocked, a setting back of the infilling would still allow the opening to be 'expressed'.

Many a door becomes warped or its architrave distorted by settlement but can easily be retained by careful adjustment to the hinges, by the planing down of the top or bottom rail to a new profile and the addition of weather stripping. The greater inclemency of Irish weather led to the introduction in that country of the so-called 'door saddle', or hinged flap, at the base that seems to have found no counterpart on the mainland, other than the weatherboard known in Scotland as a 'verge', chiefly intended to assist in the shedding of water. Grandmother's solution of a bolster at the base of the door has the great advantage of being movable. If a more architectural solution is required, external storm porches are likely to be much more disruptive visually than new internal lobbies.

Even if well oiled, hinges can become strained through overuse. There is much less risk of their being distorted if the door is taken off the hinges before being repaired. Sturdy doors can require three hinges but the degree of visibility and the position of any newcomer is all important. The third hinge on a new door is normally placed just below the top one but this cannot be acceptable as an inflexible rule on an existing one. In a number of cases older doors will have been strengthened against forced entry by the addition on the internal face of metal bands. This is common, for example, in Spitalfields.

A major new problem has arisen with the introduction under the Fire Regulations of the requirement that doors should have a half-hour or an hour resistance in a blaze. Such regulations do not normally apply to houses in single occupation except where they are part of a block of flats or more than two storeys high. Where a single unit house is to be altered the Fire Officer can make recommendations, but these can be ignored. He has far greater power over conversions to multiple residential occupation. But there is no longer any excuse for disfiguring doors by the crude application of hardboard, as used to be the case. Many Fire Officers will be satisfied by increasing the resistance of the panels alone. These can be split to make veneers, sandwiching proprietary sheets with the approved fire resistant capacity or steel plates. Fielded and panelled doors with fire resistant qualities are made commercially – for example by Longden's – and some are passably authentic in appearance. Where the rails as well as the panels have to be treated the rebate of the door will have to be recut. Intumescent paint (available in a number of colours) applied to door surfaces and intumescent sealants, which expand in a fire to block the air gap between the door and the frame, have further reduced the need to butcher the door itself. Intumescents may rub off but they are not affected by overpainting except where the number of new coats is excessive. In certain circumstances the Fire Officer may insist on the introduction of a self-closing device. It is now fortunately the case that where glass within a door has to be made resistant there are alternatives to the off-putting wired glass used in so many conversions in the Sixties.

Whether fire resistant or not, off-the-peg doors, even though proclaiming themselves to be 'traditional' should nearly always be avoided. Larger firms like Magnet Southern will take individual bespoke orders. Firms like Comyn Ching (110 Golden Lane, London EC1Y 0SS) in continuous existence since 1723 offer an enormous range of door furniture. A common mistake, however, is to fix shiny brass fittings in a vernacular context.

The bases of external door surrounds are vulnerable to impact. Protection has been afforded traditionally by the introduction of a stone bollard or spur stone to deflect carriage wheels or an iron hoop and both solutions may yet be valid if the alternative is removal of original fabric.

FURTHER INFORMATION

The SPAB's Technical Pamphlet No. 6 'Fire Safety in Historic Buildings' covers all aspects of fire protection. So, to a lesser extent, does the GLC's brochure on 'Historic Buildings and Fire Protection'.

Other useful publications include:

Alec Monk, *Keys: Their History and Collection*, Shire Publications.

J.M. Vincent, *Locks and Keys throughout the Ages*.

The great variety of historic hinges is shown in *An Anatomy of Wrought Iron 1000–1800 AD* by J. Seymour Lindsay, published by Alec Tiranti.

ADDRESSES

The Guild of Architectural Ironmongers, 8 Stepney Green, London E1, tel. (01) 790–3431. For a full list of shops selling appropriate door fittings see *Traditional Homes*, February 1986.

Made-to-measure traditional fanlights can be ordered from John Sambrook, Park House, Northlam, East Sussex TN31 6PA.

The first hearths in the present millennium were placed centrally in a room and fuelled for the most part with wood, peat or cow dung. The subsequent changes were in location and in the fuel. From being freestanding they moved quite early in the Middle Ages to the wall usually in the centre of a longer side, although occasionally and more commonly from the seventeenth to the nineteenth century in the upper rooms, splayed across an angle. Coal predominated in the cities from the eighteenth century, bringing with it a change in container from firedog to grate and a narrowing in the width of the fireplace opening and the 'throat' into the flue. Gas was introduced early and electricity late in the nineteenth century, although both were used initially for lighting and only later for heating. In the meantime central heating, abandoned with the hypercausts of the Romans, had been rediscovered in the late eighteenth century, relying initially on hot water, hot air and steam. Very often no traces at all remain of mobile forms of heating ranging from the medieval brazier to the stove developed from the eighteenth century, but clearly these could prove vital in large lofty spaces.

In the medieval 'open hall' the central hearth, albeit largely undirected except for the occasional backing of a vertical 'reredos' screen or canopy, proved efficient in the transmission of heat with no hot air being wasted up a chimney. Nevertheless the introduction of floors into such spaces from the mid sixteenth century increased the considerable nuisance occasioned by the unchannelled smoke and posed clear hazards in the reconciliation of open hearths with wooden joists. For these reasons the central hearth had passed out of fashion centuries before in the 'politer' houses. In the humble homes the introduction of smoke bays (lit and ventilated by 'fire windows') rising through the floors sometimes and normally later enclosed in smoke hoods provided the forerunners of the fireplace, flue and chimney that are now standard.

To induce economic burning, coal required a better draught, enveloping by oxygen and a draining of the ash. This led to the introduction firstly in the sixteenth century and more commonly in the eighteenth of the grate with a fire basket to hold the lumps. Before that one, and normally two, dog irons or andirons (manufactured in cast iron from the beginning of the fifteenth century) had been sufficient to support the logs, the larger versions often doubling as holders for the spit. The 'dog grate' was a verbal and functional marriage of the two mainly in use from the eighteenth century but the most widespread was the hob grate, first introduced c.1720 (*Fashionable Fireplace*, p. 22). In this example the fire basket was flanked by the two hobs, sometimes in brick but normally in cast iron or, where particular show was important, in bronze, with bars in wrought iron or steel. In the humbler homes where the fireplace doubled for cooking and heating the hobs provided a surface for the boiling of water and the preparation of food. Perhaps the most prolific and long-lived of the manufacturers whose name appears stamped on many examples is that of Carron and Company established in 1759 in Falkirk. The Dale Company of Coalbrookdale was another leader in the field.

All sorts of devices and designs were introduced to direct the draught for a coal fire and draw away the smoke which was generally considered to be more acrid than that produced by wood. The register grate introduced in the late eighteenth century incorporating a flap or 'damper' operated by a key at the base of the flue proved common throughout the nineteenth century. Its effectiveness was however challenged by Count Rumford, the physicist and first person to investigate fireplace design scientifically, whose thoughts were published in the 1790s. He preferred to rely on the narrowing of the throat with a 'smoke shelf' leading into a wider smoke chamber, the narrowing of the fireplace with splayed sides and an advanced back and the use of fire brick in place of iron (for fuller explanation see SPAB's pamphlet on 'Chimneys in Old Buildings'). The introduction of grilles drawing in external air through the floor, the wall or the cheeks of the fireplace remain common devices to encourage the updraught necessary for the emission of smoke. In some nineteenth-century cast iron surrounds the decoration is pierced and fretted

Hob grate from Thorpe Hall, near Peterborough

for the same purpose. In a convector grate circular ventilation grilles and ventilators at the base are clearly visible.

The heat and smoke from wood fires brought culinary advantages. Depending on the area of the country the great fireplace recess can contain curing chambers for bacon with hooks for carcasses (particularly in the south-west), spice cupboards and salt boxes (in particular North Yorkshire and Cumbria) and bread ovens very often shaped as a beehive, lined with brick or earthenware and sealed by doors of wood, clay or, in later examples, cast iron. Where bread ovens had two openings, the cavity below was the furnace which provided the heat from faggots taken from the fire. The bottom plate of the oven could be set on a base of river sand, the better to retain the heat. When not in use for cooking the oven was used to air clothes and to keep alive the kindling placed there overnight for next day's fire. And there still remained room in the inglenook for the settles and High Seats that offered the snuggest spot in the house. The changeover to coal in the larger openings, by reducing the area required for burning, released space for the substantial cast iron ranges that combined fire, oven and boiler. There are references to 'iron chimneys' and 'ranges' in the sixteenth century but most survivors date from the eighteenth. The first examples were 'open', those from the early nineteenth century being 'closed' with a plate covering the fire itself. Nearly all were given a finish in black lead (still obtainable under brand names such as 'Zebrite'). With a leavening of historic tolerance such ranges can still be used. Where they remain dormant the National Trust advises a finish in Manders Black Ebony paint M.757.

The intense heat of the fire demanded a durable facing for the recess. The use of bricks laid herringbone fashion has been traditional at least since the eleventh century. The vitrification of the surface by the application of salt increased its resistance. The Romans used tiles on edge. A greensand called 'firestone' found widespread application in Sussex, Kent, Surrey, and Hampshire. The earliest iron firebacks, generally cast although occasionally wrought, appear to date from the fourteenth century. Heat is either radiated, convected or conducted and iron has the added capacity to throw some radiant heat forward into the room. Glazed tiles particularly for splayed sides have enjoyed uneven favour certainly since the seventeenth century.

The complete historic fireplace has an array of ancillary equipment. There are the cranes or sways from which pots were suspended, the meat cured, and the kettle boiled; lazybacks which tipped the kettle to pour; the poker (first christened the 'fire fork'); the fire tongs with which to fuel the fire;

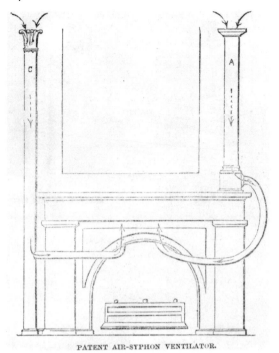

PATENT AIR-SYPHON VENTILATOR.

Nineteenth-century fireplaces could be ventilated ingeniously through side pilasters (Courtesy, Illustrated London News)

brandtongs to light one's pipe; the fire screen to shield soft complexions; the chimney board and later hinged or roller shutters which sealed off the draughty recess when it was not in use; the haster or metal-faced screen that reflected heat into out of the way corners; the iron blocks placed on the fire before being used to 'iron' the clothes; the bellows; the fender or fend iron hooked on to the wall either side of the opening; the 'curfews' or bell-shaped lids that covered the embers overnight; the jacks which rotated the spit, sometimes driven by the current of the updraught; the rack where the spit was kept when not in use; the dust covers to shield the ash; the fire pan for burning charcoal; the coal scuttle; the shovel; and, with early gas fires, dishes filled with water that were supposed to compensate for the dehydrating effects of the new-fangled fuel. Antique shops or attics can help in the reassembly of some of this array of ironmongery.

The actual fireplace itself may decay or malfunction. Among the more serious faults in the first category are any cracks in the working or back hearth, that would allow cinders to fall on to combustible material. An earlier generation will probably have extended the hearth into the room with a raised surround or curb, but when there is a reversion to natural fuels with their tendency to spit this becomes

essential. Undecorated fireclay lining to the recess can be patched and sealed by mixing new fireclay which is easily available commercially, although where the lining is modern complete replacement is probably better. Malfunctioning normally centres on the refusal of the smoke to go up the flue. Blockages may be cleared by cleaning but the problem is likely to be more intractable and require a positive inducement to a draught through the introduction of splay-sided hoods or hoppers in metal or flat sheets of toughened glass, both at the head of the recess, metal plates in the throat, the introduction of equalizing air currents from the exterior through air bricks and grilles or, as a last resort, the insertion of small extractor fans at the head of the flue. These are all matters for the professional.

Clearly a change of fuel, whether back to wood or peat or from smoking to smokeless can have an architectural impact quite apart from any effect on creature comforts (SPAB pamphlet see p. 106). Those wishing to return to more historic forms may choose to consult the Solid Fuel Advisory Service which has a display in the Building Centre at 26 Store Street, London WC1 and also has field inspectors. The National Fireplace Council can offer advice but it is primarily a manufacturers' association. In certain areas the burning of wood or non-smokeless fuel is an offence. However, there have as yet been no domestic prosecutions. Among the possible woods ash, cherry, plane, willow, hornbeam and beech all have their champions. Chestnut is said to produce a large number of sparks and this is particularly true of conifers which also emit a black smoke. Charcoal has the great advantage of being smokeless and producing great heat but it generates carbon monoxide which can be hazardous in rooms with poor ventilation.

The opening up of a lost medieval fireplace must always be a matter for caution where this involves the removal of later alterations themselves of interest. The whole point would in any case be lost unless wood was to be used. Where a lost fire surround is to be reinstated the genuine second-hand article is almost always better than the first-hand fake. The former can be purchased from fashionable shops, but normally at fashionable prices, and it is far cheaper to negotiate with demolition contractors on site. Cast-iron fireplaces in particular can be transformed by a polished matt finish, if necessary after a carefully supervised shotblasting. The fashion for stripping Georgian surrounds is however alien to genuine historic character and the placing of eighteenth-century wooden examples or parts of them in weak caustic baths can dissolve fragile reliefs in gesso or pewter and damage the wood. If later paint is to be removed try caustic putty, paintstripper or hot air guns but be careful with all three. In fixing fireplaces the National Trust advises the use of inert adhesives rather than mortar and even counsels against the application of water for cleaning lest this activates harmful salts. Nevertheless, Hannah Glass writing in the 1760s did give it as a servant's first duty of the day to open the shutters and wipe the marble surround and hearthstone with soapy water.

FURTHER INFORMATION

Christopher Gilbert and Anthony Wells-Cole's *The Fashionable Fireplace* (Temple Newsam Country House Studies No. 2, 1985) is available from Temple Newsam House, Leeds. The following publications may also prove useful:

Nicholas Hills, *The English Fireplace: Its Architecture and the Working Fire*, Quiller Press 1983.

Alison Kelly, *The Book of English Fireplaces*, Country Life 1968.

Roxana McDonald, *The Fireplace Book*, Architectural Press 1984.

J. Seymour-Lindsay, *Iron and Brass Implements of the English House* (with drawings by the author).

Lawrence Wright, *Home Fires Burning*, London 1964.

ADDRESSES

The National Fireplace Manufacturers Association, PO Box 13, Hanley, Stoke-on-Trent ST1 3RG, tel. (0782) 29031.

Yellow Pages will give the addresses of the large number of shops that now specialize in second hand fireplaces.

24 WALL PAINTINGS, PANELLING AND WALLPAPER

Wall Paintings

When thinking of wall paintings the mind turns immediately to churches. However, a small proportion of surviving Pre-Reformation examples are to be found in secular buildings.

So many major new discoveries are being made, on the average of four or five a year, that studies in the field acquire an excitement that comes from the dynamic rather than the finite. In England and Wales major surveys are under way to record surviving examples, through the Courtauld Institute and the National Monuments Record for Wales, respectively. In England Mr David Park, M.A., launched a five-year research programme in April 1980 into English Medieval Wallpaintings, which was the first of its kind since C.E. Keyser's of 1883 and Professor Tristram's of 1944–55. The present study, funded mainly by the Leverhulme Trust with assistance from the Council for the Care of Churches and the Society of Antiquaries, will record all remaining examples, secular and ecclesiastical, and all lost examples, up to a general cut-off date of 1540. The Royal Commission on Historical Monuments is recording each on colour slides and sets of the survey records and photographs will be retained at the National Monuments Record and at the Courtauld Institute with partial sets at the Council for the Care of Churches, the Redundant Churches Fund, the University of York and the University of East

Newly discovered wallpaintings from Berry Pomeroy
Castle, Devon

Anglia. An RCHM 'popular' volume by Mr Park was published in 1987. Although the major finds of recent years have been in the grander houses such as Little Moreton Hall, Cheshire, Canons Ashby, Northamptonshire, and the Ancient House at Ipswich, wall paintings are certainly found in humbler properties. It was to itinerant painters conversant with fashion that we owe the better examples, but the house owner himself would often try his hand.

Execution might have been possible for the amateur but conservation is decidedly a question for experts alone. And changing expert opinion at that – the application of resin-based varnish in the nineteenth century and wax up to the nineteen-fifties over fragile surfaces has had a disastrous effect primarily because both seal in damp and tend to darken with age. If wall paintings are in distress, or indeed concealed examples are suspected (and any old, undulating, plaster surfaces should arouse suspicion) a professional conservator should be called in. England, particularly in the persons of Mrs Eve Baker and E. Clive Rouse (now retired) and their teams, has a particular standing in the field rivalled only by Germany. Nevertheless there are no professional conservators in Wales or Scotland and in England there is so much work, partly as the result of the extra funding allocated by the Historic Buildings and Monuments Commission, that waiting lists tend

to be inescapable. The first ever professional Wallpainting Conservation Course has been run at the Courtauld Institute since Autumn 1985 and should improve matters. Conservators of course will live up to their name and will always baulk at 'touching up' even where the surviving painting is a mere shadow of its former self. This is slightly ironic for in the words of E. Clive Rouse: 'The medieval artist never intended his paintings to last for ever. Paintings were constantly being replaced as they became dilapidated or unfashionable.' Clearly it is the archaeological instinct which is paramount. In exceptional cases it is possible to remove paintings if they cannot be saved *in situ*. The surface is coated in glue and transferred to a muslin and hessian facing after which it can be detached, section by section. There are also techniques for separating layers of painting where these are all of interest and repositioning the overlays.

Once exposed, paintings should be protected from damp and direct sunlight and should not be washed or dusted. Continuous low temperatures with good ventilation are the ideal. If building works are required in the room the paintings should be covered with cellophane sheets sealed by tape applied well away from the edge of the paintings. In that early paintings are to be found normally on lime plaster, repairs to neighbouring unpainted surfaces should be in kind, with subsequent redecoration only in limewash and not with distemper or emulsion paint. Radiators or flueless gas heaters should be placed well away from the painted surfaces.

Although medieval wallpaintings command most attention there are many fascinating post-medieval examples too, which require care and protection.

Panelling

Panelling was introduced from the Middle Ages for practical reasons – it provided a further barrier to the entry of damp and condensation, and concealed it where it did occur (an ambiguous virtue) and it also conserved heat. Eighteenth-century dado rails acted as buffers to prevent furniture damaging the wall and prevented limewash whitening coloured clothes, whilst the picture rail just below the ceiling gave a fixing for the hanging of pictures or a lip for the storage of plates. In the eighteenth century such shelf-like lips were often supported on double-eyed nails. The panelling itself is generally held in position by nailed 'holdfasts' spiked into a vertical mortar joint or 'perpend'.

It is a common complaint against historic panelling that it splits and cracks on the introduction of central heating. So it can, but the result is rarely troubling. Splitting along the line of the grain and the opening of joints has the advantage of improving ventilation to the air pockets behind, reducing the likelihood of rot. Flight holes indicative of active woodworm are certainly more alarming and must be tackled (see chapter on Infestation of Timber). Where the householder applies the insecticide himself manufacturers' instructions should be strictly followed, but it may be worth repeating that an open window would prevent the build-up of fumes, that eyes should be guarded and that the panelling is best treated front and back.

Badly weakened rear surfaces can be strengthened by a new skin of dry seasoned wood, or simply by the application of a primer sealant. On dismantling do watch for 'trials', the original pencil or charcoal mock-ups on the wall behind indicating how the panelling would look. Where the front surface is unpainted and where its age does not demand that it be left in a natural colour, a wax polish is traditional and reduces a tendency to split by making the wood less dry. More shops are now selling beeswax and this can be obtained directly from James Briggs and Sons, Lion Works, Old Market Street, Manchester (tel. (061) 795–8410). There are of course many proprietary wax polishes on the market but some do contain dyes so need to be used with caution. Wax polishing once a year should be sufficient.

Wallpaper

The householder can protect historic wallpaper in obvious ways, by shielding it from direct glare, avoiding the use of chemicals and by placing acid free cartridge paper cut-outs around light switches. Conservation must be a matter for the professional and the scholar. The best source of national information both on history and conservation is the Victoria and Albert Museum (Department of Prints and Drawings). A number of companies are able to offer historic designs:

Laura Ashley Ltd, Braywick House, Braywick Road, Maidenhead. 40 Sloane Street, London SW1.

Cole and Son of Mortimer Street, 18 Mortimer St, London W1. Mr Christopher Coles Wallpaper Collection includes the blocks of Crace's founded c.1750. For free samples (01) 580–5368. Sales Order Dept. (01) 580–2288/9.

Hamilton Weston, 11 Townshend Road, Richmond, Surrey TW19 1XH, a husband and wife team with a collection of blocks for hand printing from 1690–1840 (£21—£25 per roll at November 1984 prices).

Osborne & Little, 304 Kings Road, London SW3.

A. Sanderson & Sons Ltd, 52/53 Berners St, London W1P 3AD founded 1878. Now owns many historic woodblocks including designs by William Morris, Owen Jones, Walter Crane, Voysey etc. The Sanderson Archive, of 5000 wallpaper designs, was moved to Uxbridge in 1983.

Warner & Sons, 2 Anglia Way, Chapel Hill Braintree, Essex CM7 6RS produces a small range of documented wallpapers.

Watts & Company, 7 Tufton Street, London SW1 can supply screen printed paper from designs by Pugin etc.

Zoffany, 27A Motcomb Street, London W1 now supply reproductions of some of the historic wallpapers at Temple Newsam House, Leeds.

The V & A supplies a series of wallpaper reproduction from its own collection.

FURTHER INFORMATION

The following publications may be useful:

Fiona Clark, *William Morris, Wallpapers and Chintzes*, Academy Editions 1974.

John Compton, article in *Putting back the Style*, Evan Bros. 1982, (ed. Alexandra Artley).

Eric Entwisle, *A Literary History of Wallpaper*, B.T. Batsford 1960.

Eric Entwisle, *The Book of Wallpaper*, 1954, reprinted Kingsmead 1970.

Eric Entwisle, *Wallpapers of the Victorian Era*, F. Lewis 1964.

Brenda Greysmith, *Wallpaper*, Studio Vista 1976.

Jean Hamilton, *Introduction to Wallpaper*, HMSO 1983.

C. Oman and J. Hamilton, *Wallpapers*, Sothebys/V & A 1982.

'Sanderson 1860–1985'. Catalogue of an exhibition held by Sandersons.

A.V. Sugden and E.L. Edmondson, *A History of English Wallpapers 1509–1914*, B.T. Batsford 1926. Still regarded as the classic textbook.

Anthony Wells-Cole, *Historic Paper Hangings*, catalogue of the 1983 exhibition held at Temple Newsam House, Leeds LS15 0AE.

25 ARCHITECTURAL SALVAGE

A new term does not necessarily imply a new idea. Modern conservation practice has institutionalized in the words 'architectural salvage' the unselfconscious husbandry which has been displayed for centuries. It was quite common for aristocratic families in retrenchment to strip houses being abandoned or sold in order to embellish the new mansion. An antiquarianism, apparently divorced from family considerations, prompted spectacular early essays in conservation such as the re-siting at Montacute in Somerset of the great entrance porch from Clifton Maybank in Dorset when that house was substantially demolished in 1786. William Wilkins incorporated the columns from the portico of Prince Regent's shortlived Carlton House into the front elevation of his National Gallery. Clough Williams-Ellis at Portmeirion and Sir Frederick Gibberd in his famous garden at Harlow are part of a long tradition of architectural magpies stretching back to Horace Walpole and beyond.

The growth of conservation legislation accompanied by the explosion of interest in antiques has led to a more systematic approach in the last decade. Planning authorities will often insist on the use of second-hand materials wherever possible and a number of District and County Councils have established Materials Banks open to potential restorers. There are good examples in Abingdon, Birmingham, Brighton, Cardiff, Dartmoor National Park, Lewes and Salisbury. In Derbyshire applicants for listed building consent are asked if they would be willing to donate fabric and features retrieved from demolition to the bank run by the county. Listed building consent will often be accompanied by conditions about the salvage of important items, although as it is impossible to condition a third party by such a consent particular new locations have to be specified in a roundabout way. In some counties like Cambridgeshire builders are so alive to the advantages of storing second-hand materials that a municipal store is regarded as superfluous. Most demolition contractors are well aware of the value of salvage and will sell on either to builders or exchange of cash on the site. The professional salvager will normally have the items in which he is interested entered as credits in a demolition contract with an agreement to purchase at a certain price. This gives the owner a return and the contractor an interest in their retention. It is important to remember that retrieval of materials from a demolition site without authorization is, strictly speaking, illegal. At the more sophisticated end of the market there is a flourishing export trade to America, Japan and Europe in everything from stained glass to Victorian bar fittings and reclaimed bricks. Indeed such is the discrepancy between the demand and supply that the supply to the legitimate market is being supplemented by a spate of thefts particularly of Georgian fireplaces, even doors, from houses in use. Some salvage firms are not known for the scrupulous observance of listed building consent procedures.

Salvage is not always carried out with the desire for financial reward. The great portico from the late nineteenth-century Baptist Tabernacle at Swindon was purchased by Mr Frost, a postman, in 1978 to save it from destruction although his plans to re-erect it as part of a new home have been subsequently thwarted by planning authorities. A complete nine-teenth-century chapel from Gnaton Hall at Yealmpton in Devon, the subject of a consent to demolish in 1976, was bought by a nearby landowner and re-erected in its entirety on his estate.

In 1968 Charles Brooking established the Brooking Collection of architectural components from 1700 to 1935, as an exercise in pure and applied preservation; to retain representative examples of doors and windows and other features, and to educate present day restorers. The Museum has recently been rehoused in the Georgian house of Bradstone Brook at Shalford in Surrey, in space offered by the international architectural practice of Scott Brownrigg and Turner. The Museum and reference library (with a particularly valuable run of builders' catalogues) is open by appointment and technical advice is offered at a modest fee. Plans announced in 1979 for a Museum of Architecture have so far remained just a gleam in the eye of the sponsors.

FURTHER INFORMATION

A selection of architectural salvagers:
(Many builders have their own stores of secondhand materials)

1 Architectural Antiques, Savoy Cinema, New Road, South Molton, Devon, tel. 076–95–3342.

2 Architectural Antiques of Ludlow, 140 Corve Street, Ludlow, Shropshire.

3 Architectural Heritage, Boddington Manor, Boddington, Cheltenham, Glos, tel. Coombe Hill 741 (After hours 22191). Additional showroom at Bayshill Lodge, Montpellier, Cheltenham. Open 10–5.30 by appointment. Founded 1978. Send 50p for details.

4 Architectural Salvage Index, Netley House, Gomshall, Surrey GU5 9QA, tel. (048) 641-3221. Established in 1977 by the architectural practice of Hutton and Rostron and the Architectural Press. This is a data bank of available features and materials; potential purchasers contact the owners directly. If no immediate buyer comes forward the item will be included in the lists regularly published in the *Architects Journal*. For items to be given away or sold under £10 there is no charge for entry onto the Index. Commission is charged only to sellers. The Index will not accept items removed from listed buildings without the benefit of listed building consent.

5 Bailey's Architectural Antiques, The Engine Shed, Ashburton Industrial Estate, Ross-on-Wye, Herefordshire, tel. (0989) 63015.

6 Nigel Bartlett, 67 St Thomas Street, London SE1, tel. (01) 378–7895. 'Purveyor of fine chimneypieces, garden statuary and period architectural features.'

7 Beacon Architectural Salvage, The Stable Yard, Alscot Park, Stratford-on-Avon, Warwickshire, tel. (078) 987–616.

8 Brighton Architectural Salvage, 33 Gloucester Road, Brighton, tel. (0273) 681656.

9 Conservation Building Products, Forge Lane, Cradley Heath, Warley, West Midlands B64 6AL, tel. (0384) 64219.

10 Coventry Conservation Store, 78 Whitefriars Street, Coventry, tel. (0203) 38110.

11 Crowther of Syon Lodge, Syon Lodge, Busch Corner, Isleworth, Middlesex TW7 5BH, tel. (01) 560–7978/7985. Established on its present site in 1929. Open weekdays 9–5, Saturdays and Sundays 11–4.30. Also at 6 Old Bond Street, London W1, tel. (01) 493-8688.

12 T. Crowther & Son, 282 North End Road, Fulham, London SW6, tel. (01) 385–1375/7.

The proprietors of 11 and 12 are from the same family. A large number of craftsmen are employed to repair items for sale.

13 Glover and Stacey Ltd, Malthouse, Main Road, Kingsley, Bordan Hants, tel. (0252) 549334.

14 Hale Farm Building Materials, 32 Guildford Road, Farnham, Surrey, tel. (0252) 726484.

15 Havenplan's Architectural Emporium, The Old Station, Station Road, Killarmarsh, Nr Sheffield, tel. (0742) 489972.

16 The House Hospital, 68 Battersea High Street, London SW11, tel. (01) 223-3179. Open 2-6 on weekdays, Saturdays 10-1. Telephone Anna Skrine (mornings) (01) 247-3961.

17 House of Steel Antiques, 400 Caledonian Road, Islington, London N1 1DN, tel. (01) 607-5889.

18 Langham Architectural Materials, Langham Farm, East Nynehead, Wellington, Somerset, tel. (082346) 297.

19 Liverpool Architectural Workshop, Head Street, St James's Place, Liverpool L8 1QU, tel. (051) 708-7518

20 London Architectural Salvage & Supply Company, Mark Street (off Paul Street), London EC2A 4ER, tel. (01) 739-0448/9. Established in 1978 in a substantial redundant church, itself of great architectural importance and the work of James Brook. Open 9.30-5.30 (4.30 Saturday).

21 Oakferry Limited, The Orchard, Heytesbury House, Heytesbury, Warminster, Wiltshire BA12 0HG, tel. (0985) 40014.

22 Sheffield Architectural Antiques, Ponds Forge, Sheaf St, Sheffield, tel. (0742) 586480.

23 Solopark Limited, The Old Railway Station, Station Road, Nr. Pampisford, Cambridgeshire with branch at Ipswich, tel. (0223) 834-663.

24 Townsends, 36 New End Square, NW3, tel. (01) 794-5706/7.

25 Walcot Reclamation, 108 Walcot Street, Bath, Avon BA1 5BG, tel. (0225) 66291.

26 Whiteway and Waldron, 305 Munster Road, London SW6, tel. (01) 381-3195.

For further names see *Traditional Homes* October, 1985.

The salvage of fittings from redundant churches became easier after 1974 with the establishment of the post of Furnishings Officer for each diocese. Lists of such items are published and exchanged between Officers and to outside parties. Most dioceses have their own stores although some fittings of sacramental importance such as fonts are smashed (unless they are of considerable artistic value) to avoid the risk of their being put to unseemly use. Items of great beauty can often be obtained from redundant churches for the cost of removal.

Since 1982 the Stained Glass Repository has been established at The Glaziers Hall, 9 Montague Close, London Bridge. At present only glass from the Greater London area is being salvaged but items can be resited anywhere in the country. There is no purchase charge but the new owner bears the expense of removal.

In 1900 Adolph Loos, the Viennese architect and apologist of the Modern Movement, took as his subject in 'The Story of a Poor Rich Man' a client who found himself the victim of an architect of the most purist persuasion. He was provided with the finite house, from which nothing could be added and nothing taken away. He was even directed to refuse the presents his children brought home for him from the kindergarten as they would create aesthetic confusion. Loos's homily was meant to be sardonic and it confirmed, if such confirmation was required, that every house – however ancient, however designed – cannot help but be dynamic rather than static. The real difficulties arise in accommodating the inevitable pressures for change in the most sensitive manner. The SPAB Manifesto of 1877, written by men outraged particularly at the ham-fisted and arrogant repair of churches did state that 'if it (an historic building) has become inconvenient for present use, raise another building rather than alter or enlarge the old one' and 'treat our ancient buildings as monuments of a bygone art, created by bygone manners, that modern art cannot meddle with without destroying.' Ruskin preferred collapse to adulteration. And yet absolute attitudes were soon

modified. W.R. Lethaby writing in 1925 in 'Philip Webb and His Work' gives the Society's view that if additions must be made 'they should be as unobtrusive as possible and frankly modern'; paraphrasing a gloss to the Manifesto of April 1924

To the SPAB extensions should be in the style of their own time so that no challenge is offered to the original building which is thus silhouetted by contrast with the new. The completely opposite point of view sees nothing wrong in designing in the original idiom, fusing the new and the old into a single stylistic entity and deliberately disguising the newcomer. The great cathedrals, churches and houses of this country show many examples of both schools of thought. Each has champions and unselfconscious exponents among those extending more humble homes nowadays.

At Pool's Cottage, Five Ways Road, Haseley, Coventry the casual observer would be hard put to disentangle the new from the old. At Worcester the nineteenth-century extension to the early eight-

Pool's Cottage, Fiveways Road, Haseley, Coventry, Warwickshire, plans for extension Architect, D.T. Rathbone, 1984

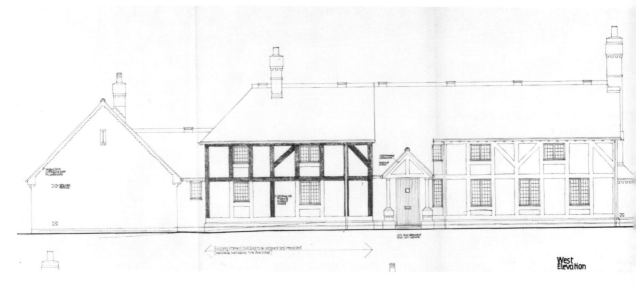

West Elevation

Britannia House, Worcester. The larger nineteenth-century extension to the recessed eighteenth-century *original of c.1725 is recognizable from a distance only through the lack of glazing bars in the windows*

37 Bilton Road, Rugby, Warwickshire. Scheme for extension by Kellett & Thompson, Chartered Architects

Oversley House, Kinwarton Road, Alcester,
Warwickshire. Architects, Austin Vernon Associates,
1983. The original chapel is that on the left

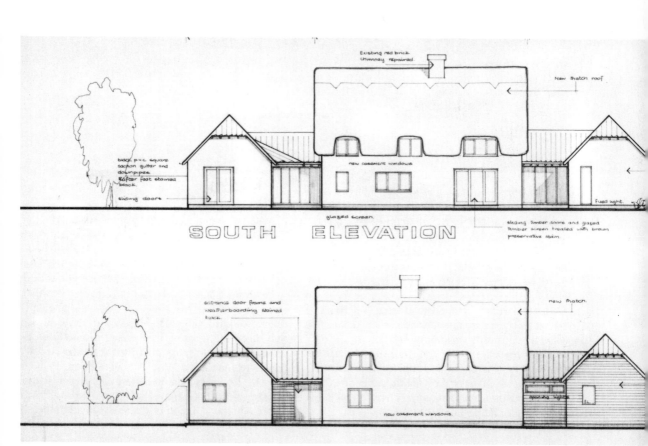

Hill Farm, Church Road, Easton, Huntingdonshire,
architects, Saunders Boston 1983. The two 'pavilions'
either side are the additions

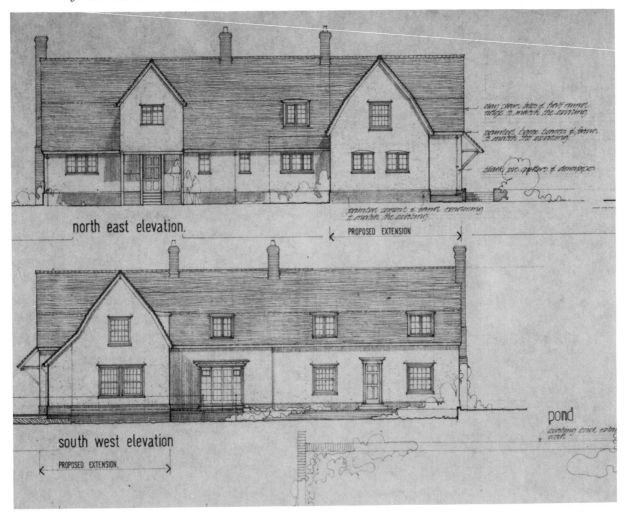

Harvest Farm, Milden, extension by Graham Jones, 1984

eenth-century original is more identifiable, but displays a deferential stylistic empathy extraordinary for a provincial Victorian architect. At Oversley House, Alcester in Warwickshire a scheme for a block of flats placed behind an existing (and modest) chapel creates a completely new sham chapel to counterbalance the existing one.

The extension to 37 Bilton Road, Rugby, a listed gentleman's villa of the mid nineteenth century, is dressed in the style of the villa but offers less of a challenge to the existing symmetry by a set-back that breaks the building line.

In other examples the same effect has been achieved by contrasting surface treatments and by changes in the roofline. At Hill Farm, Church Road, Easton the original cottage in the centre can still be 'read' independently from the two new asymmetrical

'pavilions'. Such in fact has been the method of extending cottages over the centuries, although rather more common was the addition of a crosswing at one side running across the main axis and presenting a gable to the street, or the addition of extra ground floor space to the rear covered by a long catslide roof carried down over it at a pitch. At Harvest Farm, Milden, in Suffolk the new extension has taken the form of a crosswing. Sometimes the extension in the traditional form can stray rather closer to conceit. At Paunton Court Farm, Bishops Frome, Worcester the two-storey extension is disguised as an oasthouse complete with cowl, a building type common in the area. On a number of occasions local planning authorities have strongly advised that freestanding extensions or the inelegantly termed 'granny annexes' should adopt the appearance of detached stables, pavilions or dovecotes.

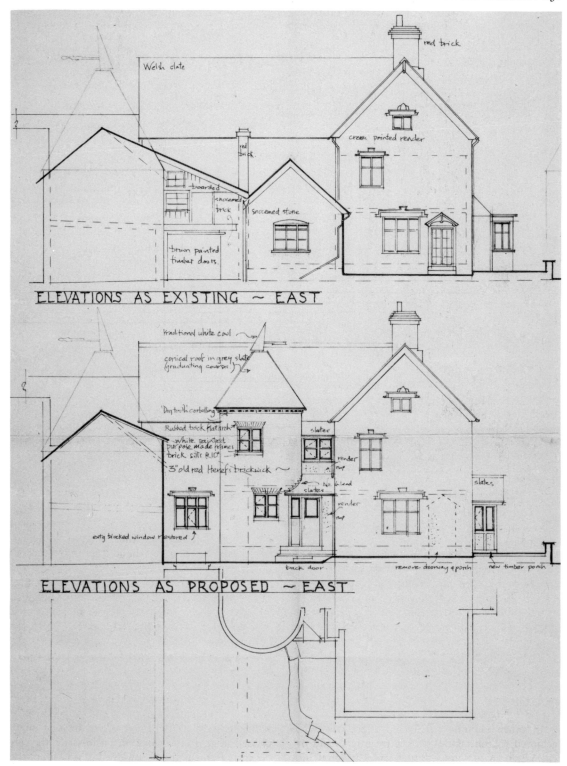

Welsh slate

red brick

cream painted render

red brick

boarded
snocemed brick

snocemed stone

brown painted timber doors

ELEVATIONS AS EXISTING ~ EAST

traditional white cowl

conical roof in grey slate (graduating courses)

'Dog tooth' corbelling

Rubbed brick flat arch

white painted purpose made frames
brick sills @ 10"

3" old red Herefs brickwick

slates

render
rwp

extg blocked window restored

new lead

slates

render
rwp

slates

back door

remove doorway & porch

new timber porch

ELEVATIONS AS PROPOSED ~ EAST

Paunton Court Farm, Bishops Frome, Worcester.
Architect, Ian Harper, 1982. The 'oast tower' extension
has now been constructed.

'Frankly modern' extension to an eighteenth-century house (now offices) at Newbury

Foregate Street, Worcester. The pair of curiously distended windows on the first floor are disconcerting aesthetically but intriguing historically

At Abingdon, Oxfordshire (formerly Berkshire) listed building consent has been granted for the removal of the 'Disraeli window' inserted in the mid nineteenth century in a way that unbalanced a fine group of Georgian stables.

And yet the window, associated with one of Briatin's most famous Prime Ministers, clearly possesses historic interest. Should it go?

In the Market Place at Blandford Forum in Dorset the Secretary of State refused consent for the removal of the Victorian shopfront to Currys (listed Grade I). This did make the eighteenth-century building appear rather lopsided but was itself an interesting attempt to enter into the classical spirit of the original design by the Bastard Brothers

The plan by the National Trust to return the eighteenth-century front elevation of Croft Castle, Herefordshire to its appearance prior to 1914 was granted consent in 1985.

Photos show the effect of the change of 1914 (photos, courtesy of The National Trust)

The alternative is to be 'frankly modern' as at Newbury, Berkshire (p. 152).

Extensions do not have to break through the existing building envelope. Attic spaces intended in timber framed cottages principally for storage and in Georgian or Victorian terrace houses for the servants have been reconditioned to provide extra accommodation for the family. In the last case extra space can be provided by re-profiling the roof to a mansard, but there are many cases where this is highly inappropriate. Almost all planning authorities in rural areas prefer the extra lighting required to be through rooflights rather than dormers. There will certainly, however, be cases where traditionally-designed dormers, perhaps with bargeboards, would look far less out of place – although there is the danger in complying with buildings regulations that they might be overscaled. The doubling up of adjacent properties to form single units can entail even less external change.

The old house may of course be too large rather than too small. It is far less easy to lay general guidelines about retrenchment. Where fabric of importance is concerned demolition should be the last, not first, resort. Demolition is not cheap (the average three-storey house costs £10 000 to demolish and the operation can attract VAT). Making good the newly-exposed external walls brings further expense and practical problems where original materials are not at hand to disguise the patching. Internal subdivision to create extra units will require planning permission but the earlier social division between the family and the servants necessitated two completely separate systems of circulation that should provide the starting point for the breaking up of the unit.

The removal of later additions because they offend is a far more subjective matter. The eccentricities of fenestration in Foregate Street, Worcester are original and it would be a return to the disgraced Victorian drive to 'improve' on the work of our predecessors to introduce a balance that never existed. There is after all the charm of the picturesque and the naive and the assurance of knowing that incompetence is timeless. Views can nevertheless differ legitimately. The local authority approved the removal of the so-called Disraeli Window added in the mid nineteenth century to one wing of the Georgian stables at Abingdon, Berkshire as part of a recent comprehensive programme of repair and conversion. On the other hand the displacement of the flamboyant Victorian shopfront from a Grade I listed Georgian building at 20 Market Place, Blandford Forum, Dorset was refused consent by the Secretary of State after a Public Inquiry. The National Trust plan to return the front elevation of Croft Castle to its appearance prior to 1914 was granted consent in 1985.

27 THE CONVERSION OF NON-DOMESTIC PROPERTIES AND COUNTRY HOUSES

By the end of this century it seems highly likely that one-fifth or more of the homes in listed properties will be housed in buildings that were not constructed as dwellings.

As planning policies are designed to discourage new and isolated houses in rural areas practically the only way to live there can be to take on the challenge of converting a disused barn or church although permission to convert may be subject to the restriction that the house can only be occupied by someone engaged in agriculture.

In the conversion of barns a number of guidelines should be followed. These are laid down in the policy broadsheet issued by SPAB in June 1984 as part of its Barns Campaign. Broadly speaking it is important that the bulk of the barn in the countryside should remain dominant and that the shell and roof be as little disturbed as possible by new apertures. Many planning authorities now insist on the avoidance of a formal domestic appearance, windows being limited wherever practical to the less public side of the building, being small and informally, though not capriciously, composed. Rooflights are invariably preferred to dormers. In Kent tall slit windows are preferred by the County Council in oast house conversions. The colour preference for window frames is black or dark brown or a coating in traditional red oxide. Although standard chimneys may well be more sympathetic in the materials they are nearly always rejected in favour of industrial metal flues as these are much smaller and less domestic. They have the support of SPAB. Although weatherboarding can often be a later replacement for earlier daubing, the standard preference is for retention and, in the case of Essex, its protection by the use of traditional tarring. Internally, the measure of success must be the degree to which the original spatial integrity is preserved. The retention of at least one bay to full height is normally insisted upon and the most suitable is that between the two matching midstrey entrances designed to light and ventilate the threshing floor; and very often the most generously glazed area in any conversion, if the doors are replaced by expanses of glass (or retained as giant shutters to such glazing). The introduction of suspended floors need not be alien to the original character of the barn; 'lofts' for the storage of hay and straw or the unthreshed crop (sometimes approached by an external stairs) are not uncommon. New floors may, however, have to be carried independently from the existing shell on the insistence of Building Inspectors and this will have the advantage of allowing original timbers to remain undisturbed. Any cutting away of principal timbers, particularly tie beams, collar beams and braces is damaging archaeologically and highly inadvisable structurally. Some existing partitions within the barn may well be of interest in their own right and could be used to advantage to create segregated spaces. 'Corn holes' usually within a single bay and given a ceiling, where the grain and chaff was stored after threshing to await the process of winnowing, have become storage rooms or toilets. The treatment of the floors often cannot be so conservative. Ironically rammed earth, lime and ash can serve for modern domestic purposes, and it is the threshing floor, recognizable through the use of wooden planks on sleepers, brick paviors or stone flags, that is more difficult to retain where this is raised to allow the cat or dog underneath to catch the rats. In larger barns there might be more than one such floor. In barns built for, or converted to, the housing of livestock, central stone gutters might survive in the floor. Clearly the retention of the whole run promises nothing but twisted ankles. Nevertheless partial retention might be possible. Other features deserve

retention, the cathole or niche, where the keys and grease for the flail were kept, the owl hole – very often in the gable – through which the scourge of the rodents would fly and the patterned ventilation holes mostly on later brick barns which can provide telling lighting effects through the introduction of recessed glazing. Where they have to be blocked recessed black bricks will maintain the affect of solid and void. In timber-framed barns a watching brief should certainly be maintained during any building works to ensure that features of interest are recorded and/or saved. The presence of grooves in the top of horizontal members on side walls, for example, could well indicate stave holes for earlier wattle and daubing later replaced by weatherboarding. In oast houses the surmounting cowl (which would date the building subsequent to the 1790s and may retain the farmer's emblem) should be retained even if fixed in position, to prevent the rotation in the winds for which it was designed. In some conversions ingenious top lighting has been arranged through the aperture. In dovecotes (of which 2000 survive) the two distinguishing features are the nestholes themselves sometimes of brick or at other times in wood and the potence or rotating stick attached to a ladder which gave access to the holes. The normal size of dovecotes is such that residential conversion without extension dictates maximum use of the internal space and thus the removal of the potence. Even in such a case the holes can be kept, as can any rat ledge that runs around the interior two thirds of the way up.

A dovecote in Bedford is to be used by a potter, the nest holes providing a readymade system of shelving. Inside stables the stall dividers could be used with imagination to provide partitioning, if necessary after resiting. Harness rooms, coachhouses and ostler's and grooms' houses probably adjoin. If a number of farm buildings are to be converted you may be puzzled to find one prominently labelled 'dairy'. Under the Window Tax such a use was exempt from the imposition and was thus prominently advertised. Again, where a number of buildings are to be tackled an open cartshed, although it sounds unsuitable for residential use, can be excellent for ancillary garaging.

It is very important to remember that residential conversion always involves compromise. Although continued agricultural use can bring with it a greater risk of fire, there are strong arguments for refusal of consent for conversion in cases where the barn is clearly capable of many more years productive unaltered use, and when the owner is being swayed by the prices which barns are now attracting from house seekers. Even where a barn has been condemned for use on health grounds by the Health and Safety Executive, or is clearly in need of repair, grant aid is possible from the Ministry of Agriculture for 'reconditioning' provided that the structure remains in agricultural use. The Ministry does not insist on compliance with any aesthetic conditions, although, as the Secretary of State has a duty under Section 11 of the Countryside Act of 1968 to have regard to the desirability of conserving the beauty and amenity of the countryside in exercising his statutory duties, a grant may be refused on conservation grounds. Under the Agriculture Improvement Scheme, which came into operation in October 1985, grants of 25 per cent up to £24 000 of eligible expenditure can be obtained to provide tourist accommodation and craft or light industrial facilities in farm buildings in Less Favoured Areas (generally uplands). Further information can be obtained from ADAS (see Notes).

Some conversions, such as farm shops, involve so little material change of use that planning permission is not required (provided that such shops are purely for the sale of farm produce). Other, non-agricultural, uses are less self-effacing but can still be sensitive. In 1982 the Council for Small Industries in Rural Areas (COSIRA) introduced a scheme of 25 per cent grants (originally 35 per cent) towards the cost of converting redundant buildings to provide work places in villages and towns with a population of less than 10 000. However, under half the country is

eligible. Redundant churches, schools and barns have all benefited under this scheme. The net cost of conversion, after the grant, is 100 per cent allowable (up to 1250 sq. ft) as a revenue item to businesses or those trading on a personal account. The Countryside Commission is empowered to give grants towards the conversion of agricultural buildings to provide visitor and information centres and the English and Welsh Tourist Board can help in conversion to farm museums, craft centres or self-catering holiday accommodation. In the Peak District and Yorkshire Dales the conversion of field barns to provide bunk houses for walkers has skilfully avoided the web of bureaucracy surrounding the creation of houses by christening the resultant buildings 'stone tents'. As such they are exempt from the regulations surrounding residential properties. Other barns have been converted to restaurants, to museums, to theatres and to churches.

Such is the demand, primarily for residential conversion, that some builders particularly in the south-east are beginning to specialize in the dismantling of 'redundant' barns for re-erection in whole or part as the shell of an otherwise wholly new property. A goodly number are now being exported to America, concealed externally by a blockwork skin and clad in cedarwood shingle. The fate is an unkind one and clearly this 'London Bridge' solution must remain the exception rather than the rule.

FURTHER INFORMATION

There is a comprehensive bibliography of articles on historic farm buildings compiled by the SPAB as part of its Barns Campaign. This is available free from the SPAB at 37 Spital Square, London E1.

One of the best of the cheaper books is J.E.C. Peters's *Discovering Traditional Farm Buildings*, Shire Publications 1981. The larger publications include Nigel Harvey's *The History of Farm Buildings in England and Wales*, David and Charles 1970 (recently reprinted).

The Essex County Council published a booklet called *Residential Barn Conversions* in 1985.

ADDRESSES

ADAS (Agricultural Development and Advisory Service), Ministry of Agriculture, Fisheries and Food, Great Westminster House, Horseferry Road, London SW1P 2AE.

Country houses have always been in multiple residential occupation however much their physical presence in the landscape was meant to denote aristocratic power. Each community was a microcosm of a strictly hierarchical society headed by the owner and his family who lorded it over retainers, scholars, priests and servants. Since the eighteenth century at least visitors of the correct social status have been welcomed and as early as 1854 Althorp was open to the general public. What has changed in this century, with the introduction of offices and hotels or conversion to houses and flats, has been not so much an increase in the number of occupants but a lessening in the social distinctions between them.

More than ever before there is now the opportunity to live as an owner/occupier or as a tenant in a great country house. The names of two men are closely associated with this growing field of enterprise, Kit Martin and Christopher Buxton. Mr Martin, trained as an architect and the son of Sir Leslie, the designer of the Royal Festival Hall, is associated particularly with the conversion of Dingley Hall, Northamptonshire and Hazells Hall, Bedfordshire to multiple residential use – both buildings formerly threatened by demolition – but he has of late expanded into Scotland, taking on the challenge of Cullen House, Banffshire in 1982 and Keith Hall near Aberdeen in 1984. Christopher Buxton's training is in business administration. His most celebrated schemes have saved Charlton House in Wiltshire (now 18 units), Kirtlington Park, Oxfordshire, Chillinglee Park, Sussex (burned out by troops in 1943) and Compton Verney in Warwickshire which he acquired for conversion for more than £500 000 in 1984. His firm, Period and Country Houses Limited, has taken on 20 houses since 1954. He has been an unsuccessful bidder for three notable 'problem houses', Barlaston Hall, Staffordshire, The Grange, Hampshire and Hylands House near Chelmsford. Both men favour the device of a management company, in which owners or lessees buy shares, to maintain the setting and common parts.

The Country Houses Association, founded in 1955 (and then known as the Mutual Householders Association) owns nine houses converted to apartments for the retired or semi-retired. The Association is a registered charity and a non-profit-making organization under the Industrial and Provident Societies Act of 1893. Residents loan the Association a fixed sum returnable less 3 per cent per annum when the apartment is vacated and relet. Each conversion is carried out with commendable determination to preserve the character of the house, the principal rooms remaining undisturbed and open to the general public, the residents very often acting as guides. Each house has its own secretary. The Association is based at Cornhill House, 41 Kingsway, London WC2.

A similar principle lies behind the Gifted Houses Scheme run by Help the Aged (32 Dover Street, London W1 2AP). In return for donating large houses for occupation by elderly people the original owner is allowed to retreat to a smaller, more manageable section of the house where he can live free from rent, rates, the cost of external repairs and insurance for the duration of his own life and that of a surviving spouse.

Multiple occupation need not be permanent. The hesitant and then meteoric rise of the concept of Timeshare (one scheme in 1976, two by 1980, 35 by 1982) has allowed many people to buy several weeks' occupation for a fixed number of years in a wide variety of listed buildings. A variation on this theme is offered by Mr Charles Maitland, the enterprising owner of Henbury Hall at Sturminster Marshall, Dorset. He offers five year bonds to purchasers who receive instead of interest an annual week's holiday at the Hall. At the end of the five years, the initial cost of the bond is refunded in full. The income is applied to the conservation of the Hall. Such spectacular growth has produced problems and following the liquidation of some schemes a British Property Timeshare Association has been established both to encourage the development of the industry and to offer independent consumer protection. Membership of the Association by Timeshare companies is not compulsory.

Far cheaper holidays, but without any entitlement

to ownership, are offered by the Landmark Trust, which has gained a unique reputation in offering holidays in more idiosyncratic listed buildings, be they Georgian follies, Victorian railway stations or something even more unusual.

If the saving of country houses had been left purely to the mechanisms of the market, many more would have been lost. There will always be a place for the labour of love.

Useful Addresses

Comprehensive lists of the societies and organizations in the world of Conservation can be found in two directories published in the Autumn of 1984, both priced £2.50: 'Heritage' published by the British Tourist Authority and obtainable from 239 Old Marylebone Road, London SW1 and the 'Environmental Directory' published by the Civic Trust (see below).

The National Amenity Societies

This bland generic term covers the five national societies which must be informed whenever application is made to demolish a listed building in whole or part in England and Wales.

(a) *The Ancient Monuments Society*, St Andrew-by-the Wardrobe, Queen Victoria Street, London EC4V 5DE, tel. (01) 236–3934.
Secretary: Matthew Saunders; Chairman: Ivor Bulmer-Thomas.

Concerned with the study and conservation of historic buildings of all ages and all types, in partnership with the Friends of Friendless Churches.

(b) *The Council for British Archaeology*, 112 Kennington Road, London SE11, tel. (01) 582–0494.
Director: Dr Henry Cleere.

The CBA's role in casework is to inform and coordinate the activities of the local societies and organizations which constitute its membership, which is institutional only. It has regional representatives.

(c) *The Georgian Group*, 37 Spital Square, London E1, tel. (01) 377–1722.

Secretary: Roger White; Chairman: William Harris.

Concerned with the study and conservation of Georgian and Classical architecture.

(d) *The Society for the Protection of Ancient Buildings* (SPAB), 37 Spital Square, London E1, tel. (01) 377–1644.
Secretary: Philip Venning; Chairman: The Duke of Grafton.

The oldest and wealthiest of the societies. Its remit is mainly buildings constructed prior to 1700 but it has a special concern with techniques and philosophies of restoration.

(e) *The Victorian Society*, 1 Priory Gardens, London W4, tel. (01) 994–1019.
Secretary: Barry Walker; Chairman: Alan Crawford.

Studies and conserves the arts and architecture of the Victorian and Edwardian period.

The work of the national amenity societies is coordinated by a Joint Committee (Secretary, Matthew Saunders) based at the offices of the AMS. The National Trust, the National Trust for Scotland, the Civic Trust and the CPRE are also members of the Joint Committee.

In Scotland it is the Scottish Civic Trust and the Architectural Heritage Society of Scotland (see below) which have the duty to reply to local authorities on any threat to listed buildings.

The Ancient Monuments Board for Scotland, the Scottish Development Department, 17 Atholl Crescent, Edinburgh EH3 8JN, tel. (031) 229–9321.

The Ancient Monuments Board for Wales, Welsh Office, Cathays Park, Cardiff CF1 3NQ, tel. (0222) 825–111.

The Architectural Heritage Fund, 17 Carlton House Terrace, London SW1, tel. (01) 930–0914.

Architectural Heritage Society of Scotland, 43b Manor Place, Edinburgh EH3 7EB, tel. (031) 225–9724.

Formerly the Scottish Georgian Society and renamed in 1985. Founded for the 'study and protection of Scottish architecture'.
Secretary: Margaret Gilfillan.

Association of Conservation Officers. The ACO is regionally based.
Chairman: Michael Pearce, Quavey, Redlynch, Salisbury, Wiltshire.

Founded in the autumn of 1981 to coordinate and inform the activities of Conservation Officers employed by local authorities.

Association for Industrial Archaeology, The Wharfage, Ironbridge, Telford, Shropshire TF8 7AW, tel. (095) 245–3522.

The leading body in the field of industrial archaeology, founded in 1973.

Association for Preservation Technology, Box 2487, Station D. Ottawa, Ontario K1P 5W6, Canada.

Although based in North America the APT is an international organization for professionals.

Association for Studies in the Conservation of Historic Buildings (ASCHB) c/o the Institute of Archaeology, 31–34 Gordon Square, London WC1H 0PY.
Honorary Secretary: Alasdair Glass.

An organization for professionals which disseminates information on repair techniques through lectures, newsletters and annual transactions.

British Association for Local History, 45 Bedford Square, London WC1B 3DP, tel. (01) 636–4066.
General Secretary: Bettie Miller.

Founded in 1982 to advance the understanding and knowledge of local history through an information service, courses, competitions, projects and publications.

British Trust for Conservation Volunteers (BTCV), 36 St Mary's Street, Wallingford, Oxfordshire OX10 0EU, tel. (0491) 39766.

Organizes conservation working holidays, runs training courses and publishes handbooks.

Building Conservation Association, Apartment 39, Hampton Court Palace, East Molesey, Surrey KT8 9BS, tel. (01) 943–2277.
Director: John Griffiths.

Founded in 1979 'to promote the proper repair, maintenance and improvement of buildings of all types and ages'. There is a permanent exhibition at the Palace open daily 9.30 am–5.30 pm, Sundays from 12 noon.

Castle Howard Textile Conservation Centre, Castle Howard, York, tel. (065–384) 333.

The Centre, operational in 1982, cleans and repairs 'costumes, lace, embroideries and household furnishings from historic houses, private collections and museums'.

Centre for the Conservation of Historic Parks and Gardens, University of York, King's Manor, York YO1, tel. (0904) 59861.

The Centre, established in 1982, is compiling an inventory of sites. It welcomes consultancy work.

Civic Trust, 17 Carlton House Terrace, London SW1Y 5AW, tel. (01) 930–0914.

The premiere body for 'the protection and improvement of the environment'. With particular concern for civic design, wasteland and the threat posed by heavy lorries. Compiles register of local amenity societies. Publishes *Heritage Outlook*. There are separate Trusts for the *North-West* (69 Rodney Street, Liverpool L1 9EX, tel. (051) 709–1550), the *North-East* (34–35 Saddler Street, Durham DH1 3NU, tel. (0385) 61181), Scotland (see Scottish Civic Trust) and Wales (see below).

Civic Trust for Wales, 46 Cardiff Road, Llandaff, Cardiff CF5 2DT, tel. (0222) 552388.

Concrete Society, Devon House, 12/15 Dartmouth Street, London SW1H 9BL, tel. (01) 222–1822.

Primarily concerned with the modern use of concrete but also interested in its earliest architectural manifestations.

Conference on Training Architects in Conservation (COTAC), 19 West Eaton Place, London SW1, tel. (01) 245–9888.
Honorary Secretary: Donald Insall.

To promote the training of architects in the skills of conserving historic buildings.

Conservation Bureau, Rosebery House, Haymarket Terrace, Edinburgh EH2 5EZ, tel. (031) 337–9595.

For the collection and dissemination of information on conservation within Scotland.

Council for the Protection of Rural England (CPRE), 4 Hobart Place, London SW1W 0HY, tel. (01) 235–9481.
Director: Robin Grove-White; Chairman: David Astor.

Council for the Protection of Rural Wales, 32 High Street, Welshpool, Powys, tel. (0938) 2525.
Director: S.R.J. Meade.

Council for Small Industries in Rural Areas (COSIRA), 141 Castle Street, Salisbury, Wiltshire SP1 3TP tel. (0722) 336255. There are 23 regional offices.

Countryside Commission, John Dower House, Crescent Place, Cheltenham, Gloucestershire GL50 3RA, tel. (0242) 521381.

Countryside Commission (Wales), 8 Broad Street, Newtown, Powys SY16 2LU, tel. (0686) 26799.

Countryside Commission for Scotland, Battleby, Redgorton, Perth PH1 3EW, tel. (0738) 27921.

Crafts Council, 12 Waterloo Place, London SW1Y 4AU, tel. (01) 930–4811.
Director: David Dougan.

Publishes the National Register of Conservation Craft Skills in the Building Industry. Formerly known as the Crafts Advisory Committee.

Department of the Environment, 2 Marsham Street, London SW1P 3EB, tel. (01) 212–3443. There are Regional Offices

English Tourist Board, 4 Grosvenor Gardens, London SW1W 0DU, tel. (01) 730–3400.

Fire Mark Society c/o Chartered Insurance Institute Library, 20 Aldermanbury, London EC2.

Fortress Study Group, 24 Walters Road, Hoo, Rochester, Kent ME3 9JR, tel. (0634) 251954.

Fountain Society, 16 Gayfere Street, London SW1, tel. (01) 222–6037. Founded 1986.

Furniture History Society, c/o The Department of Furniture, Victoria & Albert Museum, London SW7.

Garden History Society, PO Box 27, Haslemere, Surrey GU27 3DR.
Honorary Secretary: Mrs Jennie Hook.

Heritage Coordination Group, Conewood House, Crawley Ridge, Camberley, Surrey.
Honorary Secretary: Mrs Pamela Cowen.

Coordinates the activity of conservation organizations through an annual conference.

Heritage Education Trust, St Mary's College, Strawberry Hill, Waldegrave Road, Twickenham TW1 4SX, tel. (01) 892–0051.
Honorary Director: Martyn Dyer.

Established in 1982 to further the education of the public and children in historic architecture.

Heritage in Danger, 17 Duke Street, St James's, London SW1Y 6DB.
Honorary Secretary: Hugh Leggatt.

Concerned chiefly with works of art, museum objects and libraries and the associated reform of tax regimes.

Historic Buildings and Monuments Commission for England, ('English Heritage') Fortress House, 23 Savile Row, London W1X 2BT, tel. (01) 734–6010.
Chief Executive: Peter Rumble.

Chairman: Lord Montagu of Beaulieu.

Established on 1st April 1984 to take over most of the functions of the Department of the Environment in respect of historic buildings, including the management of 400 ancient monuments.

Historic Buildings Council for Scotland, 25 Drumsheugh Gardens, Edinburgh EH3 7RN, tel. (031) 226–3611–4.
Secretary: D.J. Christie.

The statutory advisers to the Secretary of State for Scotland, particularly on grants and loans towards the repair of privately owned buildings.

Historic Buildings Council for Wales, Crown Building, Cathays Park, Cardiff CF1 3NQ, tel. (0222) 825111.
Secretary: R.J. Bolus.

Statutory advisers to the Secretary of State for Wales.

Historic Farmland and Buildings Group, c/o John Weller, Verandah House, Bildeston, Suffolk IP7 7EF, tel. (0449) 740492.

Established as a result of a meeting in 1983 to record historic agricultural buildings.

Historic Houses Association, 38 Ebury Street, London SW1W 0LU, tel. (01) 730–9419.
Secretary-General: Terence Empson.

Founded in 1973 to give a centralized voice to the owners of the larger historic houses, particularly in the country.

Housing Corporation, 149 Tottenham Court Road, London W1P 0BN, tel. (01) 387–9466.

Funds and supervises registered housing associations. There are regional offices.

Institute of Advanced Architectural Studies, The King's Manor, York YO1 2EP, tel. (0904) 24919. Offers a range of conferences for the professional, particularly MA courses in Conservation Studies.

Irish Architectural Archive, Merrion Square, Dublin. Founded 1976.
Chairman: Alastair Rowan.

Landmark Trust, Shottesbrooke, Maidenhead, Berkshire, tel. (0628) 82 5925/3431.
Director: J.W. Wellfare.

A charity which rescues idiosyncratic historic buildings for use as holiday homes.

Letterbox Study Group, 11 Morven Road, Bearsden, Glasgow G61 3BU.

Men of the Stones, The Rutlands, Tinwell, Stamford, Lincs. PE9 3UD, tel. (0780) 63372.

The champions of natural stone.

Moated Site Research Group, 29 Pine Walk, Liss,

Hampshire GU33 7AT.

Researches medieval manors and halls enclosed by a moat or ditch.

National Association of Almshouses, Billingbear Lodge, Wokingham, Berkshire RG11 5RU, tel. (0344) 52922/3.

National Association of Decorative and Fine Arts Societies (NADFAS), 38 Ebury Street, London SW1W 0LU, tel. (01) 730–3041.

Coordinates 158 member societies.

National Heritage Memorial Fund, Church House, Great Smith Street, London SW1P 3BL, tel. (01) 212–5414.

Secretary: Brian Lang; Chairman: Lord Charteris.

Established in 1980 to offer assistance towards the acquisition, maintenance and preservation of land, buildings, works of art and other objects of outstanding interest. Successor to the National Land Fund.

National Monuments Record, Fortress House, 23 Savile Row, London W1, tel. (01) 734–6010.

The principal library for photos of historic buildings. Open during normal office hours. Prints can be ordered, but this generally takes from 6 to 8 weeks.

National Piers Society, 82 Speed House, Barbican, London EC2Y 8AU.

Honorary Secretary: B.J. Rushton.

National Trust, 36 Queen Anne's Gate, London SW1H 9AS, tel. (01) 222–9251.

Director: Angus Stirling.

National Trust for Scotland, 5 Charlotte Square, Edinburgh EH2 4DU, tel. (031) 226–5922.

Director: Lester Borley.

Royal Archaeological Institute, 304 Addison House, Grove End Road, St John's Wood, London NW8 9EL.

Royal Commission on Ancient and Historical Monuments in Wales, Edleston House, Queen's Road, Aberystwyth, Dyfed SY23 2HP, tel. (0970) 4381/2.

Secretary: Peter Smith.

Studies the historic monuments of Wales.

Royal Commission on Historical Manuscripts, Quality House, Quality Court, Chancery Lane, London WC2, tel. (01) 242–1198.

Maintains National Register of Archives.

Royal Commission on Historical Monuments (England), Fortress House, 23 Savile Row, London W1X 1AB, tel. (01) 734–6010.

Absorbed the Industrial Monuments Survey in 1981, the national archaeological survey of the Ordnance Survey in 1983 and the 'Survey of London' in 1986. The statutory body for the study of historic buildings in England.

Royal Commission on the Ancient and Historical Monuments of Scotland, 54 Melville Street, Edinburgh EH3 7HF, tel. (031) 225–5994/5.

Secretary: J.G. Dunbar.

Royal Fine Arts Commission, 7 St James Square, London SW1Y 4JU, tel. (01) 839–6537.

Secretary: Sherban Cantacuzino.

Statutorily appointed to advise on tendentious development proposals.

Royal Fine Arts Commission for Scotland, 9 Atholl Crescent, Edinburgh EH3 8HA, tel. (031) 229–1109.

Royal Institute of British Architects, 66 Portland Place, London W1N 4AD.

Secretary: Patrick Harrison.

The professional body for architects. The library is open to non-members. The Drawings Collection and the Heinz Gallery (for monthly exhibitions – open free) are both at 21 Portman Square, London W1.

Royal Town Planning Institute, 26 Portland Place, London W1N 4BE, tel. (01) 636–9107.

Secretary: D.R. Fryer.

The professional body for planners.

Save Britain's Heritage (SAVE), 68 Battersea High Street, London SW11 3HX, tel. (01) 228–3336.

Secretary: Ken Powell; Chairman: Sophie Andreae.

Conservation pressure group.

Scottish Civic Trust, 24 George Square, Glasgow G2 1EF, tel. (041) 221–1466/7.

Society of Architectural Historians of Great Britain, (SAHGB) c/o HBMC London Division, Room 208, Chesham House, Warwick Street, London W1.

Honorary Secretary: Frank Kelsall.

Society for the Interpretation of Britain's Heritage, 4 Holmewood Close, Kenilworth, Warks CV8 2JE.

Secretary: I.C.A. Parkin

To improve the appreciation and interpretation of the Heritage.

Thirties Society, 3 Park Square West, London NW1, tel. (01) 286–5143.

Honorary Secretary: Clive Aslet.

Founded in 1979 to promote the conservation of interwar architecture.

Tool and Trades History Society, 275 Sandridge Lane, Bromham, Chippenham, Wilts SN15 2JW. Founded 1983.

Town and Country Planning Association, 17 Carlton House Terrace, London SW1Y 5AS.

Director: David Hall.

An old-established organization, a guiding force behind the founding of the garden cities, particularly concerned with the advancement and democratization of planning.

Ulster Architectural Heritage Society, 181A Stranmillis Road, Belfast 8.
Secretary: Mrs Elizabeth Cavanagh.

International

Europa Nostra, 9 Buckingham Gate London SW1E, tel. (01) 821–1171.

International Centre for the Study of the Preservation and the Restoration of Cultural Property (ICCROM), 13 via di San Michele, 00153 Rome, Italy.

Offers courses for research workers and technicians.

International Council on Monuments and Sites (ICOMOS), UK address: 34–36 Bedford Square, London WC1, tel. (01) 636–0974.
Honorary Secretary: Mrs Jane Fawcett.

Miscellaneous

The Civic Trust can give the name and address of the secretaries of local amenity societies registered with it.

The Design Council (28 Haymarket, London SW1Y 4JU, tel. 01–839–8000) publishes an Annual Directory of some 600 British design practices.

BIBLIOGRAPHY

General Books on Conservation

Alexandra Artley (ed.), *Putting Back the Style, A Directory of Authentic Renovation,* Evans Bros 1982.

David Baker, *Living with the Past. The Historic Environment* from 3 Oldway, Bletsoe, Bedford MK44 1QG.

Jack Bowyer, *Guide to Domestic Building Surveys* 3rd Edition 1979.

Jack Bowyer (ed.), *Handbook of Building Crafts in Conservation* Hutchinson.

Jack Bowyer, *Vernacular Building Conservation,* Architectural Press 1980.

Sherban Cantacuzino and Susan Brandt, *Saving Old Buildings,* Architectural Press 1980.

Pamela Cunnington, *Care for Old Houses,* Prism Alpha 1984.

Edinburgh New Town Conservation Committee, *The Care and Conservation of Georgian Houses: A Maintenance Manual,* Architectural Press 1980. (Revised Edition planned)

Sir Bernard Fielden, *The Conservation of Historic Buildings,* Butterworth. A magisterial work intended for professionals.

John Harvey, *Conservation of Buildings,* John Baker 1972 (now out of print).

Donald Insall, *The Care of Old Buildings Today,* Architectural Press, 1972. Aimed at the professional.

Alan Johnson, *How to Restore and Improve Your Victorian House,* David & Charles 1984.

Hugh Lander, *The House Restorer's Guide,* David and Charles 1986.

Ian Melville & Ian Gordon, *The Repair and Maintenance of Houses,* Estates Gazette 1973. Extremely long textbook for surveyors: referred to in text as Melville & Gordon.

National Building Agency, *Common Building Defects, Diagnosis and Remedy,* The Construction Press 1979.

Richard Pierce and Alastair Coey, *Taken for Granted* (including chapters on The Repair and Maintenance of Historic Buildings written by Richard Oram), published by the Royal Society of Ulster Architects and the Ulster HBC 1984. An invaluable and unique conservation manual for Northern Ireland.

A.R. Powys, *The Repair of Ancient Buldings,* 1929, republished 1981. Embodies the philosophy of the SPAB.

John Prizeman, *Your House, The Outside View,* Blue Circle 1975.

Beverley Pyke, *The Good Looking House*, Redcliffe 1980.

Alan Taylor, *The Pocket Book of Home Renovation*, Evans Bros 1980.

Hermione Sandwith and Sheila Stainton, *The National Trust Manual of Housekeeping*, Allen Lane 1984.

Neville Whittaker, *The House and Cottage Handbook*, Civic Trust for the North-East 1976.

Dictionaries

Martin S. Briggs, *Everyman's Concise Encyclopaedia of Architecture* 1959, reprinted 1969.

James Stevens Curl, *English Architecture, An Illustrated Glossary*, David & Charles 1977.

John Fleming, Hugh Honour, Nikolaus Pevsner, *Penguin Dictionary of Architecture*.

Eric Gee, *A Glossary of Building Terms used in England from the Conquest to c.1550*, published by the Frome Historical Research Group (The Hermitage, Gentle Street, Frome, Somerset BA11 1JA). Referred to in the text as Gee.

Paul Marsh, *Illustrated Dictionary of Building*, Construction Press 1982.

Glen Pride, *Glossary of Scottish Building*, 1975, available from the Scottish Civic Trust (see Useful Addresses).

John S. Scott, *Penguin Dictionary of Building*, 3rd Edition 1984.

Howard Colvin, *Biographical Dicitonary of British Architects 1600–1840*, John Murray 1978.

Rupert Gunnis, *Dictionary of British Sculptors, 1660–1851* Abbey Library.

John Harvey, *English Medieval Architects, A Biographical Dictionary down to 1550*, Alan Sutton Publishing, reprinted with additions October 1984.

Standard Texts

M.W. Barley, *The English Farmhouse and Cottage*, 1961.

R.W. Brunskill, *The Illustrated Handbook of Vernacular Architecture*, 1971.

N.W. Brunskill, *Traditional Buildings of Britain*, 1981 (paperback 1985)

Alec Clifton Taylor, *The Pattern of English Building*.

A. Fenton and B. Walker, *The Rural Architecture of Scotland* 1981

Eric Mercer, *English Vernacular Houses*, 1975.

Peter Smith, *Houses of the Welsh Countryside*.

Craftsmen

Craftsmen in all aspects of building conservation advertise regularly in the relevant press and in the Yellow Pages. There are, however, compendium lists available in a number of publications.

Guidebook to Restorers. New edition to be published by the Guild of Master Craftsmen Publications, Parklands House, Keymer Road, Burgess Hill, West Sussex, which now has exhibition space at Castle Place, High Street, Lewes.

Handbook of English Crafts and Craftsmen, June Lewis, Robert Hale 1978.

Traditional Homes, Trades and Services Directory, to be published at regular intervals with updated computer printouts of specified categories in the magazine of that name (Schweppes House, Grosvenor Road, St Albans, Herts AL1 3TN), and in loose-leafed form.

The Scottish Development Agency (Rosebery House, Haymarket Terrace, Edinburgh EH12 5EZ) publish a directory of craftsmen for Scotland (*The Scottish Conservation Directory*). The SDA's and RIAS' *Scottish Architects in Conservation* also covers contractors and craftsmen. The appendix to Jack Bowyer's *Vernacular Building Conservation* (see p. 164) includes an appendix of craftsmen and suppliers.

There are a number of county based craft guilds (for example, in Dorset) that can advise on craftsmen in the locality.

Conservation officers at District and County Councils should also be able to help.

The Crafts Council and COSIRA (see Useful Addresses) both maintain registers of craftsmen, in the latter case regionally based. The Register of Artists and Craftsmen maintained by the Council for the Care of Churches (83 London Well EC2) is of interest to the owners of secular buildings as well.

Interiors

James Ayres, *The Shell Book of the Home in Britain*, Faber & Faber 1981. On the decoration, design and construction of vernacular interiors 1500–1850.

Geoffrey Beard, *Craftsmen and Interior Decoration in England 1660–1820*, Bartholomew 1981.

John Cornforth, *English Interiors 1790–1848, The Quest for Comfort*, Barrie & Jenkins 1978.

John Fowler & John Cornforth, *English Decoration in the 18th Century*, Barrie & Jenkins.

Peter Thornton, *17th Century Interior Decoration in England, France and Holland*, Yale 1979.

Keeping up to Date

A number of organizations run courses for non-professionals. In 1985 the SPAB (See Useful Addresses) held what is hoped will prove the first of a regular weekend course on the Repair of Old Houses for laymen. It already runs an annual week-long course for professionals in October. There are longer courses run by the Architectural Association at 36 Bedford Square, London WC1 and at other schools of architecture, for example at the Universities of Manchester and Leicester. The Weald and Downland Open Air Museum at Singleton, Chichester, West Sussex holds a summer workshop on the Repair of Traditional Buildings. The Building Conservation Trust with display space at Hampton Court Palace has a permanent exhibition on the repair of properties of all ages. The Building Centres, at Store Street just off Tottenham Court Road and in Cambridge and Southampton have exhibitions by suppliers on all forms of building materials. The Research and Technical Advisory Service (RTAS) of the HBMC can handle external enquiries.

The magazines *Traditional Homes* (Schweppes House, Grosvenor Road, St Albans, Herts AL1 3TN), *Period Home* (90B High Street, Tenterden, Kent TN30) and *Heritage Outlook* (Civic Trust, 17 Carlton House Terrace, London SW1) are very useful for keeping in touch. The first-named is now producing an annual *Traditional Home Repairs*, first issue, January 1986.

The largest collection of books on architecture, old and new, is held at the:

British Architectural Library at the Headquarters of the RIBA, 66 Portland Place, London W1.

It is still at present open to non-members. Opening hours: Monday until 5 pm; Tuesday, Wednesday and Thursday until 8 pm; Friday until 7 pm; Saturday until 1.30 pm. The Periodicals Index in the Library covers the last 65 years. The Drawings Collection at 21 Portman Square, London W1 is open by appointment during the mornings only.

INDEX